BASICS OF

NONLINEARITIES
IN MATHEMATICAL SCIENCES

Anthem Studies in Science, Technology and Mathematics

Other titles in the series:

Sinha, Dilip Kumar and Adhikari, Sanat Kumar *Basics of Tertiary Calculus* (2006)

Reiman, Istvan *International Mathematical Olympiad Vol I, 1959–1975* (2005)

Reiman, Istvan *International Mathematical Olympiad Vol II, 1976–1990* (2005)

Reiman, Istvan *International Mathematical Olympiad Vol III, 1991–2004* (2005)

BASICS OF
NONLINEARITIES
IN MATHEMATICAL SCIENCES

Dilip Kumar Sinha

Anthem Press

Anthem Press
An imprint of Wimbledon Publishing Company
www.anthempress.com

This edition first published in UK and USA 2006
by ANTHEM PRESS
75-76 Blackfriars Road, London SE1 8HA, UK
or PO Box 9779, London SW19 7ZG, UK
and
244 Madison Ave. #116, New York, NY 10016, USA

British Library Cataloguing in Publication Data
A catalogue record for this book is available from the British Library.

Library of Congress Cataloging in Publication Data
A catalog record for this book has been requested.

1 3 5 7 9 10 8 6 4 2

ISBN 1 84331 1702 8 (Hbk)

Cover illustration: Sonal Mansata

Typeset by Compuset International, India

Printed in India

contents

preface

Nonlinear studies, by and large, have emerged in a variety of disciplines such as physical, chemical, biological, social and technological sciences, and in particular, differential equations. As trends go, there is every likelihood that an undergraduate curriculum in areas of mathematics, science, technology and even social sciences should start reflecting a qualitative approach, mainly through differential equations. Hence, this book is intended not only for students of mathematics, but also for a wider readership.

The genesis of this book can be described essentially as an outgrowth of my postgraduate teaching. I am especially confident of the content, thanks to the classroom notes my students assiduously took down over the years and later passed on to me to structure this volume.

I must confess, I have had the privilege of sitting through the valuable lectures of leading personalities, such as Prof Rene Thom, Delegue de l'Academie des Sciences, France, Prof E C Zeeman, Warwick University, UK, Prof D J Chillingworth, University of Southampton, UK and Prof Michael A B Deakin, University of Monash, Australia, on catastrophes and bifurcations, at the Jadavpur University, Kolkata. I must also mention about my own exposure and interactions with the faculty at ICTP, Trieste, Italy, under the leadership Prof E C Zeeman, on a course on 'dynamical system'.

Problems have been set in the book with a view to engage students' creativity as well as exercise their mental prowess. Proofs of some theorems have been left out, but an inquisitive reader can look for hints in the Appendices.

Finally, I must thank the leadership of Wimbledon Publishing Company Limited for publishing a book of this genre and Mr Prantik Basu in particular for his editorial support. The book would not have been a reality if I did not have the support and co-operation from the members of my family.

26 January 2006   Dilip Kumar Sinha
Kolkata, India

preamble

It is now a truism that nonlinearity is everywhere around us. But what is nonlinearity? We know of linearity through Ohm's law, which essentially shows a linear dependence between physical parameters. Let us take a look at a clock pendulum, in which the period of oscillation does not depend in any way on the amplitude, provided we move close to the point of equilibrium. But if the pendulum is swung with greater amplitude, the period of oscillation becomes dependent on the amplitude. It looks that large amplitude brings into play a new physical reality, which doesn't manifest itself at small amplitudes, and, in fact, which now becomes predominant. We say that here we have nonlinear waves that move with large and often, very large amplitudes. If we now delve into the past, we meet several linear relationships. It is only during the past few decades that scientists have started grappling with something different from linearities and we agree to call them nonlinearities. Nonlinear science is a recent and premature coinage. We often use the terms "nonlinear system" or often "nonlinear dynamics". The emerging field of mathematical sciences, not to be looked upon as a menagerie of nonlinearities, provides in its variety of components e.g. physical sciences, life sciences, ecological sciences, social sciences etc, different contemporary phases of nonlinear science or nonlinear dynamics or nonlinear systems.

The origin of pursuits on nonlinearities dates back to the later part of the nineteenth century. Honestly speaking, J. Henri Poincare laid the foundation of such a genre of studies in his work (1878–1910) precisely through his "Celestial Mechanics" to be followed by the Russian mathematician Alexander Mikhailovich Liapunov and a bit later, by the American mathematician G. D. Birkhoff, through his work (1908–1944). Mechanics was the forte of other French mathematicians Lagrange and Laplace. Dynamics, in particular, used to be the term to refer to nonlinear science in its early phase. What else can dynamics be other than what it refers to the study of time-evolving processes? There has to be a compelling system of equations to describe the processes which may be called as 'dynamical systems'. Nonlinear systems, then, should be about dynamical processes with a physical existence. As trends show, we need to describe the system by ordinary differential equations (ode), for systems characterized by continuity and by maps, for discrete systems. Nonlinear science is yet to attain maturity and the bulk of it is still in mathematics rather in mathematical sciences, where basic mathematics finds a torrent of good applications.

Although ode's dominate the mathematical content here, the slant is towards qualitative behaviour of ode's. 'Nonlinear Theory of Oscillations' is a classical treatise in this direction. Something of this kind would have been pursued but a qualitative approach is what is needed and followed in this book. Yet, for the sake of motivation in familiar terms, we begin with oscillations of a simple pendulum. As we move on, we come across a variety of terms such as orbits, trajectories, phase-portraits etc as somewhat synonymous to paths, graphs, profiles, which we know.

In the historical development of differential equations, one finds two distinct trends—the first one is obviously the desperate attempt(s) to obtain solutions in closed forms and if not, in terms of power series. The second trend seeks to bypass the first one and seeks to obtain qualitative information about the behaviour of solutions. The architect of the qualitative theory of nonlinear equations is the French mathematician Jules Henri Poincare around 1880, while studying the stability of orbits in his monumental work "Les Méthodes Nouvelle de la Mécanique Céleste". In the study of linear differential equations which flourished more than 200 years, there is, by and large, a complete account of theories and techniques. We can't say this about nonlinear differential equations. We know that we cannot but be interested in nonlinear differential equations. The usual tendency at this juncture should be to look for linearisation of these equations, but aren't these approximating devices? We often cite problems such as that of an undamped pendulum, represented by

$$\frac{d^2\theta}{dt^2} + \frac{g}{l}\sin\theta = 0$$

and if there be a damping force proportional to the velocity of the bob, the equation turns out to be

$$\frac{d^2\theta}{dt^2} + \frac{k}{m}\frac{d\theta}{dt} + \frac{g}{l}\sin\theta = 0 \text{ where the symbols have familiar meanings.}$$

If we would like to linearise this, we can replace $\sin\theta$ by θ, and then, we are able to solve the first equation. We justify the approximation by assuming small oscillations. Another nonlinear equation is provided by the theory of a vacuum tube, represented by

$$\frac{d^2x}{dt^2} + \mu(x^2 - 1)\frac{dx}{dt} + x = 0, \text{ where } \mu \text{ is a constant.}$$

This is the well known van der Pol equation. We can write such equations in several forms. We can introduce a variable y given by

$$\frac{dx}{dt} = y \ \text{ so that } \ \frac{dy}{dt} = f(x,y)$$

In the language of mechanics, we can take x as the displacement and $\frac{dx}{dt}$ as the velocity and these two together define the state of the system. These values of x and y are called its phases and this plane of x-y is called the phase plane. A simple generalization can be sought as

$$\left.\begin{array}{l} \dfrac{dx}{dt} = f(x,y) \\[2mm] \dfrac{dy}{dt} = g(x,y) \end{array}\right\} \quad \text{where } f(x,y) \text{ and } g(x,y) \text{ are well-chosen functions.}$$

The above set (or the system) has the unique solution

$$\left.\begin{array}{l} x = x(t) \\ y = y(t) \end{array}\right\} \text{ subject to conditions } x(t_0) = x_0 \text{ and } y(t_0) = y_0$$

The last set defines a curve in the phase plane known as the path of the system where we use the words 'orbit' and 'trajectory' as synonymous to path.

Alexander Mikhailovich Liapunov (1857–1918) laid the foundation of studies on stability. His classic work published in 1892 in Russian is, of course, available in English entitled "Stability of Motion". He was not only a great mathematician, but also a mechanical engineer. It was reported that he died in the aftermath of the Soviet revolution. Like Poincare, his starting point in regard to stability studies was the concept of energy. Indeed, he made use of the idea that if the energy of a physical system attains a local minimum at a certain equilibrium point, then that point is stable. This idea was generalized by Liapunov. Thus, stability of equilibrium points is said to be characterized in the sense of Liapunov. Intuitively speaking, an equilibrium point is stable if all solutions, beginning at close by points continue in the neighbourhood; otherwise, it is unstable. As mentioned earlier, it is asymptotically stable if all solutions not merely stay close by but also tend to be equilibrium points as time approaches infinity. As a physical example, let us get back to the example of an oscillating pendulum so as to obtain the genesis of the choice of the function, called the Liapunov function. The pendulum equation is given by, with damping, $\dot{\theta} = v$, and $\dot{v} = -\omega^2 \sin\theta - cv$ where c is constant.

Let us define the energy of the pendulum as $V(\dot{\theta}, \theta) = \frac{1}{2} m(l\dot{\theta})^2 + mgl(1 - \cos\theta)$. When the damping is neglected i.e. $c = 0$, the system is conservative so that there is no dissipation of energy. Therefore, $V = $ constant throughout the motion of the system i.e. $\frac{dV}{dt} = 0$ along the trajectories of the system. Since $V(\dot{\theta}, \theta) = c$ forms a closed curve around $\theta = 0$ for small c, we can say that $\theta = 0$ is a stable equilibrium point. But, when the damping is present, the energy will surely dissipate during the motion of the system i.e. $\frac{dV}{dt} \leq 0$ along the trajectories of the system i.e. V cannot remain constant indefinitely throughout the motion. Hence, one can take V to be decreasing till it reaches zero, which means that the trajectory tends to $\theta = 0$ as $t \rightarrow \infty$. So, by analyzing, in a way, the derivative of V along the trajectories of the system can be determined. In fact that was the genesis of thought processes that led Liapunov to explore, instead of energy, some functions to be possibly of use in determining the stability or otherwise of the system. Formally, we shall take up these aspects later on.

In sum, we can say, as it has become discernible by now, that we move back and forth between dynamics and strictly mathematical nuances, so as to look, for purposes of motivation, for concepts of dynamics.

motivation

2.1 Nonlinear dynamics

Nonlinear dynamics, as mentioned earlier, has to draw necessarily upon dynamical processes and there lies the motivation to its consideration through appropriate examples. We consider a simple (nonlinear) example of dynamics, given by a pendulum moving in a vertical plane (Fig. 2.1). We take a constant downward gravitational force equal to the mass m of the bob. The mass of the rod supporting the bob is not taken into account. We also assume, first, for reasons of simplicity, that there is no frictional (or viscous) force resisting the motion, proportional to the speed of the

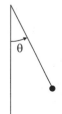

Fig. 2.1: Pendulum

bob. Let l be the constant length of the rod. The bob of the pendulum, as is well-known, moves along a circle of radius l. If $\theta(t)$ be the counter clockwise angle from the vertical to the rod at time (t), then the angular velocity of this is $\dfrac{d\theta}{dt}$ and the velocity is $l\dfrac{d\theta}{dt}$. The downward gravitational force has the component $-mg\sin\theta(t)$ tangent to the circle. This is the force on the bob that produces the motion. Therefore, the total force tangent to the circle, at time t is $-mg\sin\theta$, while the acceleration of the bob tangent to the circle is $l\dfrac{d^2\theta}{dt^2}$

Hence, from Newton's law,

$$\frac{d^2\theta}{dt^2} = -\frac{g}{l}\sin\theta \tag{1}$$

which we can write as $\dfrac{d^2\theta}{dt^2} + \omega^2\sin\theta = 0$ where $\omega^2 = \dfrac{g}{l}$

Let us solve this equation (1), given the initial conditions

$$\theta(0)=\alpha, \dot{\theta}(0)=\beta \tag{2}$$

Let us introduce a new dependent variable v so that the second order system differential equation given by (1) reduces to the set of first order differential equations as:

$$\frac{d\theta}{dt}=v, \quad \frac{dv}{dt}=-\omega^2\sin\theta \tag{3}$$

To get an idea of v and θ, we have from (3),

$$\frac{dv}{d\theta} = -\frac{\omega^2\sin\theta}{v}$$

Integrating, $\dfrac{v^2}{2}=\omega^2\cos\theta + \text{constant}$, which can be simplified as

$$v^2 - 2\omega^2\cos\theta = a \tag{4}$$

where a is constant.

Thus, we can have in the $(v\text{-}\theta)$ plane, a sketch of (4). This is referred to as its path which is obviously symmetrical about the θ-axis. Similarly, the graph is symmetrical about the v axis. The shape of the graph depends on the constant a given by

$$a = \beta^2 - 2\omega^2\cos\alpha$$

We now distinguish five cases :

(I) $a < -2\omega^2$

(II) $a = -2\omega^2$

(III) $-2\omega^2 < a < 2\omega^2$

(IV) $a = 2\omega^2$

(V) $a > 2\omega^2$

Case I: $a < -2\omega^2$

$$v^2 = a < 2\omega^2 \cos\theta - 2\omega^2 = 2\omega^2 (\cos\theta - 1) \le 0$$

In this case there are no real values of v for any real value of θ. Hence, there is no path.

Case II: $a = -2\omega^2$

$$a = 2\omega^2 \cos\theta - 2\omega^2 = 2\omega^2 (\cos\theta - 1)$$

The only points in the $(v\text{-}\theta)$ plane satisfying this equation are $(2n\pi, 0)$ where n is any integer; therefore the path obviously consists of isolated points on the θ-axis.

Case III: $-2\omega^2 < a < 2\omega^2$

We can write (4) as $v = \pm\sqrt{2\omega^2 \cos\theta + a}$ (5)

Let us consider first quadrant where

$$v = \sqrt{2\omega^2 \cos\theta + a}$$ (6)

Since $\cos\theta$ is maximum at $\theta = 0$, the value $v = \sqrt{2\omega^2 \cos\theta + a}$ on the v axis is also a maximum. Let this be the point A shown in the path, (Fig. 2.2).

Since $\cos\theta$ decreases as θ increases from 0 to π, v also decreases as θ

increases. v is zero at a point B, say, where $\theta = \arccos^{-1}\left(-\dfrac{a}{2\omega^2}\right) < \pi$. Since the graph is symmetrical about θ and v axes, we have the curve $ABCD$. For different values of a i.e. for different initial values, we can get similar elliptical curves like $ABCD$. As $\cos\theta$ is periodic with the period 2π, there will be some elliptical paths around points $(2n\pi, 0)$ where

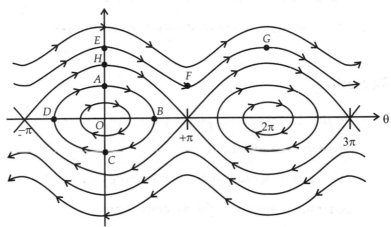

Fig. 2.2: Phase plane curves for an undamped simple pendulum

n is an integer.

If we take a to be close to $-2\omega^2$ then the points A and B will be very close to the origin O. With the increase of values of a, intercepts on the axes will increase. The slope of the curve is clearly undefined at the points where the graph crosses θ axis.

Case IV: $a = 2\omega^2$

In this case $v = \omega\sqrt{2(1+\cos\theta)} = 2\omega\cos\dfrac{\theta}{2}$

The graph is obviously a part of a cosine function with its maximum value 2ω at the point H and it is zero at $\theta = \pi$. To obtain the rest of the curve, we note that graph is symmetrical and $\cos\theta$ is periodic. Its slope is also given by $\dfrac{dv}{d\theta} = -\dfrac{\omega^2\sin\theta}{v}$; if n is an odd integer, the slope is $\pm\omega$ at $(n\pi, 0)$.

Case V: $a > 2\omega^2$

$\because |\cos\theta| \le 1$, v can never be zero.

The slope is zero at $\theta = n\pi$ where n is a non negative integer, vide, the points F, G, H.

We again use symmetry if we are to have graphs in all the other quadrants.

Remarks

1. Figure 2.1 represents phase-plane curves, for the motion of the pendulum with no resistance to motion.

   Let us look at it from the energy point of view. The sum total of kinetic and potential energies of the system is given by

   $$V(\dot\theta, \theta) = \frac{1}{2} m (l\dot\theta)^2 + mgl(1 - \cos\theta)$$

   Now, we have, earlier, the equation

   $$v^2 - 2\omega^2 \cos\theta = a$$

   Multiplying by $\frac{1}{2} ml^2$ and adding mgl, we have

   $$V(\dot\theta, \theta) = \frac{1}{2} ml^2 a + mgl = V(\beta, \alpha)$$

   which shows that the energy remains constant on each of the curves of the figure. Such curves can thus be called energy curves.

2. We come back to our old question: is it possible, by now, to obtain the solution of the non-linear equation? The answer is partly yes; we can do the latter in numerical terms but we shall not do this now.

3. We have met the equation $\dfrac{dv}{d\theta} = -\dfrac{\omega^2 \sin\theta}{v}$

   Obviously, this equation provides the direction of the field at each point of the phase, except where $-\dfrac{\omega^2 \sin\theta}{v}$ becomes indeterminate. These are, no doubt, peculiar points, often called singular points or singularities; for example, here these are

$(n\pi, 0)$ n being any integer. We shall learn more about them in the light of what are critical points.

4.   We have so far not considered nonlinearity, which we do in the next article. Let us accommodate this by having a damping (or frictional) force resisting the motion of the pendulum. This force is taken as $c\dfrac{d\theta}{dt}$, c being a non-negative constant, the force being directed tangentially to the arc, representing the motion of the pendulum.

2.2 Nonlinearity in the motion of a pendulum

The equation of motion is given by

$$\ddot{\theta}(t) = -c\dot{\theta}(t) - \omega^2 \sin\theta(t) \tag{1}$$

$$\left(\dot{\theta} = \frac{d\theta}{dt}, \ddot{\theta} = \frac{d^2\theta}{dt^2}\right); \text{ this is equivalent to } \left.\begin{array}{l} \dot{\theta} = v \\ \dot{v} = -cv - \omega^2 \sin\theta \end{array}\right\} \tag{2}$$

We have, therefore,

$$\frac{dv}{d\theta} = \frac{-cv - \omega^2 \sin\theta}{v} \tag{3}$$

We take the initial values as $\theta(0) = \alpha, \dot{\theta}(0) = \beta$

Here equation (3) cannot be solved analytically in familiar ways. But we can get an idea of the motion by drawing the path (Fig. 2.3). Here the slope is obviously less than in the above case (without damping). The equilibrium points of (2) are given by

$\dot{\theta} = 0, \dot{v} = 0 \Rightarrow \theta = n\pi$ ($n = 0$, any integer)

$v(\pi) = 0$

We may proceed to obtain a series solution of (3)

Let us seek the solution in the form of power series by

$$v(\theta) = a_0 + a_1(\theta - \pi) + a_2(\theta - \pi)^2 + \dots \tag{4}$$

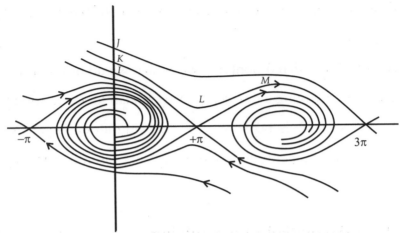

Fig 2.3 : Phase plane of a simple pendulum with damping

Let us put this in the given equation to obtain the values of $a_0, a_1, a_2, \ldots$

Let $x = \theta - \pi$ (5)

then $v\left(\dfrac{dv}{dx} + c\right) = \omega^2 \sin x$ (6)

We now seek a solution of (6) in the form

$$v(x) = a_1 x + a_3 x^3 + a_5 x^5 + \ldots$$ (7)

Substituting (7) in (6)

$$\left(a_1 x + a_3 x^3 + \ldots\right)\left(c + a_1 + 3a_3 x^2 + \ldots\right) = \omega^2\left(x - \frac{x^3}{3!} + \frac{x^5}{5!} - \ldots\right)$$

Equating coefficients of like powers of x we obtain a set of equations from which the constants can be obtained $a_1^2 + ca_1 - \omega^2 = 0$

So, $a_1 = \dfrac{-c \pm \sqrt{c^2 + 4\omega^2}}{2}$ (8)

It gives one positive value and one negative value of a_1

If we differentiate (7), we can obtain the slope at $x = 0$ or at $x = \pi$, assuming the differentiation to be justified. Clearly a_1 is the slope at $x = 0$ $(\theta = \pi)$ and so we find, because of (8), two slopes of the graph.

Similarly, equating the coefficient of x^3

$$3a_1a_3 + (c+a_1)a_3 = \frac{\omega^2}{3!}$$

or $$a_3 = -\frac{\omega^2}{6(c+4a_1)}$$

Similarly,

$$a_5 = -\frac{\omega^2 - 360a_3{}^2}{120(c+6a_1)}$$

So, (7) is obtained.

In order to have an indication of the behaviour of this damped system, we go back to the equation (3) given by

(3) $$\frac{dv}{d\theta} = \frac{-cv - \omega^2 \sin\theta}{v}$$

For the un-damped system, we have

(9) $$\frac{dv}{d\theta} = -\frac{\omega^2 \sin\theta}{v}$$

Clearly (3) and (9) have the same set of singularities. Further, comparing (3) and (9), the slopes for both the systems differ by a constant and in fact, that for the damped system is less than that in the undamped . This is true for every point in the phase–plane. We shall get back to the graph(s) later on.

Remark

The time 't' does not appear explicitly in the equation and hence, the equation is called *autonomous*. We need to know something more in order to study the behaviour of equation (3). Another nonlinear system with two variables, appropriately chosen below, becomes amenable so that phase-portraits of the paths/orbits/trajectories, whatever we say, may be obtained.

The system known, as Lotka-Volterra system, is drawn from the dynamics of population ecology. The system is, mathematically, given by

$$\frac{dH}{dt} = (a_{11} - a_{12}P)H \tag{5}$$

$$\frac{dP}{dt} = (-a_{21} + a_{22}H)P$$

where a's are constants

Dividing one by the other, we obtain

$$\frac{dH}{dP} = \frac{(a_{11} - a_{12}P)H}{(-a_{21} + a_{22}H)P}$$

or, $$\frac{(-a_{21} + a_{22}H)}{H} dH = \frac{(a_{11} - a_{12}P)}{P} dP$$

or, $$-\frac{a_{21}}{H} dH + a_{22}dH = \frac{a_{11}}{P} dP - a_{12}dP$$

Integrating,

$$a_{21} \log H - a_{22}H + a_{11} \log P - a_{12}P = \text{constant}$$

or, $$\log\left(\frac{P^{a_{11}} H^{a_{21}}}{c}\right) = (a_{22}H + a_{12}P)$$

which are paths in $(H - P)$ plane, c being a constant.

These can be shown to be a family of closed curves in $H - P$ plane.

The above systems have remarkably common features, so much so, that the variables either $\frac{\theta}{\omega}$ or $\frac{H}{P}$ while changing with time can become stationary or steady. This can be obtained mathematically by putting $\frac{d(\cdot)}{dt} = 0$, wherever it may occur. We also say that the earlier nonlinear autonomous system has equilibria at the points $(\theta, \omega) = (n\pi, 0), n = 0, \pm 1, \pm 2, \ldots$

Similarly, the other nonlinear autonomous system (5) has equilibria at (0,0), $\left(\dfrac{a_{11}}{a_{12}}, \dfrac{a_{21}}{a_{22}} \right)$. We shall later study the behaviour of such systems about points of equilibria.

2.3 Another look at nonlinearity

Although we have not been able to get the variables in exact terms, which we often seek, for nonlinear systems considered above, yet we could have some understanding of solution curves which portraits imply. It must have been obvious by now that we need to recall methods of curve tracing or sketching. We continue this so as to obtain some more insights into what nonlinearities are all about, of course, with implications.

System 1

$$\frac{dx}{dt} = -y + x\left(1 - x^2 - y^2\right)$$

$$\frac{dy}{dt} = x + y\left(1 - x^2 - y^2\right) \tag{1}$$

Let us proceed in a different way. We move over to polar coordinates by putting,

$x = r\cos\theta$, $y = r\sin\theta$, so that

$r^2 = x^2 + y^2$; $r^2\dot{\theta} = x\dot{y} - y\dot{x}$

Now, $r\dot{r} = x\dot{x} + y\dot{y}$

$$= x^2\left(1 - r^2\right) + y^2\left(1 - r^2\right)$$

$$= \left(1 - r^2\right)\left(x^2 + y^2\right) = r^2\left(1 - r^2\right)$$

$$\dot{r} = r\left(1 - r^2\right)$$

$$\therefore \quad \left.\begin{array}{l} \dfrac{dr}{dt} = r\left(1 - r^2\right) \\[2mm] \dfrac{d\theta}{dt} = -1 \end{array}\right\}$$

Integrating,

$$\left. \begin{array}{l} r = \dfrac{1}{\sqrt{1+c_0 e^{-2t}}} \\[4mm] \theta = -t + t_0 \end{array} \right\}$$

where c_0 is a constant

$$x = \dfrac{1}{\sqrt{1+c_0 e^{-2t}}} \cos(-t + t_0)$$

$$y = \dfrac{1}{\sqrt{1+c_0 e^{-2t}}} \sin(-t + t_0)$$

If $c_0 = 0, r = 1, \theta = -t + t_0$

$$x^2 + y^2 = 1$$

which is a circular path in the anti-clockwise direction.

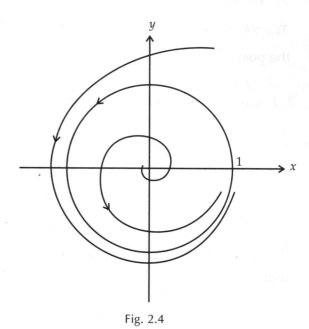

Fig. 2.4

If $c_0 < 0$, then $r > 1$, but $r \to 1$ as $t \to \infty$

Also, if $c_0 > 0$, then $r < 1$, but $r \to 1$ as $t \to \infty$

This shows that there exists a closed path $r = 1$ and all other paths approach $r = 1$, from outside and inside. This closed path as $t \to \infty$, is shown in Fig. 2.4.

System 2

It is known that evolution of biological populations takes place. We can associate what is called a biomass as the quantitative measure of a biological population. If x be this number, changes in x often take place, as is well known, at certain discrete moments $t_1, t_2, \ldots$ corresponding to the birth of a new generation, related, perhaps, to the seasons. x_0 is the initial value of x at time t_0. We take that the change of the variable x at a given time t_{k+1} $(k = 0, 1, 2, \ldots)$ is determined by its value at time t_k and by abiotic conditions. If

x_k be the value of x at time t_k, we have the difference equation of the type $x_{k+1} - x_k = f(x_k, \mu)$ where $f(x_k, \mu)$ is a function to be chosen appropriately in terms of the position say, μ. Malthus, way back in 1798, chose a linear dependence.

A logistic version by Verhulst leads to the difference equation

$$x_{k+1} - x_k = (a - bx_k)x_k$$

$$\Leftrightarrow \quad x_{k+1} = \{(a+1) - bx_k\}x_k$$

Obviously, if $a > 0$, $x = \dfrac{a}{b}$ is the equilibrium, i.e. if $x_0 = \dfrac{a}{b}$ then $x_k = \dfrac{a}{b}$ for all k. Also if $(a+1-bx_k) < 0$ then $x_{k+1} < 0$ for which the reality of the model fails. Hence, we assume that

$$x_k \le \frac{a+1}{b}$$

Let us put now $y = \dfrac{b}{a+1}x$, and $\lambda = a+1 > 0$

Then

$$y_{k+1} = \lambda y_k (1 - y_k) \text{ for } k = 0, 1, 2, \ldots, \quad y_0 \in [0,1].$$

$$\because x_k = \frac{a+1}{b}, y_0 < 1.$$

That $0 < \lambda < 4$, follows from $0 < y_k < 1$, as $0 < y_k < 1$ i.e $\{\lambda y(1-y) \le 1\}$ for all $y \in [0,1]$ and also from the fact that the maximum of the function $y(1-y)$, in $(0,1)$ is $\dfrac{1}{4}$ is evident.

Remarks

1.   We can study the behaviour of solutions y_k for different values of λ vide appendix II. These, as may be seen later, tell about, in particular, the stability of the

system, nature of the orbits etc. In this context and elsewhere, as well the word neighbourhood' (or briefly, nbd) around a critical point, say $(0,0)$ is intended to be the set of all points (x,y), lying within some distance (fixed and positive) of $(0,0)$.

2.   We have talked about evolution in biological or ecological terms; the simplest model of evolution predicts the exponential growth of the population. The state of the system is described by points in the first quadrant of the plane, say, (x,y). Locally the curve, called also a manifold, of the possible states, say, $(x > 0, y > 0)$ of a system is called phase space. The evolution of the state is described in terms of dynamics by the motion of the points in the phase space. Obviously, the velocity of this motion depends only on the present state. The evolution is thus motion of the phase point. Our study will be essentially about the trajectory of this moving point in the phase space. One can look upon the decomposition of the phase space into trajectories as the phase-portraits of the system.

3.   An important breakthrough which Poincare could obtain was to limit the study of two-dimensional autonomous ode's to that of a line onto itself. So, a linear map and the like, need recapitulation. How can we define a system in terms of mapping in this context? An evolutionary system is defined by a mapping $f : M \rightarrow M$ sending a phase point x belonging to the phase space M, to a new phase point $f(x)$ of the same space. The space trajectory in this case consists of a sequence of points, $x, f(x), f(f(x)), \ldots$ which represent the state of the system. Poincare's map is another lead concept by Poincare, which plainly speaking, seeks to associate, to an initial point, i.e. a segment, with the next point of intersection of its trajectory with the segment. We shall take it up later, in details.

recapturing linear ordinary differential equations

3.1 A fresh look at fundamental properties

In the earlier chapters, we have talked about trajectories, phase-portraits etc. By trajectories, we have meant essentially solution curves and we have had, indeed portrayals of phases by plotting simply trajectories from initial states, covering usually the large part of $x-y$ plane. A trajectory, we should recall, does not give any position $\{x(t), y(t)\}$ at time t, rather it does, in a way, hide t's, whatever be this. We describe this by saying that the trajectory gives only the *qualitative* but not quantitative features. Further, in such contexts, we are concerned with points of equilibria. The region close to such points and also those far away from such points are those which determine the behaviour of this system. But we cannot proceed till we are in a position to know, pre-emptively whether *localities* or *globalities* of behaviour, if we agree to use such terms, exist; and whether these are unique or whether they are characterized by the dependencies such as continuity, discreteness etc. In this chapter, we would like to recapitulate the fundamental properties that ode's have in general, and what they have to have more, if locality or globality is to be reckoned. We do this spadework here in mathematical terms, with a view to developing the study of qualitative behaviour of solutions in subsequent chapters. Obviously, there are commonalities, which we simply state without proof; the new aspects are, of course, being attended to.

3.2 Statements

Given the equation $\dfrac{dx}{dt} = f(x,t) \cdots\cdots (1)$ and given the initial state at $t = t_0$, we take that the system is defined for $t > t_0$. Let us now state the conditions of its existence and uniqueness of the system given by (1) where $x(t_0) = x_0$. In the study of the quantitative behaviour of system, we consider local existence and uniqueness of the solution. Let us state, without proof, this in the form of the following theorem :

I. Theorem I

Let $f(x,t)$ be a piecewise continuous in t and satisfy the Lipschitz condition given by $\| f(x,t) - f(y,t) \| \le L \| x - y \| \cdots\cdots (2)$ (L is called Lipschitz constant) (unique parameter), such that $(x, y) \in B = \{ x \in R^n \mid \| x - x_0 \| \le r \}, t \in [t_0, t_1]$

Then there exists some $\delta > 0$ such that the system (1) with $x(t_0) = x_0$ has a unique solution over $[t_0, t_0 + \delta]$

3.3 Definitions

1. A function satisfying (2) is called Lipschitz in x.

    For simplicity, we consider the case when f depends on x only. The function $f(x)$ is said to be locally Lipschitz in a domain $D \subset R^n$ (open and connected set) if each point of D has a neighbourhood (nbd) D_0 such that f satisfies the condition (2) for all points in D_0 with some Lipschitz constant say L_0. We say that f is Lipschitz in a set W if it satisfies (2) for all points in W with some Lipschitz constant L_0.

2. A locally Lipschitz function in a domain D is not necessarily Lipschitz in D for the Lipschitz condition may not hold uniformly with the same constant L for all points in D. Nevertheless, in every compact (closed and bounded) sub-sets of D, a locally Lipschitz function in a domain D is Lipschitz.

3. A function $f(x)$ is said to be globally Lipschitz if it is Lipschitz on R^n.

Remark

The above definitions can also be extended to the function $f(x,t)$ provided the Lipschitz condition holds uniformly for all t in a given interval of time; $f(x,t)$ can then be called locally Lipschitz in (x,t) on $[a,b] \times D \varepsilon R \times R^n$ if each point $x \in D$ has a nbd. D_0 such that f satisfies (2) on $[a,b] \times D_0$, with the same Lipschitz constant L_0. We say that $f(x,t)$ is locally Lipschitz in x on $[t_0, \infty] \times D$, if it is locally Lipschitz in x on $[a,b] \times D$ for every compact interval $[a,b] \subset [t_0, \infty]$.

The function $f(x,t)$ is said to be Lipschitz on $[a,b] \times W$ if it satisfies (2) for all $t \in [a,b]$ and for all points in W with the same Lipschitz constant L.

In particular, if $f: R \to R$ then the Lipschitz condition can be written as $\dfrac{|f(x) - f(y)|}{|x - y|} \le L$. Geometrically this means that on a plot of $f(x)$ versus x, a straight line joining any two points of $f(x)$ cannot have a slope whose absolute value is greater than L. Therefore, a function $f(x)$ having an infinite slope at some point, is not locally Lipschitz at that point.

As an example, $f(x) = x^{\frac{1}{3}}$, it is not locally Lipschitz at $x = 0$ for $f'(x) = \dfrac{1}{3} x^{-\frac{2}{3}}$ which tends to ∞ as $x \to 0$. But $|f'(x)|$ is bounded over some interval, say k. If $f'(x)$ is bounded by a constant k over the interval then $f(x)$ is Lipschitz on the same interval when we take $k = L$ as the Lipschitz constant.

II.   Theorem II (Global existence and uniqueness)

Let $f(x,t)$ be piecewise continuous in t and let it satisfy $\|f(x,t)-f(y,t)\| \le L\|x-y\|$, where x and $y \in R^n, \forall\, t \in [t_0, t_1]$. Then the equation $\dfrac{dx}{dt} = f(x,t)$ with $x(t_0) = x_0$ has a unique solution over $[t_0, t_1]$.

III.   Theorem III

Let, $f(x,t)$ be piecewise continuous in t and locally Lipschitz in x for all $t \ge t_0$ and for all x in a domain $D \subset R^n$. Let W be a compact subset of D; $x_0 \in W$ is also supposed to be known; every solution of $\dot{x} = f(x,t), x(t_0) = x_0$ lies entirely in W. Then there is a unique solution that is defined for all $t \ge t_0$.

3.4 Some deductions

Some properties of locally and globally Lipschitz functions :

PROPERTY 1: Let two functions $f(x,t)$ and $\dfrac{\partial f(x,t)}{\partial x}$ be continuous on $[a,b] \times D$ for some domain $D \in R^n$ then f is locally Lipschitz in $[a,b] \times D$.

Proof: Let $x_0 \in D$. Let r be so small that the domain $D_0 = \{x \in R^n\,/\,\|x - x_0\| \le r\}$ is contained in D; the set D_0 is convex and compact . By continuity, $\dfrac{\partial f}{\partial x}$ is bounded on $[a,b] \times D_0$. Let L_0 be a bound for $\left\|\dfrac{\partial f}{\partial x}\right\|$ on $[a,b] \times D_0$. Therefore, by definition, f is Lipschitz in $[a,b] \times D_0$ with the Lipschitz constant L_0.

PROPERTY 2: If $f(x,t)$ and $\dfrac{\partial f(x,t)}{\partial x}$ are continuous in $[a,b] \times R^n$ then f is globally Lipschitz in x on $[a,b] \times R^n$. $\left[\dfrac{\partial f}{\partial x}\right]$ is uniformly bounded on $[a,b] \times R^n$.

Remark

Let us determine the Lipschitz constant

Let $f:[a,b]\times D\to R^n$ be continuous for some domain $D\in R^n$. It is also supposed that $\dfrac{\partial f}{\partial x}$ exists and is continuous on $[a,b]\times D$. If, for a convex set $W\in D$, there is a constant $L\geq 0$ s.t. $\left\|\dfrac{\partial f(x,t)}{\partial x}\right\|\leq L$ on $[a,b]\times W$. Then $\|f(x,t)-f(y,t)\|<\|x-y\|$ for all $t\in[a,b]$ and for all $x\in W, y\in W$.

This shows that we can calculate the Lipschitz constant if we know $\dfrac{\partial f(x,t)}{\partial x}$.

linear systems :
qualitative behaviour

As mentioned earlier, we continue with the study of linear systems along with some of its features so that some indications about the behaviour of non-linear systems become obvious. Poincare defined in 1885 'behaviour' in some contexts where notions of critical points of a system need to be considered. As a step in this direction, we have already touched upon briefly, the study of few trajectories associated with linear systems. The other allied concepts are 'node', 'centre', 'focus' and 'saddle point'. We introduce them first as a prelude to study the qualitative behaviour of linear systems.

Let us recall, for reasons of simplicity, problems involving two unknown functions $x(t)$ and $y(t)$ where both $\dfrac{dx}{dt}$ and $\dfrac{dy}{dt}$ are expressed in terms of x and y.

We describe a solution by plotting the locus of the point $\{x(t), y(t)\}$. We have come to know what trajectories are and we also know that the set of points occupied by a trajectory is the orbit or the trace. There is a subtle difference between an orbit and a trajectory in that the latter is associated with the specific parameter, say t. We shall see a bit later that the parameterisation provides the trajectory with an orientation, indicated by arrows in relevant figures. The plane associated with a differential equation is called *phase plane*. The solution curves given by $\{u(t), v(t)\}$ as t increases from $-\infty$ to $+\infty$ are, of course, the trajectories. If we have the equation, for example, $u'' + u = 0$, the phase plane orbits are circles with the origin at their centre and so we, here, get the associated parameter t distinguishing between an orbit and a trajectory.

The origin (0,0) in the phase plane is called *critical point* for the given equation. Let us now study critical points. These are obtained by putting $\dfrac{dx}{dt} = 0$ and $\dfrac{dy}{dt} = 0$. These are also called stationary points or points of equilibria. We begin with their naive descriptions followed by formal definitions accompanied, of course, by their geometrical representations.

4.1 Overview of Critical Points

For reasons of simplicity, we take the origin (0,0) as a critical point. We take this as an isolated initial point.

1. Centre

If (0,0) is a centre then surrounding it we have an infinite number of closed paths. These paths are close to (0,0) but it is not approached by any path as $t \to +\infty$ or $t \to -\infty$.

Definition : The isolated point $O(0,0)$ is called a *centre* if $\exists$ a nbd of (0,0) which contains a countably finite number of closed paths, each of which has (0,0) in its interior and which are such that the diameters of the paths approach zero as we move towards O but it is not approached by any path as $t \to +\infty$ or $t \to -\infty$ (See Fig. 4.1)

Fig. 4.1

Example : $\dfrac{dx}{dt} = y$

$$\dfrac{dy}{dt} = -x$$

$$\dfrac{dy}{dx} = \dfrac{-x}{y} \Rightarrow ydy + xdx = 0 \Rightarrow x^2 + y^2 = \text{constant}$$

$\therefore$ The path is a circle, *vide*, Fig. 4.1(a)

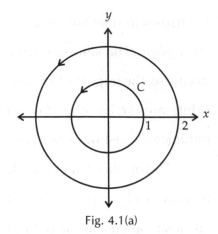

Fig. 4.1(a)

2. Saddle Point

Let O be a critical point having the following characteristics, *vide* Fig. 4.2:

(1)   it is approached by two half line paths AO and BO as $t \to +\infty$ and these two paths form the geometrical path AB.

(2)   it is approached by two half line paths CO and DO as $t \to -\infty$ and these two paths form the geometrical path CD.

(3)   in the four domains R_1, R_2, R_3, R_4 there are infinitely many semi-hyperbolas which approach O as $t \to +\infty$ or $t \to -\infty$

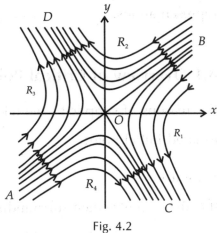

Fig. 4.2

Definition: The isolated critical point $O(0,0)$ is called a *saddle point (vortex point)* if $\exists$ a *nbd* in which the following conditions are satisfied:

(a)   there exist two paths which approach $O(0,0)$ from pairs of opposite directions as $t \to +\infty$ and $\exists$ two paths also approaching and entering $O(0,0)$ from opposite directions as $t \to -\infty$

(b)   in each of the four domains R_1, R_2, R_3, R_4 there are infinitely many paths (semi-hyperbolas).

It is thus a point which traces such a path which not only approaches O but does so in such a way that the lines through O tend to definite directions as $t \to +\infty$ or $t \to -\infty$. There are rectilinear paths AO, BO, CO, DO, as in Fig. 4.3.

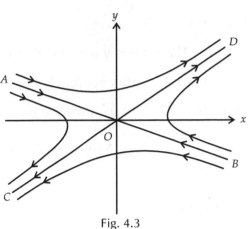

Fig. 4.3

3. Node

Definition : The isolated critical point $O(0, 0)$ is called a *node* if $\exists$ a nbd vide, Fig. 4.4 of (0,0) such that every point P in this nbd has the following properties :

(a) P is defined for all $t > t_o$ and for $t < t_o$, for some $t < t_o$.

(b) P approaches $O(0, 0)$ as $t \to +\infty$ or $t \to -\infty$.

(c)   all other paths look like parabolas with each of them approaching O, and with slopes approaching that of the line AB.

Example : $\dfrac{dx}{dt} = x$

$\dfrac{dy}{dt} = -x + 2y$

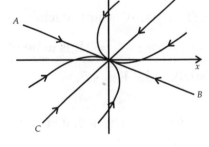

Fig. 4.4

Solution : $x = c_1 e^t$

$y = c_1 e^t + c_2 e^{2t}$

(i)   For $c_1 = 0$, $x = 0$, $y = c_2 e^{2t}$

Hence the paths are the positive y-axis or the negative y-axis according as $c_2 >$ or < 0. These paths approach and enter $O(0,0)$ as $t \to -\infty$.

(ii)   For $c_2 = 0$, $x = c_1 e^t$, $y = c_1 e^t$

∴ The path is $y = x$> or <0 according as c_1> or <0.

Both the paths approach and enter (0,0).

(iii)   If $c_1 \neq 0, c_2 \neq 0$, then we have

$y = x + \left(\dfrac{c_1}{c_2} \right) x^2$ which are parabolas arbitrarily close to

(0,0) without neither approaching (0,0) nor entering

(0,0)

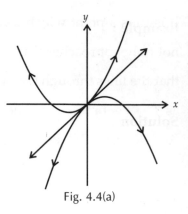

Fig. 4.4(a)

The slope of the tangent to the path through $(x, y) (\neq (0,0))$ is given by

$$\frac{dy}{dx} = \frac{-x + 2y}{x}$$

Solving this, we find $y = x + cx^2$

Hence, by definition, the critical point is a node, as shown in Fig. 4.4(a)

4. Spiral Point (Focal Point or Focus)

Such a point is approached in a spiral like manner by infinite families of paths as $t \to +\infty$ or $t \to -\infty$. It is to be observed that such paths approach $O(0,0)$ but do not enter $O(0,0)$, vide, Fig. 4.5.

Definition : The isolated critical point $O(0,0)$ is said to be a *spiral point* if ∃ a nbd of $O(0,0)$ such that any point P in this nbd has the following properties:

(a) P is defined for all $t > t_0$ and also for some $t < t_0$.

(b) P approaches $O(0,0)$ as $t \to +\infty$ or $t \to -\infty$

(c) P approaches $O(0,0)$ in a spiral like manner winding round (0,0) for an infinite number of times as $t \to +\infty$ or $t \to -\infty$.

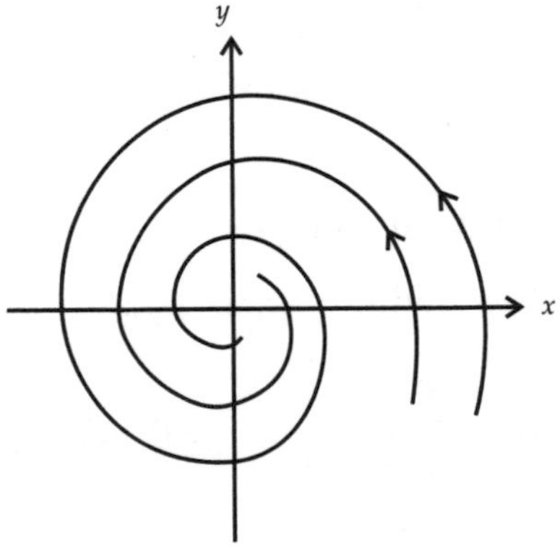

Fig. 4.5

Example : $\dfrac{dx}{dt} = ax - y$

$\dfrac{dy}{dt} = x + ay$

Solution : $x = r\cos\theta,\ y = r\sin\theta$

$r^2 = x^2 + y^2$

$r\dot{r} = x\dot{x} + y\dot{y}$

$r^2\dot{\theta} = (x\dot{y} - y\dot{x})$

$\therefore\ \dfrac{dr}{d\theta} = ar \Rightarrow \dfrac{dr}{r} = a\,d\theta$

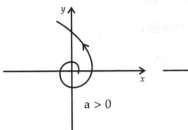

a > 0   a < 0

Fig. 4.5(a)   Fig. 4.5(b)

$\Rightarrow r = ce^{a\theta}$ where c is a constant

which are spirals as shown in Figs. 4.5(a) & 4.5(b)

Remarks

1. Having described what a critical point is all about, let us now proceed to analyse the behaviour of linear systems by using their phase-portraits of a given system, even topologically. In fact, the problem is yet to be solved for

$\dfrac{dx}{dt} = P(x, y)$

$\dfrac{dy}{dt} = Q(x, y)$

where P and Q are polynomials of degree two, One may recall that this is the problem of David Hilbert whose work on identification of unsolvable problems is a classic one, referred to in mathematical antiquity.

2. In what follows, let us seek in different ways what insight can be obtained about linear systems in respect of their qualitative behaviour. A question, why we should keep on harping on linear systems, non-linearity being our objective may arise.

Another query: is there any linkage between behaviours of linear and nonlinear systems? In general, not. But amidst points of equilibria (or critical points), some linkages may be discernible in some situations or examples. Let us now see if the idea of characteristic equations, eigen values etc. be of use. In this regard, we shall associate the critical roots described above with the nature of eigen values; we may use words 'local', 'global' or even 'stable', 'unstable', without being too technical about them, which we shall do later.

4.2 Qualitative behaviour of linear systems

Let us begin with a simple system given by

$$\left.\begin{array}{l} \dfrac{dx}{dt} = P(x,y) \\[3mm] \dfrac{dy}{dt} = Q(x,y) \end{array}\right\} \tag{1}$$

We take (x_0, y_0) a point in the phase plane, as the equilibrium or critical (or stationary/steady/singular) point so that $P(x_0, y_0) = 0$, $Q(x_0, y_0) = 0$.

In particular, (1) gives rise to, for linear systems

$$\left.\begin{array}{l} \dfrac{dx}{dt} = a_{11}x + a_{12}y \\[3mm] \dfrac{dy}{dt} = a_{21}x + a_{22}y \end{array}\right\} \tag{2}$$

where a_{ij} $(i, j = 1, 2)$ are constants. Obviously (0, 0) is the critical point of (2).

We can write (2) as

$$\dot{\vec{x}} = A\vec{x} \tag{3}$$

where A is a 2×2 real matrix.

In order to study the nature of trajectories of (2) in the nbd of (0,0), we look for the solution of (2) in the form

$$x = \alpha_1 e^{\lambda t}, \ y = \alpha_2 e^{\lambda t} \tag{4}$$

where λ is to be obtained from the characteristic equation

$$\begin{vmatrix} a_{11} - \lambda & a_{12} \\ a_{21} & a_{22} - \lambda \end{vmatrix} \tag{5}$$

Given an initial state $\vec{x}_0$, we can write the solution of (3) as

$$x(t) = M \exp(J_r t) M^{-1} x_0$$

where J_r is the real Jordan form of A and M is a real nonsingular matrix such that

$$M^{-1} A M = J_r$$

Let (λ_1, λ_2) be the roots of the characteristic equation given by (5). We now distinguish the roots or the eigen values.

From (4), we have

$$x(t) = x_0 e^{\lambda_1 t}, \ y(t) = y_0 e^{\lambda_2 t} \tag{6}$$

Eliminating t between these equations we have

$$y = c x^{\lambda_2 / \lambda_1} \tag{7}$$

where $c = \dfrac{y_0}{(x_0)^{\lambda_2 / \lambda_1}}$

The family of curves that emanate from (7) is the phase portrait of the system, assuming c to take up arbitrary values in the x-y plane. The nature of the phase portrait, particularly its slope, obviously depends on the signs of λ_1 and λ_2. We consider the following cases depending on the signs of λ_1 and λ_2.

Case I : $\lambda_1 < 0, \lambda_2 < 0$

Both x and $y \to 0$ as $t \to \infty$.

Let us take, without any loss of generality, $\lambda_2 < \lambda_1 \cdot e^{\lambda_1 t} \to 0$, being faster than $e^{\lambda_2 t} \to 0$, we may call for convenience, λ_2 as the fast root while λ_1, the slow root. The trajectory tends to (0,0) of the x-y plane along the curve (7) which has a ratio $\dfrac{\lambda_2}{\lambda_1}$, its slope being given by

$$\frac{dy}{dx} = c \frac{\lambda_2}{\lambda_1} x^{\left[\left(\frac{\lambda_2}{\lambda_1}\right) - 1\right]} \tag{8}$$

Since $\left[\dfrac{\lambda_2}{\lambda_1} - 1\right] > 0$, the slope $\to 0$ as $|x| \to 0$ and the slope $\to \infty$ as $|x| \to \infty$. So, the trajectory while moving towards the origin becomes tangent to x-axis; but moving towards infinity, it becomes parallel to the y-axis.

The typical portrait is given in Fig. 4.6:

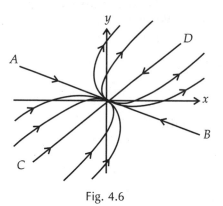

Fig. 4.6

The critical point $O(0,0)$ is the node, described earlier but it can be said to be a stable node because of its approach towards the point.

On the other hand, if λ_1 and λ_2 are positive, trajectory will be basically the same but directions would be reversed, for both $e^{\lambda_1 t}$ and $e^{\lambda_2 t} \to 0$ as $t \to -\infty$.

Case II : $\lambda_1 > 0$ and $\lambda_2 \leq 0$ i.e. $\lambda_2 > \lambda_1 > 0$

Then $e^{\lambda_1 t} \to \infty$ while $e^{\lambda_2 t} \to 0$ as $t \to \infty$.

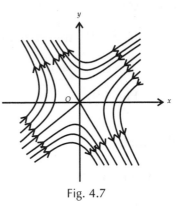

Equation (7) has then a negative exponent. The trajectories are shown in Fig. 4.7

The two stable trajectories are those which approach the origin as $t \to \infty$ while the other two trajectories can be shown to be unstable. The equilibrium point is thus a saddle.

Fig. 4.7

Case III : $\lambda_1 = 0$ and $\lambda_2 \geq 0$

Then $x = x_0, y = y_0 e^{\lambda_2 t}$

Now $e^{\lambda_2 t} \to \infty$ or $\to 0$ according as $\lambda_2 >$ or < 0, as $t \to \infty$

Hence, in totality, the critical point is either unstable or stable (not in the way we have talked about earlier).

Case IV : Complex conjugate roots: $\lambda_{1,2} = \alpha \pm i\beta$

$$\therefore \quad \begin{cases} x = x_0 e^{(\alpha + i\beta)t} \\ y = y_0 e^{(\alpha - i\beta)t} \end{cases}$$

$$\therefore \quad x = x_0 e^{\alpha t} \left(\cos \beta t + i \sin \beta t \right)$$

$$y = y_0 e^{\alpha t} \left(\cos \beta t - i \sin \beta t \right)$$

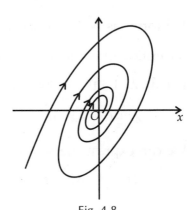

If $\alpha > 0$ and $\beta \neq 0$, the critical point is unstable, $\left(e^{\alpha t} \to \infty, \cos \beta t \to \infty \right)$

On the other hand, if $\alpha < 0$ and $\beta \neq 0$ the critical point is a stable focus.

Fig. 4.8

If $\alpha > 0$ and $\beta \neq 0$, the critical point is stable and is clearly a centre. The portion, in general, is a spiral, as shown in Fig. 4.8

Case V : The roots are multiple : $\lambda_1 = \lambda_2 = \lambda \neq 0$.

If $\lambda < 0$, the critical point is a node (stable) and for $\lambda > 0$, it is the opposite i.e. an unstable node. (See Fig. 4.9)

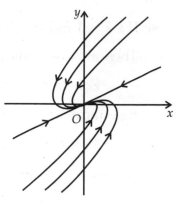

Fig. 4.9

Remark

We have mentioned the nature of points *vis a vis* the nature of roots of the equilibrium. By using the reference to Jordan's form J_r of A and other requirements $\left(e.g.\, M^{-1}\, AM = J_r\right)$, we could have mentioned eigen values, and the like for describing the critical roots and we could have had accordingly phase portraits, to which we shall return, with some in-depth treatment on the eigen values.

4.3 More about qualitative behaviour of linear systems (around a critical point) : Phase-portraits from a different approach

We can represent any (two dimensional) linear system by $\dot{x} = Ax$ $\qquad$ (1)

where $x = \begin{bmatrix} x_1 \\ x_2 \end{bmatrix}$, and $A = \begin{bmatrix} a_{11} & a_{12} \\ a_{21} & a_{22} \end{bmatrix}$.

We form, as before, the characteristic equation in λ where $\bar{x} = \bar{x}_r\, e^{\lambda t}$. We take origin as the critical or equilibrium point around which we shall study the behaviour of the system. Let λ_1, λ_2 be the roots of the characteristic equation (i.e. its eigen values) given by

$$\lambda^2 - (a_{11} + a_{22})\lambda + (a_{11}a_{22} - a_{21}a_{12}) = 0.$$

We can express the solution of (1), as mentioned earlier, in the form given by

$$x(t) = M \exp(J_r t) M^{-1} x_0 \qquad (2)$$

where J_r is the real form of A and M is a real nonsingular matrix such that

$$M^{-1}AM = J_r.$$

In particular, for two dimensions, depending on the nature of the eigen values of A, the real form of J_r can be of three types : $\begin{bmatrix} \lambda_1 & 0 \\ 0 & \lambda_2 \end{bmatrix}$, $\begin{bmatrix} \lambda & k \\ 0 & \lambda \end{bmatrix}$ and $\begin{bmatrix} \alpha & -\beta \\ \beta & \alpha \end{bmatrix}$ where k is either zero or one. J_r is the Jordan form.

If we now take $M = [v_1 \, v_2]$ where v_1 and v_2 are the real eigen vectors associated with λ_1, λ_2 and we make a change of coordinates $z = M^{-1}x$, we have the set of differential equations as $\dot{z}_1 = \lambda_1 z_1$, $\dot{z}_2 = \lambda_2 z_2$.

In fact, $z_1(t) = z_{10}e^{\lambda_1 t}$, $z_2(t) = z_{20}e^{\lambda_2 t}$.

where z_{10} and z_{20} are the initial values.

Eliminating, $z_2 = cz_1 \dfrac{\lambda_2}{\lambda_1}$ (3)

where $c = \dfrac{z_{20}}{(z_{10})^{\lambda_2 / \lambda_1}}$

The shape of phase portrait depends on the signs of λ_1 and λ_2.

Case I : Eigen values distinct and real

Let us consider first the case when both the eigen values are negative i.e $\lambda_2 < \lambda_1 < 0$.

Both the exponential terms $e^{\lambda_1 t}$ and $e^{\lambda_2 t}$ tend to zero as $t \to +\infty$, but since $\lambda_2 < \lambda_1$ and tends to zero faster than $e^{\lambda_1 t}$, we say, as before, that λ_2 is the fast eigen value and λ_1 is the slow eigen value. v_2 is similarly called the fast eigen vector and v_1 is slow eigen vector.

In $z_1 - z_2$ plane, the trajectory tends to the origin of the $z_1 - z_2$ plane along the curve given by (3).

Now $\dfrac{dz_2}{dz_1} = c \dfrac{\lambda_2}{\lambda_1} z_1 \left(\dfrac{\lambda_2}{\lambda_1} - 1 \right)$

Since $\left(\dfrac{\lambda_2}{\lambda_1} - 1 \right)$ is +ve, the slope of the curve approaches 0 as $|z_1|$ tends to 0 and approaches ∞, as $|z_1|$ tends to infinity.

As the trajectory approaches the origin, it becomes tangent to the $|z_1|$ axis and as it approaches infinity, it becomes parallel to the z_2 axis. These observations enable us to sketch the typical family of trajectories of (3), as shown in Fig. 4.10.

Going back to the $x_1 - x_2$ coordinates, the family of the trajectories are as shown in Fig. 4.11. In the $x_1 - x_2$ plane the equilibrium point $x = 0$ is a stable node.

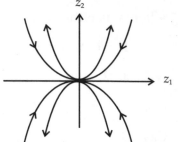

Fig. 4.10

When λ_1 and λ_2 are both positive, the phase portrait will be the same except that the directions will be reversed, since the exponential terms $e^{\lambda_1 t}$ and $e^{\lambda_2 t}$ grow exponentially as t increases. The corresponding equilibrium point $x = 0$ for $\lambda_2 > \lambda_1 > 0$ then becomes unstable node.

With eigen values of opposite signs $(\lambda_2 < 0 < \lambda_1)$ $e^{\lambda_1 t} \to \infty$ and $e^{\lambda_2 t} \to 0$ as $t \to \infty$.

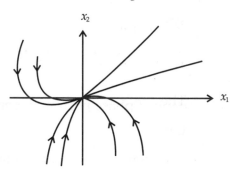

Fig. 4.11

But we call λ_2, a stable eigen value and λ_1, an unstable eigen value. The exponent $\dfrac{\lambda_2}{\lambda_1}$ in equation (3) is –ve, the trajectories have hyperbolic sheets which become tangent to the z_1 axis as $|z_1| \to \infty$ and become tangent to the z_2 axis as $|z_1| \to 0$. The two trajectories along the z_2 axis are stable trajectories, since they approach the origin as $t \to \infty$ while the two trajectories along the z_1 axis are unstable trajectories since they approach to ∞ as $t \to \infty$. The equilibrium point is a saddle point.

Fig. 14.12(a) and 14.12(b) are phase orbits of a saddle point in (modal) co-ordinates (z_1, z_2) and in original coordinates (x_1, x_2)

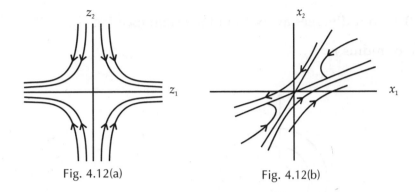

Fig. 4.12(a)   Fig. 4.12(b)

Case II

Complex eigen values : $\lambda_{1,2} = \alpha \pm i\beta$; in terms of modal coordinates z_1 and z_2, the system is given by

$$\left.\begin{array}{l} \dot{z}_1 = \alpha z_1 - \beta z_2 \\ \dot{z}_2 = \beta z_1 + \alpha z_2 \end{array}\right\} \tag{4}$$

The corresponding transformation given by $z = M^{-1}x$

Let $z_1 = r\cos\theta$, $z_2 = r\sin\theta$

$$r = \sqrt{z_1^2 + z_2^2}, \qquad \theta = \tan^{-1}\frac{z_2}{z_1}$$

$$r\dot{r} = z_1\dot{z}_1 + z_2\dot{z}_2, \qquad r^2\dot{\theta} = \dot{z}_1 z_2 - \dot{z}_2 z_1$$

Substituting in (4) $\dot{r} = \alpha r$

$$\dot{\theta} = \beta \tag{5}$$

The solution of (5) is $r(t) = r_0 e^{\alpha t}$

$$\theta(t) = \theta_0 + \beta t$$

(where r_0 and θ_0 are values of r and θ at $t = 0$)

which is a logarithmic spiral in z_1–z_2 plane.

Depending on the values of α, the trajectories take different forms.

If $\alpha < 0$ then trajectory converges towards origin as shown in Fig. 4.13. If

$\alpha > 0$ then it diverges away from the origin (See Fig. 4.14). If $\alpha = 0$ trajectory is a circle of radius r_0.

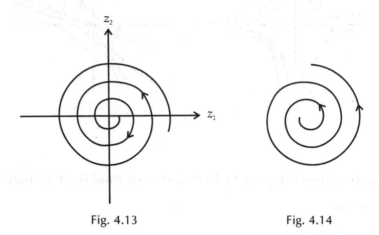

Fig. 4.13   Fig. 4.14

Fig. 4.15(a), 4.15(b), 4.15(c) are the trajectories in the x_1–x_2 plane. The equilibrium point $x=0$ is called a stable focus if $\alpha < 0$, unstable focus if $\alpha > 0$ and a centre if $\alpha = 0$.

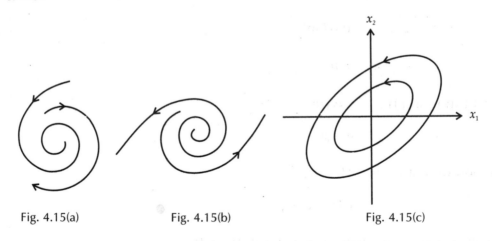

Fig. 4.15(a)   Fig. 4.15(b)   Fig. 4.15(c)

Case III

Non zero multiple eigen values

$$\lambda_1 = \lambda_2 = \lambda \, (\neq 0)$$

In terms of change of coordinates given by

$$\left.\begin{array}{l} \dot{z}_1 = \lambda z_1 + k z_2 \\ \dot{z}_2 = \lambda z_2 \end{array}\right\} \qquad (6)$$

where k is a constant. Its solution is given by

$$\left.\begin{array}{l} z_1(t) = e^{\lambda t}\left(z_{10} + z_{20} t\right) \\ z_2(t) = e^{\lambda t} z_{20} \end{array}\right\} \qquad (7)$$

where z_{10} and z_{20} are initial values of z_1 and z_2.

Now eliminating t, we get the trajectory as

$$\frac{z_1}{z_2} = \left[\frac{z_{10}}{z_{20}} + \frac{k}{\lambda}\log\left(\frac{z_2}{z_{20}}\right)\right] \qquad (8)$$

If $k \neq 0$, then we have the following phase portraits for $\lambda < 0$ and for $\lambda > 0$, vide, Fig. 4.16(a) and 4.16(b)

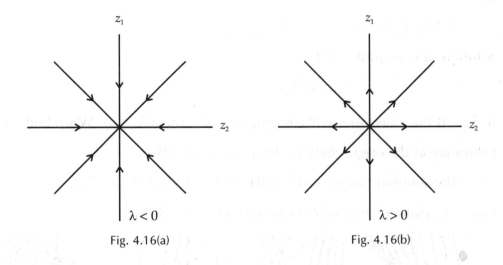

Fig. 4.16(a)   Fig. 4.16(b)

These are portraits similar to those for a stable node. The equilibrium point $x=0$ is called a stable node is $\lambda < 0$ and unstable node is $\lambda > 0$. It is to be noted that the phase portraits do not have the asymptotic behaviour. [See Figs. 4.17(a); (b) and (c)]

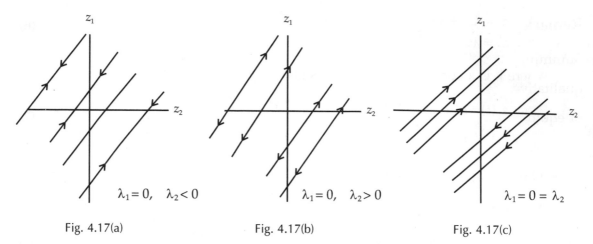

Fig. 4.17(a)   Fig. 4.17(b)   Fig. 4.17(c)

Case IV : One or both the eigen values are zero.

Where one or both eigen values of A are zero, the phase portraits are said to be degenerate when $\lambda_1 = 0$, $\lambda_2 \neq 0$. The equation in the modal coordinates are given by

$$z_1 = 0 \, , \; z_2 = \lambda_2 z_2$$

Solutions are given by $z_1(t) = z_{10}$

$$z_2(t) = z_{20}e^{\lambda_2 t}$$

If $\lambda_2 < 0$ the trajectories will converge and diverge if $\lambda_2 > 0$. When both the eigen values are at the origin, then we have $\dot{z} = z_2$, $\dot{z}_2 = 0$.

The solutions are given by $z_1(t) = z_{10} + z_{20}t$, $z_2(t) = z_{20}$.

In $x_1 - x_2$ plane phase portraits are given by Figs. 4.18.

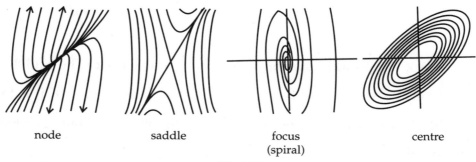

node   saddle   focus   centre
                                                  (spiral)

Fig. 4.18

Remark

Summing up, we see that the system can have, qualitatively six portraits, associated with different types of equilibrium:

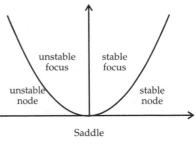

Fig. 4.19

Stable nodes, unstable nodes, saddle point, stable focus (spiral), unstable focus (spiral), centre.

So, we can have the following write-up as the eigen values (roots of the characteristic equation) λ_1, λ_2 along with the nature of critical (equilibrium) points (See Fig. 4.19).

I. Roots λ_1, λ_2 real and distinct

(a) $\lambda_1 < 0$ and $\lambda_2 < 0$; the critical point is asymptotically stable (a stable nodal point)

(b) $\lambda_1 > 0$ and $\lambda_2 > 0$; the critical point is unstable (an unstable nodal point)

(c) $\lambda_1 > 0$ and $\lambda_2 < 0$; the critical point is unstable (a saddle point)

(d) $\lambda_1 = 0$ and $\lambda_2 > 0$; the critical point is unstable

(e) $\lambda_1 = 0$ and $\lambda_2 < 0$; the critical point is stable but not asymptotically.

II. Roots are complex: $\lambda_1 = \alpha + i\beta,\ \lambda_2 = \alpha - i\beta$

(a) $\alpha < 0$ and $\beta \neq 0$; the critical point is asymptotically stable

(a stable focal or spiral point)

(b) $\alpha > 0$ and $\beta \neq 0$; the critical point is unstable (an unstable focal or spiral point)

(c) $\alpha = 0$ and $\beta \neq 0$; the critical point is stable (a vortex point) but not asymptotically

III. Roots multiple: $\lambda_1 = \lambda_2$

(a) $\lambda_1 = \lambda_2 < 0$; the critical point is asymptotically stable (a stable nodal point)

(b) $\lambda_1 = \lambda_2 > 0$; the critical point is unstable (an unstable nodal point)

(c) $\lambda_1 = \lambda_2 = 0$; the critical point is stable.

One may also remark that there may be a case where all the points in the phase-plane are stable critical points.

4.4 Illustrative Examples

Example 1

Discuss the behaviour of $\ddot{x} + x = 0$

$$\therefore \ \dot{y} = -x$$

$$\dot{y} = -x$$

Comparing this with the form $\dot{x} = a_{11}x + a_{12}y$

$$\dot{y} = a_{21}x + a_{22}y$$

we get $a_{11} = 0, a_{12} = 1, a_{21} = -1, a_{22} = 0$

$$\begin{vmatrix} a_{11} - \lambda & a_{12} \\ a_{21} & a_{22} - \lambda \end{vmatrix} = \begin{vmatrix} -\lambda & 1 \\ -1 & -\lambda \end{vmatrix} = 0$$

$$\Rightarrow \lambda^2 + 1 = 0 \ \Rightarrow \lambda = \pm i$$

Then the roots are purely imaginary; hence the critical point is stable but not asymptotically (a vortex point)

Example 2

Discuss the behaviour of $\dot{x} = 4y - x$

$$\dot{y} = -9x + y$$

We get $a_{11} = -1, a_{12} = 4, a_{21} = -9, a_{22} = 1$

$$\begin{vmatrix} -1 - \lambda & 4 \\ -9 & 1 - \lambda \end{vmatrix} = 0$$

$$\Rightarrow -(1+\lambda)(1-\lambda)+36=0$$

$$\Rightarrow -(1-\lambda^2)+36=0$$

$$\Rightarrow \lambda^2+35=0$$

$$\Rightarrow \lambda=\pm\sqrt{35}i$$

Here the roots are purely imaginary; hence critical point is stable but not asymptotically (vortex point).

Example 3

Investigate the behaviour of $\dot{x}=x-2y$
$$\dot{y}=-3x+2y$$

We get $a_{11}=-1,\ a_{12}=-2,\ a_{21}=-3,\ a_{22}=2$

$$\begin{vmatrix} -1-\lambda & -2 \\ -3 & 2-\lambda \end{vmatrix}=0$$

$$\Rightarrow (1-\lambda)(2-\lambda)-6=0$$

$$\Rightarrow 2-3\lambda+\lambda^2-6=0$$

$$\Rightarrow \lambda^2-3\lambda-4=0$$

$$\Rightarrow \lambda^2-4\lambda+\lambda-4=0$$

$$\Rightarrow (\lambda+1)(\lambda-4)=0$$

$$\Rightarrow \lambda=-1,\ 4$$

The roots are real and distinct but are of opposite signs. Hence critical point is unstable, and a saddle point.

Example 4

For what values of parameter α the system $\quad \dot{x} = y$,

$$\dot{y} = (\alpha - 1)x - \alpha y \quad \text{is stable ?}$$

Here, $a_{11} = 0$, $a_{12} = 1$, $a_{21} = \alpha - 1$, $a_{22} = -\alpha$

$$\begin{vmatrix} -\lambda & 1 \\ \alpha - 1 & -\alpha - \lambda \end{vmatrix} = 0$$

$$\Rightarrow \lambda(\alpha + \lambda) - (\alpha - 1) = 0$$

$$\Rightarrow \lambda^2 + \alpha\lambda - (\alpha - 1) = 0$$

$$\Rightarrow \lambda^2 = \frac{-\alpha \pm \sqrt{\alpha^2 + 4(\alpha - 1)}}{2} = \frac{-\alpha \pm \sqrt{\alpha^2 + 4\alpha + 4 - 8}}{2}$$

$$= \frac{-\alpha \pm \sqrt{(\alpha + 2)^2 - 8}}{2}$$

$$\lambda_1 = \frac{-\alpha + \sqrt{(\alpha + 2)^2 - 8}}{2}, \lambda_2 = \frac{-\alpha - \sqrt{(\alpha + 2)^2 - 8}}{2} \quad \text{or}$$

$$\lambda_1 = \frac{-\alpha + \sqrt{\alpha^2 - 4(1 - \alpha)^2}}{2}, \lambda_2 = \frac{-\alpha - \sqrt{\alpha^2 - 4(1 - \alpha)^2}}{2}$$

If λ_1 and λ_2 are real then

$$(\alpha + 2)^2 - 8 > 0 \quad \text{or} \quad \alpha^2 + 4(\alpha - 1) > 0 \Rightarrow \alpha^2 > 4(\alpha - 1)$$

If $\alpha = 1$, then λ_1 and λ_2 are real. But $\lambda_1 = 0, \lambda_2 = -1 < 0$

Hence the solution is stable but not asymptotically.

If $\alpha = 0$, then λ_1 and λ_2 are purely imaginary; then the solution is stable but not asymptotically.

If $0 < \alpha < 1$, then $\alpha > 0$, and $1-\alpha > 0$ then $\lambda_1 + \lambda_2 = -\alpha < 0$ and $\lambda_1 \lambda_2 = 1 - \alpha > 0$

$\therefore \quad \lambda_1 < 0, \lambda_2 < 0$, the solution is asymptotically stable.

In other cases, the solutions are unstable.

Exercise

1. Let us conceive of a critical point being approached and also entered by a path as $t \to \infty$ (or as $t \to -\infty$) if the four half-line paths through origin make up the line AB and CD. Let there be paths, which look like parts of parabolas approaching the critical point with slope approaching that of line AB. Draw the sketch.

2. Let us think of the critical point approached and entered by two half-line paths as $t \to +\infty$ and two similar half-line paths as $t \to -\infty$. Let these paths lie on two lines AB and CD. How many regions are there between the four line-line paths? Let each of these regions contain a family of paths which look like (rectangular) hyperbolas; they do not approach the critical point as $t \to \infty$ but are asymptotic to one or another half-line paths; as $t \to +\infty$ or $t \to -\infty$. Draw a sketch on the lines described.

3. Discuss the behaviour of critical point $(0,0)$ for the following equations —

    (i) $\dot{x} = 4y - x$; $\dot{y} = -9x + y$

    (ii) $\dot{x} = x - 2y$; $\dot{y} = 2y - 3x$

    (iii) $\dot{x} = x - y$; $\dot{y} = 2x + 3y$

    (iv) $\dot{x} = -2x + y$; $\dot{y} = -x - 4y$

4. Classify the critical point of each of the systems

    (a) $\dfrac{dx}{dt} = 2x + 4y$; $\dfrac{dy}{dt} = x + 3y$

    (b) $\dfrac{dx}{dt} = -3x + 2y$; $\dfrac{dy}{dt} = -3x + 4y$

5. Establish the nature of the critical point (0,0) from each of the systems

   (a) $\dfrac{dx}{dt} = x - y$; $\dfrac{dy}{dt} = 2x + 3y$

   (b) $\dfrac{dx}{dt} = 4y - x$; $\dfrac{dy}{dt} = -4x + y$

   (c) $\dfrac{dx}{dt} = x - 2y$; $\dfrac{dy}{dt} = 2y - 3x$

6. For what values of the parameter α is the system $\dot{x} = \alpha x + y$, $\dot{y} = -x$ stable?

7. In the plane of parameters α and β, find the regions where the zero solution of the system

$$\frac{dx}{dt} = \alpha x + (\beta - 2\alpha\beta - 1)y ; \qquad \frac{dy}{dt} = x - \beta y \quad \text{is stable.}$$

8. What sort of critical point do you have if it is approached in a spiral-like manner by a family of paths that wind around it in an infinite number of times as $t \to +\infty$ (or as $t \to -\infty$)?

   Obtain the differential equation of the paths. Sketch a few of the paths. How do they behave as $t \to +\infty$ (or as $t \to -\infty$)? What can you say, from such behaviour patterns, about the stability or otherwise of the critical point?

9. Does the differential equation $\dfrac{d^2x}{dt^2} = 2x^3$ have a phase-portrait? What is the nature of the critical point in regard to its stability or otherwise? Where is it?

10. Discuss the behaviour of the critical point of the system

$$\frac{dx}{dt} = -x, \qquad \frac{dy}{dt} = -2y$$

Are these same as those of the system

$$\frac{dx}{dt} = 4y ; \qquad \frac{dy}{dt} = -x \quad ?$$

Do they differ? If so, how?

11. Solve for x and y, in general terms, for the system

$$\frac{dx}{dt} = x, \qquad \frac{dy}{dt} = -x + 2y$$

What is the critical point of the system?

Study the behaviour of the system around the critical point. Draw a sketch of the paths for all possible cases. What is the nature of the critical point?

Does the slope of the tangent to the path through (x, y) indicate anything new about the solution curve?

12. Find the general solution of the system

$$\frac{dx}{dt} = 4y, \qquad \frac{dy}{dt} = -x$$

stability studies

Nonlinear dynamics if it is to reflect dynamical processes or features, can ill afford to miss study of stability or otherwise of systems. The concept of stability is in many ways natural; complexity is with what the nonlinear phenomena in nature abound and stability is, in a way, a mathematical variant, preferred to for in-depth studies. In the previous chapters, we have somewhat loosely made adjectival use of the term, 'stable', without, of course, erring about it or being too technical about it. Now we study this with a bit of sophistication.

The concept of stability or otherwise, centres around the study of equilibrium of critical (or stationary) points that we have considered. We also know how critical is the role of these points in differential equations and their applications in a variety of systems, physical, social, biological, ecological etc. Naively speaking, we can speak of equilibrium to be stable if solutions in the nbd do not move away for all future time. It is difficult to clinch a *state* exactly but only approximately in order that an equilibrium is meaningful. Most often, we consider the notion of stability in the sense of the Russian mathematician

Alexander Mikhailovich Liapunov (often written Lyapunov) in his celebrated work 'Theory of Motion Stability' (1892) after Poincare. Liapunov drew upon energy, an important concept of dynamics, as this motivated for the choice of mathematical entities. Let us begin with formal definitions of stability and its types.

5.1 Definitions

Definition 1

Let $\bar{x} \in W$ be an equilibrium of the differential equation

$$\dot{x} = f(x) \tag{1}$$

where $f : W \to E$ is a C^1 map from an open set W of the vector space E into E. Then $\bar{x}$ is a *stable* equilibrium if for every neighbourhood (nbd) S of $\bar{x}$ in W, there is an nbd S' of $\bar{x}$ in S such that every solution $x(t)$ with $x(0)$ in S' is defined and in S for all $t>0$, as shown in Fig. 5.1.

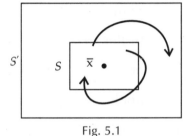

Fig. 5.1

Definition 2

If, besides the properties in Definition 1, if we add

$\lim_{t \to \infty} x(t) = \bar{x}$, then $\bar{x}$ is *asymptotically stable*, as shown in Fig. 5.2

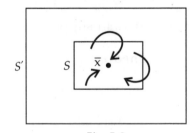

Fig. 5.2

Definition 3

An equilibrium $\bar{x}$ that is not stable is called *unstable*. This implies that there is a nbd S of $\bar{x}$, such that for every nbd S' of $\bar{x}$, there is at least one solution $x(t)$ starting at $x(0) \in S'$ that does not lie entirely in S, as shown in Fig. 5.3

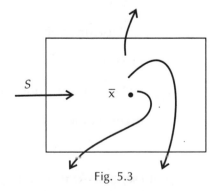

Fig. 5.3

Remarks

1. An equilibrium which is asymptotically stable is, of course, stable. We call this a *sink*. But an equilibrium that is stable but not asymptotically stable for the equation.

    $$\dot{x} = Ax$$

    is the origin and, as we have seen earlier, A has purely imaginary eigen values. This is shown in Fig. 5.4

    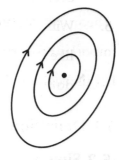

    Fig. 5.4

2. Unlike a sink, a *source* is an example of an unstable equilibrium, to which we shall return later.

3. In Remark (1) we have an outstanding example, which can be shown to be a sink or source, even if there be a very small (linear) disturbance to this so as to have a nonlinear character (often designated nonlinear harmonic oscillator)

4. In view of the above, can we explore for an equilibrium point to be either unstable or asymptotically stable? Yes, it is possible for a hyperbolic equilibrium point. What's that? In support of this, we state without proof, following theorem:

    Theorem

    Let $W \subset E$ be an open set and let $f : W \to E$ to be continuously differentiable. Let $f(\bar{x}) = 0$ and $\bar{x}$ to be the stable equilibrium point of the equation $\dot{x} = f(x)$.

    Then, no eigen value of $Df(x)$ has positive real part. We can now say that an equilibrium point $\bar{x}$ is *hyperbolic* if the derivative $Df(x)$ has no eigen value with zero real part.

    As a sequel, one can raise questions about the behaviour of equilibrium if the eigen values of $Df(x)$ have nonzero real parts. It is to be noted, at this stage, that if these real parts are all negative, the hyperbolic equilibrium point $\bar{x}$ is, of course, a sink; if they happen to be all positive, $\bar{x}$ is called a source. If both signs occur, $\bar{x}$ is a saddle point which is unstable, because of the above theorem.

5.   With the above definitions, broadly in general terms, and remarks, as well, we would like to take up studies on behaviour of systems, found as Liapunov's ideas. Let us do more necessary preliminaries for the purpose.

5.2 Simple types of equilibrium

Let us have, as before, consider the system

$$
\left.
\begin{aligned}
\frac{dx}{dt} &= P(x,y) \\
\frac{dy}{dt} &= Q(x,y)
\end{aligned}
\right\}
\tag{1}
$$

Now $P(x,y)$ and $Q(x,y)$ have the same meanings, as on earlier occasions, with (0,0) as its critical point. Let Ω be any region with (0,0) as the isolated critical point. Let C be a path of (1). Let us have

$$
\left.
\begin{aligned}
x &= f(t) \\
y &= g(t)
\end{aligned}
\right\}
\tag{2}
$$

as the parametric representation of the solution of (1).

Let $D = \sqrt{f^2(t) + g^2(t)}$ be the distance between the critical point (0,0) and any point R on the path C. The critical point (0,0) is called stable if given a $\varepsilon > 0$, $\exists$ number δ, such that for every path C for which, $D(t_0) < \delta$, for some $t = t_0$, then $D(t) < \varepsilon$.

$D(t_0) < \delta$ means at $t = t_0$, the point R lies within the circle of radius δ with (0,0) as centre and the case with $D(t) < \varepsilon$, means that the point R lies on the circle of radius ε

that is, the stability of (0,0) means that every path like C which is inside the circle k_1 at $t = t_0$ will continue to be inside the circle k_2 of radius ε for $t > t_0$. In other words, every path C stays close to (0,0), as we want it to be and is well within the distance ε after it gets close enough.

An isolated critical point (0,0) of the system (1) is said to be asymptotically stable

(i)   if it is stable

(ii)   if $\exists$ a number $\delta > 0$ s.t. $D(t_0) < \delta$ for some t_0 then,

$$\lim_{t \to \infty} f(t) = 0$$

$$\lim_{t \to \infty} g(t) = 0$$

Remark

With these ideas, let us have, in the next section, a stricter presentation of stability or otherwise, for autonomous systems. We do this, to begin with, for autonomous systems and that, too, in the context of fundamental properties of equations, stated earlier

5.3 Criteria for behaviour of autonomous systems

Let the autonomous system be

$$\dot{x} = f(x) \qquad \left(\dot{x} = \frac{dx}{dt} \right)$$

where $f : D \to R^n$ is a locally Lipschitz map from a domain $D \subset R^n$ to R^n. Without any loss of generality, we can have $x = 0$ to be the equilibrium point of (1) i.e. $f(0) = 0$. The equilibrium point $x = 0$ of (1) is (a) stable, if for each $\varepsilon > 0$, there is $\delta = \delta(\varepsilon) > 0$ such that $\|x(0)\| < \delta \Rightarrow \|x(t)\| < \varepsilon$, $\forall t \geq 0$; (b) asymptotically stable if it is stable and δ can be chosen such that $\|x(0)\| < \delta \Rightarrow \lim_{t \to \infty} x(t) = 0$; (c) unstable, if it is not stable.

Remark

In geometrical terms, a trajectory starting in a δ of the origin will not leave the ε nbd. For example, we had earlier the system for the pendulum given by :

$$\dot{\theta}=\omega$$

$$\omega=-a\sin\theta-b\omega$$

This has two equilibrium points $(\theta=0, \omega=0)$ and $(\theta=\pi, \omega=0)$. If we ignore the frictional term i.e. $b=0$, the trajectories in the nbd of the first equilibrium are closed orbits. Thus, given a nbd (circle) with the equilibrium point as the centre, one can have trajectories well within this nbd. The $\varepsilon-\delta$ criteria are satisfied. But we cannot say about the part (b). In other words, the trajectories starting off the equilibrium point do not tend to this point; rather they stay within their closed orbits. If, on the other hand, we take into account the friction (with $b>0$), the origin will assume a distinct nature and we can then proceed to verify if the above criteria are satisfied (the nature of the critical point and the rest of the statement are left as exercises.) Do trajectories starting close to the equilibrium point tend to it as $t\to\infty$? What can be said about the other equilibrium point $x=\pi$? Is then $\varepsilon-\delta$ requirement satisfied? No, but why? The equilibrium point at $x=\pi$ is a saddle point. Thus we, through this example, deal with stability and asymptotic stability of equilibrium points using the phase portrait. In all fairness, we ought to generalize this but we instead of doing so, let us seek some other ways, as shown by Liapunov, through his important theorem called by his name, Liapunov's theorem. This will also take care of the global existence of the solution of (1) which is in no way assured by the local Lipschitz portrait of f.

5.4 Liapunov's method

Historically, the method has a genesis. In the widely-cited book 'Theory of Motion of

Stability', Laipunov introduced the ideas of 'perturbed motion', 'characteristic numbers' etc. which have obviously a contemporary flair in nonlinear dynamics. He solved the problem of stability in critical cases by introducing functions of two kinds, the history for autonomous differential equation and the other, for non-autonomous differential equation. He could thereby dispense with the so-called 'linearization'. We need some preliminaries.

Definition 1

A function $V(x_1, x_2 ..... x_n)$ is said to be *positive definite* in an ε-neighbourhood $\left(\sum_{i=1}^{n} x_i^2 \le \varepsilon \right)$ of the origin of coordinates if it is positive at all points of this nbd except at the origin of coordinates where it is zero; in symbols, this means

$$V(x_1, x_2, \cdots, x_n) > 0 \text{ if } \sum_{i=1}^{n} x_i^2 > 0$$

$$V(0,0,\cdots,0) = 0$$

For example, $V = x_1^2 + x_2^2 + x_3^2$ is positive definite in the (x_1, x_2, x_3) space.

Definition 2

If $V(x_1, x_2 ..... x_n)$ is negative with $\sum_{i=1}^{n} x_i^2 > 0$ and being zero at the origin of coordinates, it is called *negative definite*.

Remarks

1.   We can extend the above definition for a function $V(t, x_1, x_2, ..., x_n)$. We can call this to be positive definite in a neighbourhood of the origin of coordinates for all $t \ge t_0$, $(t_0 > 0)$, if there exists a t-independent positive definite function

$W(x_1, x_2......x_n)$ such that $V(t, x_1, x_2.....x_n) \geq W(x_1, x_2.....x_n)$ for all values of the arguments and $V(t,0,0,....)=0$.

2.   As it has become discernible by now, we move back and forth between ideas of dynamics and strictly mathematical ones, so as to look, for, as motivation, concepts of dynamics. This is in keeping with what mathematicians like Poincare, Liapunov and others did in the course of historical developments of the topics. We now fall back upon energy concepts and let us see what it can offer in this context. Let $E(x)$ be the sum of kinetic and potential energies of a system in dynamics; for reasons of simplicity, we go back to the notion of pendulum. We choose the reference state to be such that $E(0)=0$, i.e. its potential energy is zero. Then,

$$E(x) = \int_0^{x_1} a \, \cos\theta \, d\theta + \frac{1}{2}x_2^2 = a(1 - \cos x_1) + \frac{1}{2}x_2^2$$

Taking $b=0$ (no friction) i.e. the system to be conservative i.e. no dissipation of energy, we can take $E=c$ (constant) during the motion of the system, i.e. $\frac{dE}{dt}=0$ along the trajectories of the system. Now, $E(x)=c$ can be taken as a closed orbit around $x=0$ for small c; we may also say that $x=0$ is an equilibrium point and a stable one, too. If further $b>0$, energy will decay during the motion of the system so that mathematically, $\frac{dE}{dt} \leq 0$ along the trajectories of the system. Also E cannot remain constant during the motion, because of friction and so it keeps on decaying till it values to zero so that eventually the trajectory approaches $x=0$ as $t \to \infty$. Can we, therefore, think analogously in terms of function that will ensure stability of the equilibrium point? Liapunov, in 1892, really sought for such a function and hence, the genesis of what is called a Liapunov function.

5.5 More about Liapunov's method

With the above remarks, let us present formally the method. In general, let us have the system of differential equations as given by

$$\frac{dx_i}{dt} = f_i(t_1, x_1, x_2, \ldots x_n) \quad (i = 1, 2, \ldots x) \tag{1}$$

Let $V(t, x_1, x_2 \ldots x_n)$ be a continuously differentiable function of its arguments. Then the total derivative of $V(t_1, x_1, x_2 \ldots x_n)$ with respect to t, calculated along the paths or solutions of (1) is given by

$$\frac{dV}{dt} = \frac{\partial V}{\partial t} + \sum_{i=1}^{n} \frac{\partial V}{\partial x_i} \frac{dx_i}{dt} = \frac{\partial V}{\partial t} + \sum_{i=1}^{n} \frac{\partial V}{\partial x_i} f_i(t, x_1, x_2 \ldots x_n) \tag{2}$$

We have taken 't' to appear explicitly in the RHS of (2) and if 't' has not been there, the system is autonomous. Let us present it more formally as follows:

Let $V : D \to R$ be a continuously differentiable defined in a domain $D \subset R^n$ containing the origin. The time derivative of V along the trajectories of

$$\dot{x} = f(x)$$

is given by

$$\dot{V}(x) = \sum_{i=1}^{n} \frac{\partial V}{\partial x_i} \dot{x}_i = \sum_{i=1}^{n} \frac{\partial V}{\partial x_i} f_i(x)$$

$$= \begin{bmatrix} \frac{\partial V}{\partial x_1} & \frac{\partial V}{\partial x_2} & \ldots & \frac{\partial V}{\partial x_n} \end{bmatrix} \begin{bmatrix} f_1(x) \\ f_2(x) \\ \ldots \\ f_n(x) \end{bmatrix} = \frac{\partial V}{\partial x} f(x)$$

Let us state Liapunov's stability theorem for non-autonomous systems. This is stated as follows:

If the system of differential equations (1) is such that there exists a function

$V(t_1, x_1, x_2, \ldots x_n)$ which is positive definite in an ε-nbd of the origin of coordinates for $t \geq t_0$ and whose derivative $\dfrac{dV}{dt}$ calculated along the trajectories or solution curves of the system of (1) is nonpositive, then the zero solution of the system is stable.

For autonomous systems, in keeping with earlier notations, we present Liapunov's theorem in a bit different way.

Let $x = 0$ be an equilibrium point $x = 0$ of

$$\dot{x} = f(x) \tag{i}$$

and let $D \subset R^n$ be a domain containing $x = 0$. Let $V : D \to R$ be a continuously differentiable function such that

$$V(0) = 0 \text{ and } V(x) > 0 \text{ in } D \ldots \{0\} \tag{ii}$$

$$\dot{V}(x) \leq 0 \text{ in } D \tag{iii}$$

Then $x = 0$ is stable. However, if

$$\dot{V}(x) \leq 0 \text{ in } D \ldots \{0\}$$

then $x = 0$ is asymptotically stable.

The proof is omitted here and is given partly in a later chapter.

Remarks

1. For the sake of completeness, we may also state Liapunov's theorem on asymptotic stability for autonomous system, as done for the first form.

    If an autonomous system of differential equation

    $$\frac{dx_i}{dt} = f_i(x_1, x_2, \ldots x_n) \quad (i = 1, 2, \ldots n) \tag{3}$$

    is such that there exists a function $V(x_1, x_2, \ldots x_n)$ which is positive definite in an ε-nbd of the origin of co-ordinates and whose derivative $\dfrac{dV}{dt}$ calculated along the trajectories/solution curves of the system (3) is negative definite, the zero solution $x_1 = 0$, $(i = 1,2,.....n)$ is asymptotically stable.

2.   Having considered stability or asymptotic stability of system (autonomous or non-autonomous), it remains as yet to state something about instability of the system. The simplest way, of course, may be to say if none of the above is okayed, the system is definitely unstable. But, for mathematically tenable purposes, let us set forth the following Chetaev's theorem on stability :

If, for a system of equations,

$$\frac{dx_i}{dt} = f_i(t, x_1, x_2.....x_n) \quad (i = 1,2,.....n)$$

there exists a function V that satisfies :

(i)   there is a $V > 0$ region (i.e., the region where V assumes only positive values, is bounded)

(ii)   the derivative $\frac{dV}{dt}$, in the $V > 0$ region, calculated along the paths/solution curves (if any) of the system is positive definite; the zero solution of the system is unstable .

3.   It is evident that one can deal with Liapunov's theorem without being able to solve the simple differential equations.

4.   How to go about with the findings of Liapunov's function? There is no hard and fast rule to find Liapunov's function. If the right hand side of the first system does not contain it, we should look for Liapunov function that does not depend on explicitly either. Indeed one has to go for trial and error method. Let some hunch be acquired through such exercises.

5.6 Seeking Liapunov's function

I.   Given a system of equations

$$\frac{dx}{dt} = \alpha x^3 + by$$

$$\frac{dy}{dt} = -cx + dy^3$$

can we look for the Liapunov function of the system in the form

$$V(x, y) = F_1(x) + F_2(y)$$

where $F_1(x)$ and $F_2(y)$ are differentiable functions to be determined?

$$\text{Now, } \frac{dV}{dt} = F_1'(x)\dot{x} + F_2'(y)\dot{y}$$

$$= F_1'(x)\left(ax^3 + by\right) + F_2'y\left(-cx + dy^3\right)$$

If $\dfrac{dV}{dt}$ is to have the same form as $V(x, y)$ then

$$F_1'(x)by - F_2'(y)cx = 0$$

Separating the variables, we have

$$\frac{F_1'(x)}{cx} = \frac{F_2'(y)}{by} = \text{constant} = \frac{1}{2}(\text{say})$$

$$\therefore \; F_1(x) = cx^2, \; F_2(y) = by^2$$

which give $V(x, y) = cx^2 + by^2$

II.   **Revisiting the example of pendulum**

As shown earlier, the equation of motion is equivalent to

$$\left. \begin{array}{l} \dfrac{d\theta}{dt} = \omega \\[2mm] \dfrac{d\omega}{dt} = -u \; \sin\theta \end{array} \right\}$$

Let the Liapunov function be given by

$$V(\theta, \omega) = a(1 - \cos\theta) + \frac{1}{2}\omega^2$$

$V(0, 0) = 0$, $V(\theta)$ is positive definite over the domain $-2\pi < \theta < 2\pi$

Now, $\dfrac{dV(\theta, \omega)}{dt} = a\,\dot\theta\,\sin\theta + \omega\dot\omega$

From the above,

$$\therefore \dot V(\theta, \omega) = a\,\dot\theta\,\sin\theta + \omega\dot\omega - b\omega^2$$

$V(\theta, \omega)$ is negative semi-definite; it is *not* negative definite since $\dot V(\theta, \omega) = 0$, for $\omega = 0$ whatever be θ.

$\therefore$ The origin is *stable*, although the phase portrait brings out the asymptotic stability of the origin (where, of course, *b>0).*

Remarks

1.   We can have a fresh look at the behaviour of the nonlinear pendulum problem from the standpoint of eigen values. Let us write the equation of the motion of the pendulum as

$$\theta = -\frac{k}{m}\theta - \frac{1}{l}\sin\theta \tag{1}$$

k being constant.

Let there be a new variable ω given by

$$\omega = \dot\theta \quad (\omega \text{ angular velocity}) \tag{2}$$

The equation (1) is equivalent to

$$\left.\begin{aligned} \dot\theta &= \omega \\ \dot\omega &= -\frac{1}{l}\sin\theta - \frac{k}{m}\omega \end{aligned}\right\} \tag{3}$$

This is a nonlinear autonomous equation in R^2 and has equilibrium at the points $(\theta,\omega)=(n\pi,0)$, where $n=\pm1,\ \pm2,\ \pm3,\ ...$

Let us take up only $(0,0)$.

The derivative at (θ,ω) of the vector field $f(\theta,\omega)$ is given by

$$\mathrm{D}f(\theta,\omega)=\begin{pmatrix} 0 & 1 \\ -\dfrac{\cos\theta}{l} & -\dfrac{k}{m} \end{pmatrix}$$

$$\therefore \mathrm{D}f(0,0)=\begin{pmatrix} 0 & l \\ -\dfrac{1}{l} & -\dfrac{k}{m} \end{pmatrix}$$

It has eigen values given by $\dfrac{1}{2}\left\{-\dfrac{k}{m}+\left[\left(\dfrac{k}{m}\right)^2-\dfrac{4}{l}\right]^{1/2}\right\}$

which could have been obtained otherwise from the characteristic equation.

The real part $-\dfrac{k}{2m}$ is negative, of course k being taken positive and mass is positive. Thus, the equilibrium point $(\theta=0,\omega=0)$ is a sink. We can conclude that, for all sufficiently small initial angles and velocities, the pendulum approaches towards the equilibrium position $(0,0)$. This is, of course, in keeping with reality. But is it not a paradox? Does the pendulum come to rest at all while oscillating? Arguably, the pendulum does not come to rest, its motion is too small to be visible. Perhaps, one can account for this, because of the initial simplification we have done in formulating it in mathematical terms.

2. The same example provides the basis, in a way, of the approach of Liapunov about his function. Going back to its simpler form, the pendulum (with damping) has the equation

$$\dot{\theta}=\omega$$
$$\dot{\omega}=-a\sin\theta$$

With a bit of generalization for damping, the equation is given by

$$\ddot{\theta} + k(\theta, \dot{\theta})\dot{\theta} + \theta = 0$$

which can be split up (or is equivalent) to the form

$$\dot{\theta} = \omega$$
$$\dot{\omega} = -\theta - k(\theta, \dot{\theta})\omega$$

Let $k \geq 0$ and $k \in C^{(1)}$. On any trajectory, $\theta = \phi(t), \omega = \psi(t)$, let us choose the function $V(\theta, \omega)$ given by

$$V = \frac{1}{2}(k^2 + \omega^2)$$

so that

$$\frac{dV}{dt} = \theta\dot{\theta} + \omega\dot{\omega} = -k(\theta, \dot{\theta})\omega^2 < 0$$

which we have met earlier.

This shows that V is decreasing; so V is bounded for $t \geq 0$. Therefore θ and ω are also bounded. The existence of the solution is well assured. Since V is decreasing and not negative, V tends to a limit, say, V_0 for all large t; but θ and ω tend to ∞. Can we now say that idea of 'energy' was lurking somewhere in the mind of Liapunov while formulating the function in his name?

Exercise

1. What can you say about nature of the critical point (0,0) of the system

$$\frac{dx}{dt} = 2x + 4y$$

$$\frac{dy}{dt} - 2x + 6y\ ?$$

Is it stable or otherwise? Justify your answer.

2. In the plane of parameters α and β, find the regions where the zero solution of the system of equations

$$\frac{dx}{dt} = \alpha x + (\beta - 2\alpha\beta - 1)y$$

$$\frac{dy}{dt} = x - \beta y$$

is stable.

study of equilibria: another approach $\boxed{6}$

In this chapter, instead of continuing with Liapunov's studies on study of equilibria, which, of course, we shall do in a later chapter, we go back to linear systems along with their critical points, wherever they occur. The main purpose is to acquaint ourselves with a technique that makes study of nonlinear systems dependent on linear systems. We speak of this as 'linearization'. There is no dearth of ways to do so. However, we restrict ourselves to one approach; for this makes use of what we have learnt and what provides a better foundation for treatment on stability or otherwise of nonlinear systems. For reasons of simplicity, we begin with a simple type of linear system of the kind treated earlier.

6.1 A few words about autonomous systems

It is not that the word 'autonomous' is being mentioned for the first time, but we have done it earlier somewhat naively. We represent, as before, the system as

$$\left.\begin{array}{l} \dfrac{dx}{dt} = f(x,y) \\[4mm] \dfrac{dy}{dt} = g(x,y) \end{array}\right\} \tag{1}$$

where the variable (x,y) on the right-hand side do not contain t (usually, the time) explicitly but they do so implicitly because x and y are taken as functions of 't'. We describe the system (1) as 'autonomous' which, means 'self-governing'. We can write from (1)

$$\frac{dy}{dx} = \frac{g(x,y)}{f(x,y)} \tag{2}$$

which defines the slope, assuming $f(x,y) \neq 0$.

Incidentally, before we proceed, we should take $f(x,y)$ and $g(x,y)$ to be both continuously differentiable functions of x and y. We can obtain the trajectory by integrating (2), if at all integrable. But let us look at its behaviour.

Let the system (1) have (x_0,y_0) as its critical point. We seek to study its behaviour around (in nbd of) its state of equilibrium i.e. (x_0,y_0). We know how to go about with this if both $f(x,y)$ and $g(x,y)$ happen to be linear. How to have an inkling of the procedure? Why shouldn't we try with Taylor's expansion of both $f(x,y)$ and $g(x,y)$, around the equilibrium point i.e. $f(x_0,y_0)=0$; $g(x_0,y_0)=0$

Of course, we need to assume $(f,g) \in C^1$, in the nbd of (x_0,y_0), that $f(x,y)$ and $g(x,y)$ have continuous partial derivatives in the nbd of (x_0,y_0).

Doing the expansion as stated, in the immediate neighbourhood of (x_{0y},y_0) and so restricting ourselves to first order terms, we can write (1) as

$$\left.\begin{array}{l} \dfrac{dx}{dt} = ax + by \\[4mm] \dfrac{dy}{dt} = cx + dy \end{array}\right\} \tag{3}$$

where $\begin{bmatrix} a & b \\ c & d \end{bmatrix} = \begin{bmatrix} f_x(x_0,y_0) & f_y(x_0,y_0) \\ g_x(x_0,y_0) & g_y(x_0,y_0) \end{bmatrix}$ 　　　　　(4)

We cannot say anything now about what may happen at points or in regions far away from the critical point (x_0,y_0). But can it be established that characterization of the behaviour of (1) will be the same as that of (3) with (4)? The answer is yes. We again emphasise this in the close nbd of (x_0,y_0). Let us refrain from proving this formally. But we would not leave it without seeing to it that it is plausible. Let us then make some relevant and appropriate remarks. We take it that (1) has the unique (local) solution, given $(f,g) \in C^1$. What else does one require for $f(x,y)$ and $g(x,y)$? First, if there be a solution bounded for $t>0$, it does so for all positive t. Second, a critical point is nowhere on the trajectory, which we represent by $x = \xi(t), y = \eta(t)$ (neither ξ, η being constants). In a region having no critical points, no two orbits, can cross nor can an orbit cross itself.

Another vital remark: If $\lim_{t \to \infty}(x,y) = (x_1,y_1)$ exists, then (x_1,y_1) can be taken as a *stationary* point. We shall deal with what are called periodic orbits separately because of their significance, but we should note now that a periodic solution corresponds to a simple closed orbit.

If we express the system (1) as

$$\frac{d}{dt}\begin{pmatrix} x-x_0 \\ y-y_0 \end{pmatrix} = \begin{pmatrix} A & B \\ C & D \end{pmatrix}\begin{pmatrix} x-x_0 \\ y-y_0 \end{pmatrix}$$ 　　　　　(5)

then A, B, C, D are functions of (x,y) satisfying

$$\lim_{(x,y) \to (x_0,y_0)}\begin{bmatrix} A & B \\ C & D \end{bmatrix} = \begin{bmatrix} f_x(x_0,y_0) & f_y(x_0,y_0) \\ g_x(x_0,y_0) & g_y(x_0,y_0) \end{bmatrix}$$ 　　　　　(6)

Establishing the truth of these remarks is not at all difficult. The first three follow readily from the considerations of existence and uniqueness of solutions of (1). To establish that (x_1, y_1) is a stationary point when $\lim_{t \to \infty}(x,y) = (x_1, y_1)$ exists, we assert that (x_1, y_1) is not a stationary point. This implies that at least one of the inequalities $f > 0$, $f < 0$, $g > 0$, $g < 0$ holds at (x_1, y_1). Let us take, without any loss of generality, $f(x,y) = -2\alpha < 0$; the same for others. If $t \geq t_0$ with t_0 being sufficiently large, we have $f(x,y) = -\alpha$ on the trajectory, as f is continuous. Hence, $\dfrac{dx}{dt} \leq -\alpha$ for $t \geq t_0$. Therefore, $x(t) \to -\infty$ contradicts the hypothesis $x(t) \to x_1$. Hence, the result.

To see if (5) and (6) are true, we make use of Taylor's convergent expansions of f and g about (x_0, y_0) which will suffice.

Remarks

1.   We need to conclude by stating why we say a critical point to be isolated. It is said to be so if we can have a nbd in the form of a disk that contains the critical point and none else. That a critical point of (1) is isolated can also be established using the previous results.

2.   The above procedure enables to linearize

$$\frac{dx}{dt} = f(x,y) \text{ and } \frac{dy}{dt} = g(x,y)$$

and once 'linearization' is done, we can speak about its behaviour in terms of centre, node, focus, spiral (stable or otherwise). We sum up the technique in the next section.

6.2 Nonlinear systems: Linearization technique

Let us consider the following set of nonlinear equations given by

$$\left. \begin{array}{l} \dot{x} = f(x,y) \\ \dot{y} = g(x,y) \end{array} \right\} \tag{1}$$

Now, let (x_0, y_0) be the critical point of (1). Then

$$f(x_0, y_0) = g(x_0, y_0) = 0 \tag{2}$$

Let us put $\left. \begin{array}{l} x = x_0 + x' \\ y = y_0 + y' \end{array} \right\}$

Then (1) reduces to $\dot{x}' = f(x_0 + x', y_0 + y')$

$$= f(x_0, y_0) + x'(f_x)_{(x_0, y_0)} + y'(f_y)_{(x_0, y_0)}$$

$$= x'(f_x)_{(x_0, y_0)} + y'(f_y)_{(x_0, y_0)} \qquad \text{[using (2)]}$$

and similarly, $\dot{y}' = (g_x)_{(x_0, y_0)} x' + (g_y)_{(x_0, y_0)} y'$

$$\therefore \quad \begin{bmatrix} \dot{x}' \\ \dot{y}' \end{bmatrix} = \begin{bmatrix} f_x & f_y \\ g_x & g_y \end{bmatrix} \begin{bmatrix} x' \\ y' \end{bmatrix} \tag{3}$$

$\therefore$ The relevant matrix corresponding to the characteristic equation is $\begin{bmatrix} f_x & f_y \\ g_x & g_y \end{bmatrix}$

Hence, the study of the nonlinear system reduces to the study of the linear system :

$$\left. \begin{array}{l} \dot{x}' = ax' + by' \\ \dot{y}' = cx' + dy' \end{array} \right\} \tag{4}$$

where $\begin{bmatrix} a & b \\ c & d \end{bmatrix} = \begin{bmatrix} f_x(x_0, y_0) & f_y(x_0, y_0) \\ g_x(x_0, y_0) & g_y(x_0, y_0) \end{bmatrix}$

Now the characteristic equation is

$$\begin{vmatrix} a - \lambda & b \\ c & d - \lambda \end{vmatrix} = 0$$

$$\Rightarrow \quad \lambda^2 - (a+d)\lambda + (ad - bc) = 0$$

$$\Rightarrow \quad \lambda^2 + p\lambda + q = 0 \quad \text{where} \quad p = -(a+d) \qquad q = ad - bc$$

6.3 Illustrative examples

Example 1

Investigate the critical point(s) of the system

$$\frac{d^2x}{dt^2} + a\frac{dx}{dt} + b\sin x = 0$$

for its stability or otherwise.

Solution

The given equation can be written as

$$\left.\begin{aligned}\dot{x} &= y \\ \dot{y} &= -ay - b\sin x\end{aligned}\right\} \qquad (1)$$

The critical points (equilibrium solutions) of (1) are given by

$$\dot{x} = 0 = \dot{y}$$

i.e. $y = 0, x = k\pi$ where $k = 0, \pm 1, \pm 2, \ldots\ldots$

Let us investigate for stability the critical point $x = 0, y = 0$ which correspond to $k = 0$.

We have $\sin x = x - \dfrac{x^{-3}}{3!} + \ldots\ldots$

Using this expansion, (1) can be written as

$$\left.\begin{aligned}\dot{x} &= y \\ \dot{y} &= -bx - ay\end{aligned}\right\} \qquad (2)$$

The characteristic equation is

$$\begin{vmatrix} -\lambda & 1 \\ -b & -a-\lambda \end{vmatrix} = 0$$

$$\Rightarrow \quad \lambda^2 + a\lambda + b = 0$$

$$\Rightarrow \quad \lambda - \frac{-a \pm \sqrt{a^2 - 4b}}{2}$$

If $a > 0$ and $b > 0$ then the roots have negative real parts and consequently, the critical point $x = 0, y = 0$ is asymptotically stable in the first approximation.

Let us now investigate for stability the point $(\pi, 0)$ which corresponds to $k = 1$

We now use the expansion

$$\sin x = -(x - \pi) + \frac{(x - \pi)^3}{3!} - \cdots\cdots$$

Let us use the transformation

$$\left.\begin{array}{l} x = x' + \pi \\ y = y' \end{array}\right\}$$

Then equation (1) reduces to

$$\dot{x}' = y'$$
$$\dot{y}' = -ay' - b\sin(x' + \pi)$$
$$= bx' - ay'$$

Thus the characteristic equation is

$$\begin{vmatrix} -\lambda & 1 \\ b & -a - \lambda \end{vmatrix} = 0$$

If $a > 0$ and $b > 0$ the roots of the equation are real and have different signs. Consequently, for this system, the critical point $(\pi, 0)$ is unstable.

Example 2

Show that van der Pol's equation

$$\ddot{x} - \varepsilon(1 - x^2)\dot{x} + x = 0$$

has one singular point at $(0,0)$ and determine its nature

Solution

van der Pol's equation can be written as

$$\left.\begin{array}{l} \dot{x} = y = f(x,y) \\ \dot{y} = \varepsilon(1-x^2)y - x = g(x,y) \end{array}\right\} \tag{1}$$

The critical points will be obtained by solving the equations

$$f(x,y) = 0$$
$$g(x,y) = 0$$

which show that (0,0) is the only singular point.

Now $f_x = 0, f_y = 1 \qquad g_x = -2xy\varepsilon - 1$

$$g_y = \varepsilon(1-x^2)$$

At the point (0,0)

$$f_x = 0, f_y = 1$$
$$g_x = -1, \quad g_y = \varepsilon$$

Thus the system (1) can be characterized as

$$\begin{bmatrix} \dot{x} \\ \dot{y} \end{bmatrix} = \begin{bmatrix} 0 & 1 \\ -1 & \varepsilon \end{bmatrix}\begin{bmatrix} x \\ y \end{bmatrix}$$

The characteristic equation is

$$\begin{vmatrix} -\lambda & 1 \\ -1 & \varepsilon - \lambda \end{vmatrix} = 0$$

$$\Rightarrow \quad \lambda^2 - \varepsilon\lambda + 1 = 0$$

$$\Rightarrow \quad \lambda = \frac{\varepsilon \pm \sqrt{\varepsilon^2 - 4}}{2}$$

Let us now consider the following cases.

Case I

If $\varepsilon \leq -2$ then the eigen values are real and negative. Therefore (0,0) is a stable node.

Case II

If $-2 < \varepsilon < 0$ then the eigen values are complex with negative real parts. Therefore (0,0) is a stable focus.

Case III

If $\varepsilon = 0$ then the eigen values are purely imaginary. Thus (0,0) is a centre.

Case IV

If $0 < \varepsilon < 2$ then the eigen values are complex with positive real part. Thus (0,0) is an unstable focus.

Case V

If $\varepsilon \geq 2$ then the eigen values are real and positive. Thus (0,0) is an unstable node.

Example 3

Find the singular points of equation

$$\ddot{x} + \dot{x} - x^2 - 2x^3 = 0$$

and determine their nature.

Solution

The given equation can be written as

$$\left. \begin{array}{l} \dot{x} = y \\ \dot{y} = 2x^3 + x^2 - x \end{array} \right\} \tag{1}$$

The singular points are given by

$$\dot{x} = 0 = \dot{y}$$

i.e. the singular points are $(0,0), \left(\dfrac{1}{2}, 0 \right), (-1,0)$

Here $f(x,y)=y,\quad g(x,y)=2x^3+x^2-x$

$$\therefore\quad f_x=0,\qquad\qquad f_y=1$$
$$g_x=6x^2+2x-1\qquad g_y=0$$

At the point $(0,0)$, the linearized equations are $\begin{pmatrix}\dot{x}\\\dot{y}\end{pmatrix}=\begin{pmatrix}0&1\\-1&0\end{pmatrix}\begin{pmatrix}x\\y\end{pmatrix}$

At the point $(-1,0)$ $\qquad f_x=0,\qquad f_y=1$
$$g_x=-1\qquad g_y=0$$

Thus the characteristic equation for $(0,0)$ is

$$\begin{vmatrix}-\lambda&1\\-1&-\lambda\end{vmatrix}=0$$

$\therefore$ Both the roots are purely imaginary.

$\therefore$ $(0,0)$ is a stable centre

The characteristic equation for $\left(\dfrac{1}{2},0\right)$ is

$$\begin{vmatrix}-\lambda&1\\\dfrac{3}{2}&-\lambda\end{vmatrix}=0$$

$$\Rightarrow\quad \lambda^2-\frac{3}{2}=0,\text{ i.e. }\lambda\;=\;\pm\sqrt{\frac{3}{2}}$$

Thus the roots are real and of opposite signs. So the critical point $\left(\dfrac{1}{2},0\right)$ is a saddle point (unstable).

The characteristic equation for $(-1,0)$ is

$$\begin{vmatrix}-\lambda&1\\3&-\lambda\end{vmatrix}=0$$

$$\Rightarrow\quad \lambda=\pm\sqrt{3}$$

The roots are real and of opposite signs. Hence $(-1,0)$ is a saddle point (unstable)

Example 4

Examine the nature of the critical points of the system

$$\left.\begin{array}{l} \dot{x} = x(x+y-1) \\ \dot{y} = y(x-y+3) \end{array}\right\} \qquad (1)$$

Solution

Here
$$\begin{array}{l} f(x,y) = x(x+y-1) = x^2 + xy - x, \\ g(x,y) = y(x-y+3) = xy - y^2 + 3y \end{array}$$

The critical points of the system are given by $\dot{x} = 0 = \dot{y}$

i.e. $$\left.\begin{array}{l} x(x+y-1) = 0 \\ y(x-y+3) = 0 \end{array}\right\} \qquad (2)$$

Solving (2), we get the critical points of (1).

The critical points are (0,0), (0,3), (1,0), (-1,2)

Now $f_x(x,y) = (x+y-1) + x = 2x + y - 1$

$f_y(x,y) = x$

$g_x(x,y) = y$

$g_y(x,y) = x - 2y + 3$

$$\therefore \quad \begin{pmatrix} a & b \\ c & d \end{pmatrix} = \begin{pmatrix} f_x & f_y \\ g_x & g_y \end{pmatrix} = \begin{pmatrix} 2x+y-1 & x \\ y & x-2y+3 \end{pmatrix}$$

For the point (0,0)

$$\begin{pmatrix} a & b \\ c & d \end{pmatrix} = \begin{pmatrix} -1 & 0 \\ 0 & 3 \end{pmatrix}$$

Thus the characteristic equation for the critical point (0,0)

$$\begin{vmatrix} -1-\lambda & 0 \\ 0 & 3-\lambda \end{vmatrix} = 0$$

$\Rightarrow \quad (\lambda+1)(\lambda-3)=0$

$\Rightarrow \quad \lambda=3,-1$

Both the roots are real, distinct and of opposite signs. Hence, the critical point (0,0) is unstable and the critical point is a saddle.

For the point (0,3)

$$\begin{pmatrix} a & b \\ c & d \end{pmatrix} = \begin{pmatrix} 2 & 0 \\ 3 & -3 \end{pmatrix}$$

The characteristic equation for the critical point (0,3) is

$$\begin{vmatrix} 2-\lambda & 0 \\ 3 & -3-\lambda \end{vmatrix} = 0$$

$\Rightarrow \quad (\lambda-2)(\lambda+3)=0$

$\Rightarrow \quad \lambda=2,-3$

Thus, as in the above, the critical point is an unstable saddle.

For the point (1,0)

$$\begin{pmatrix} a & b \\ c & d \end{pmatrix} = \begin{pmatrix} 1 & 1 \\ 0 & 4 \end{pmatrix}$$

The characteristic equation for the critical point (1,0) is

$$\begin{vmatrix} 1-\lambda & 1 \\ 0 & 4-\lambda \end{vmatrix} = 0$$

$\Rightarrow \quad \lambda=1,4$

$\therefore$ Both the roots are real, positive and distinct.

Thus the critical point (1,0) is an unstable node.

For the point (–1, 2)

$$\begin{pmatrix} a & b \\ c & d \end{pmatrix} = \begin{pmatrix} -1 & -1 \\ 2 & -2 \end{pmatrix}$$

∴ The characteristic equation for the critical point (1,0) is

$$\begin{vmatrix} -1-\lambda & -1 \\ 2 & -2-\lambda \end{vmatrix} = 0$$

$$\Rightarrow \quad (\lambda+1)(\lambda+2)+2=0$$

$$\Rightarrow \quad \lambda^2+3\lambda+4=0$$

$$\Rightarrow \quad \lambda = \frac{-3\pm i\sqrt{9-4\times1\times4}}{2\times1} = \frac{-3\pm i\sqrt{7}}{2}$$

Both the roots are complex conjugate with negative real parts. Thus the critical point

(−1, 2) is a stable focus.

Exercise

1. Investigate the nature of the critical point(s) of the system

$$\frac{dx}{dt} = -2x+3y+xy$$

$$\frac{dy}{dt} = -x+y-2xy^2$$

2. Investigate the behaviour of the critical point(s) of the system

$$\frac{dx}{dt} = x+4y-x^2$$

$$\frac{dy}{dt} = 6x-y+2xy$$

3. Investigate the stability of the critical point ($x=0$, $y=0$) of the system

$$\frac{dx}{dt} = -x+y+2x^4-y^6$$

$$\frac{dy}{dt} = x-3y+11y^4$$

4. Find the points of equilibrium of

$$\ddot{x} + \dot{x} - x^2 - 2x^3 = 0$$

and determine their nature.

What are the phase-portraits? Given that $x(0)=0$, show that the motion will be oscillatory if

$$\frac{-(5-\sqrt{10})}{6} < x(0) < \frac{1}{2}$$

5. Investigate the behaviour of the zero solution of system

$$\frac{dx}{dt} = y - 3x^3$$

$$\frac{dy}{dt} = -x - 7y^3$$

6. Discuss the behaviour of the zero solution of

$$\frac{dx}{dt} = x - xy^4$$

$$\frac{dy}{dt} = y - x^2 y^3$$

7. What can you establish about the nature of the critical points of the system

$$\frac{dx}{dt} = -xy^4$$

$$\frac{dy}{dt} = yx^4 \ ?$$

8. What can be said about the zero solution of the system

$$\frac{dx}{dt} = \frac{1}{3}y - x - \frac{7}{2}x^3$$

$$\frac{dy}{dt} = -x - \frac{1}{2}y - \frac{5}{2}y^3 \ ?$$

nonlinear vis a vis linear systems

As mentioned earlier, we haven't as yet any method or technique to grapple with nonlinearities except those enabling us to determine the behaviour of linear systems around critical points. We have indicated somewhat cursorily about them earlier, without stating assumptions and theorems which usually accompany any mathematical statement. Let us plan to do this now, beginning precisely with nonlinear (real) autonomous systems.

7.1 Fundamentals of nonlinear systems

Let us have the nonlinear (real) system in the form given by

$$\left.\begin{aligned} \frac{dx}{dt} &= f(x,y) \\ \frac{dy}{dt} &= g(x,y) \end{aligned}\right\} \tag{1}$$

We take, as before, $f(x,y)$ and $g(x,y)$ to be continuous functions along with their derivatives. Having said so, about $f(x,y)$ and $g(x,y)$, we can write, after expansions

$$\left.\begin{array}{l} \dfrac{dx}{dt} = \left[\dfrac{\partial f}{\partial x}\right]_{(0,0)} x + \left[\dfrac{\partial f}{\partial y}\right]_{(0,0)} y + \text{higher order terms in } x \text{ and } y \\[4mm] \dfrac{dy}{dt} = \left[\dfrac{\partial g}{\partial x}\right]_{(0,0)} x + \left[\dfrac{\partial g}{\partial y}\right]_{(0,0)} y + \text{higher order terms in } x \text{ and } y \end{array}\right\} \qquad (2)$$

(the constant terms on the R.H.S. are (0,0), each of $f(0,0)$ and $g(0,0)$ being so.)

which we , further, express as

$$\left.\begin{array}{l} \dfrac{dx}{dt} = a_{11}x + a_{12}y + f_1(x,y) \\[4mm] \dfrac{dy}{dt} = a_{21}x + a_{22}y + g_1(x,y) \end{array}\right\} \qquad (3)$$

where functions $f_1(x,y)$ and $g_1(x,y)$ are terms of the higher degrees in x and y. In order that we put the set of equations in the form of a linear system, we require that

$$\left.\begin{array}{l} \lim\limits_{(x,y)\to(0,0)} \dfrac{f_1(x,y)}{\sqrt{x^2+y^2}} = 0 \\[5mm] \lim\limits_{(x,y)\to(0,0)} \dfrac{g_1(x,y)}{\sqrt{x^2+y^2}} = 0 \end{array}\right\} \qquad (4)$$

with $f_1(x,y)$ and $g_1(x,y)$ being continuous along with their partial derivatives for all (x,y).

As we may recall, for the system, we should also have

$$\begin{vmatrix} a_{11} & a_{12} \\ a_{21} & a_{22} \end{vmatrix} \neq 0 \qquad (5)$$

where $a_{11} = f_x(0,0)$, $a_{12} = f_y(0,0)$, $a_{21} = g_y(0,0)$ and $a_{22} = g_y(0,0)$

It is well known that (4) and (5) are fulfilled if

$$\left| \frac{\partial(f,g)}{\partial(x,y)} \right| \neq 0 \text{ (often referred to as Jacobian)}$$

Remark

On account of (4), we can say that the nonlinear terms $f_1(x,y)$ and $g_1(x,y)$ tend to 0 more rapidly than the linear terms $(a_{11}x + a_{12}y)$ and $(a_{21}x + a_{22}y)$. Hence, one can well guess that the behaviour of (the paths as well) the system in the nbd of $(0,0)$ would be similar to the behaviour (of the paths, too) of the corresponding linear system given by

$$\left. \begin{aligned} \frac{dx}{dt} &= a_{11}x + a_{12}y \\ \frac{dy}{dt} &= a_{21}x + a_{22}y \end{aligned} \right\} \tag{6}$$

This amounts to saying that (6) is obtained by doing away with the nonlinear terms represented by $f_1(x,y)$ and $g_1(x,y)$. Does it enable us to say that the equilibrium point $(0,0)$ of the nonlinear system of equation (1) should in no way differ from that of the linear system given by equation (6)? The answer is 'yes' and is given by the following theorem, which we now just state without proof.

7.2 Theorem

Given the nonlinear system

$$\left. \begin{aligned} \frac{dx}{dt} &= a_{11}x + a_{12}y + f_1(x,y) \\ \frac{dy}{dt} &= a_{21}x + a_{22}y + f_2(x,y) \end{aligned} \right\} \tag{1}$$

where a_{ij} $(i,j=1,2)$'s and f_1 and g_1 satisfy

$$\begin{vmatrix} a_{11} & a_{12} \\ a_{21} & a_{22} \end{vmatrix} \neq 0 \qquad (2)$$

and $\displaystyle \lim_{(x,y)\to(0,0)} \frac{f_1(x,y)}{\sqrt{x^2+y^2}} = \lim_{(x,y)\to(0,0)} \frac{g_1(x,y)}{\sqrt{x^2+y^2}} = 0$ $\qquad (3)$

the corresponding linear system is

$$\left.\begin{array}{l} \dfrac{dx}{dt} = a_{11}x + a_{12}y \\[2mm] \dfrac{dy}{dt} = a_{21}x + a_{22}y \end{array}\right\} \qquad (4)$$

obtained from (1), by removing the terms $f_1(x,y)$ and $g_1(x,y)$, and has the same critical point (0,0) as that of (1) and the behaviours of the critical point of both the systems (1) and (4) are same. The critical point (0,0) is often described as a simple critical point.

Remarks

1. This theorem enables us to get at the nature of the critical point of the nonlinear system, that of the linear system being taken from techniques and methods treated in earlier chapters; for example, by obtaining the characteristic equation for the linear system i.e.

    $$\lambda^2 - (a_{11} + a_{22})\lambda + (a_{11}a_{22} - a_{12}a_{21}) = 0$$

    and its eigen values. We should recall the nature of the trajectories depending on the nature of roots of the equation.

2. As per the above theorem, we ought to expect the type of the critical point to be the same as types of the linear system; the paths of the nonlinear system may

apparently differ, solely because of the character of the nonlinear system from the paths of the corresponding linear system. It is to be pointed out that stability (or asymptotic stability or instability) is well taken care of by criteria (often called the Liapunov's criteria) mentioned along with the nature of critical points. We restate this as follows for the sake of completeness.

Liapunov's criteria (theorem):

If both the roots of the characteristic equation of the linear system are real and negative or conjugate complex with negative real points, then the critical point of the linear system is not only asymptotically stable but also the same with the nonlinear system.

If the roots are purely imaginary, than even if the critical point be stable, the critical point of the nonlinear system may not be necessarily so. It may so happen that the critical point of the nonlinear system be asymptotically stable; stable but in no way asymptotically stable or unstable.

Finally, if either of the roots of the characteristic equation is real and positive or if the roots are conjugate complex with positive real parts then not only the critical point of the corresponding linear system is unstable but also an unstable critical point of nonlinear system.

We shall establish this in simple terms with the help of Liapunov's criteria.

3.   Some properties relating to (1) and (2), it may be recalled, have been mentioned previously.

4.   The above process of reducing a nonlinear system to a linear system is referred to as linearization, as also shown in Fig. 7.1(a) and 7.1(b).

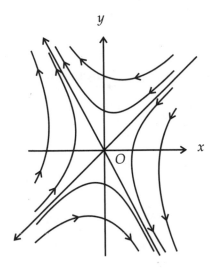

Fig 7.1(a) : Linear system

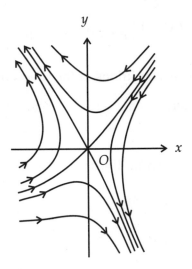

Fig 7.1(b) : Nonlinear system

5.   The above theorem, as is obvious from (5), tells about the types of the critical points (0,0) of the nonlinear system.

7.3 Direct application of theorem (7.2)

$$\frac{dx}{dt} = -2x + 3y + xy$$

$$\frac{dy}{dt} = -x + y - 2xy^2$$

Solution

$$\begin{vmatrix} a_{11} & a_{12} \\ a_{21} & a_{22} \end{vmatrix} = \begin{vmatrix} -2 & 3 \\ -1 & 1 \end{vmatrix} = 1 \neq 0$$

Further, using polar coordinates,

$$\frac{|f_1(x,y)|}{\sqrt{x^2 + y^2}} = \frac{|r^2 \sin\theta \cos\theta|}{r} \leq r$$

$$\frac{|g_1(x,y)|}{\sqrt{x^2 + y^2}} = \frac{|2r^3 \sin^2\theta \cos\theta|}{r} \leq 2r^2$$

$$\therefore \quad \frac{f_1(x,y)}{r} \text{ and } \frac{g_1(x,y)}{r} \rightarrow (0,0) \text{ as } r \rightarrow 0$$

Hence, conditions of the theorem are satisfied. (0,0) is a simple critical point of the given system.

The corresponding linear system is

$$\frac{dx}{dt} = -2x + 3y$$
$$\frac{dy}{dt} = -x + y$$

The characteristic equation is given by

$$\begin{vmatrix} -2-\lambda & 3 \\ -1 & 1-\lambda \end{vmatrix} = 0$$

i.e $\lambda^2 + \lambda + 1 = 0$

$$\Rightarrow \lambda_1, \lambda_2 = \frac{-1 \pm \sqrt{3}i}{2}$$

The critical point of the linear system is a spiral point and hence, that of the nonlinear system is a spiral point, too.

7.4 Illustrative example

For what value of α will the zero solution be stable for the autonomous system

$$\dot{x} = \alpha x + y$$
$$\dot{y} = -x \ ?$$

Solution

Here the characteristic equation is

$$\begin{vmatrix} \alpha - \lambda & 1 \\ -1 & -\lambda \end{vmatrix} = 0$$

$$\Rightarrow \quad \lambda^2 - \lambda\alpha + 1 = 0$$

$$\Rightarrow \quad \lambda_1 = \frac{\alpha + \sqrt{\alpha^2 - 4}}{2},$$

$$\lambda_2 = \frac{\alpha - \sqrt{\alpha^2 - 4}}{2},$$

Different cases

Case I

If $|\alpha| > 2$, then both the roots are real

Again if $|\alpha| > 2 \Rightarrow \alpha < -2$ or $\alpha > 2$

If $\alpha < -2$, then both the roots are '−ve'

∴ the zero solution is asymptotically stable.

If $\alpha > 2$, then both of λ_1 and λ_2 will be '+ve'; then the critical point will be unstable

Case II

If $|\alpha| = 2$, i.e. $\alpha = -2, 2$

Then $\lambda_1 = \lambda_2 = \dfrac{\alpha}{2}$

If $\alpha < 0$, then both $\lambda_1, \lambda_2 < 0$

The solution will be asymptotically stable.

$|\alpha| = 2$ and $\alpha < 0 \Rightarrow \alpha = -2$

Hence if $\alpha = -2$, then also the solution will be asymptotically stable.

Case III

If $|\alpha| < 2$, then λ_1, λ_2 are complex conjugate; if $\alpha < 0$, λ_1, λ_2 have '−ve' real parts i.e. the solution will be asymptotically stable if $\alpha < 0$ and $|\alpha| < 2$ i.e. for $-2 < \alpha < 0$

Case IV

If $\alpha = 0$, then the roots are purely imaginary. So the critical point is stable but not asymptotically.

7.5 Linearization

As we have already come to know, by now, the process of replacing a nonlinear system by a linear system, subject of course, to some conditions, is called linearization. Our main concern about these systems has been around critical point(s). The nature of such points remains, by and large, the same . Can they be different when linearized? Can there be other process(es) to go about linearization? Do they shed better understanding about the behaviour of nonlinear system through linearization? We shall seek first, through some examples, answers to some of these questions. This will be accompanied or even followed up by some forms of results, expressed in general terms.

Two non-linear systems : a striking feature

Let us have two non-linear systems

$$\left.\begin{array}{l} \dfrac{dx}{dt} = -y - x^3 \\[2mm] \dfrac{dy}{dt} = x \end{array}\right\} \tag{1}$$

and

$$\left.\begin{array}{l}\dfrac{dx}{dt}=-y-x^2 \\[2mm] \dfrac{dy}{dt}=x\end{array}\right\} \tag{2}$$

The point $(0,0)$ is a critical point for each of the systems (1) and (2).

In each case, the corresponding linear system is

$$\left.\begin{array}{l}\dfrac{dx}{dt}=-y \\[2mm] \dfrac{dy}{dt}=x\end{array}\right\} \tag{3}$$

The characteristic equation of the system (1) is given by $\lambda^2+1=0$ with the pure imaginary roots $\pm i$. Thus the critical point $(0,0)$ of the linear system is a centre.

Remarks

1. It can be established (not done now) that, the roots of the characteristic equation being purely imaginary, even if the linear system shows the critical point to be a centre, the non-linear system from which it is derived, has a spiral point as its critical point.

    As a sequel to this, let us consider another example to show that even if the linear variant of a nonlinear system leads to the critical point becoming a centre, it may not be absolutely so. Let consider the R^2 system given by

    $$\frac{dx}{dt}=-y-ax\sqrt{x^2+y^2}$$

    $$\frac{dy}{dt}=x-ay\sqrt{x^2+y^2}$$

    (*a* being a constant)

The linear version of the given system is

$$\frac{dx}{dt} = -y$$

$$\frac{dy}{dt} = x$$

which gives the critical point $(0,0)$ a centre.

Let us use polar coordinates (r,θ) so as to transform the given system to (by putting $x = r\cos\theta$, $y = r\sin\theta$)

$$\dot{r} = ar^2$$

$$\dot{\theta} = 1$$

Its solution is $r(t) = \dfrac{1}{\dfrac{1}{r(0)} + at}$

$$\theta(t) = \theta(0) + t$$

If $a \neq 0$, the critical point $(0,0)$ is not a centre of the nonlinear system; we may see later on that for $a > 0$, the critical point is called an *attractor*.

2.   We have so far come across systems where the nonlinear systems are reducible to linear systems with simple critical points. This may not occur when the nonlinearties are of involved types e.g.,

$$\frac{dx}{dt} = 2xy$$

$$\frac{dy}{dt} = y^2 - x^2$$

Such systems do not have simple critical points.

3.   Having shown some aspects of linearization, on which we fall back upon for dealing with nonlinear systems, let us consider another way of linearizing nonlinear systems. We can show it through an example, where we consider critical points other than the simpler one(s).

4. Let us now make some remarks if we generate the process of 'linearization' as mentioned above. In general terms, we write a system in the form of the nonlinear system as

$$\dot{x} = f(x) \tag{1}$$

where $x = (x_1, x_2 \cdots x_n)$

We assume this as autonomous. If we linearize in the nbd of a critical point of (1), we get

$$\dot{y} = Ay \tag{2}$$

where A is a constant $n \times n$ matrix, assuming the critical point to have been translated to the origin. We also suppose that $\det A \neq 0$. A is a non-linear matrix, and we often speak of, in such cases, the critical point to be non degenerate. Next we form the characteristic equation:

$$\det(A - \lambda I) = 0 \tag{3}$$

so that we get the eigen values $\lambda_1, \lambda_2 \cdots \lambda_n$.

We can show (not now) that there exists a real, non-singular matrix such that $T^{-1}AT$ is in the Jordan form which has also been mentioned earlier.. Further, if the n eigen values are different, then $T^{-1}AT$ is said to be in diagonal term with the eigen values as diagonal elements. If, however, there are some equal eigen values, the linear transformation $y = Tz$ can further simplify the above system as

$$T\dot{z} = ATz$$

or $\dot{z} = T^{-1}ATz \tag{4}$

We can integrate (4); the Jordan normal form being simple, we get $y = Tz$

7.6 Linearization: Another approach

Let us get back to the nonlinear system which we dealt with in the second chapter. The set of equations is given by

$$\left.\begin{array}{l} \dfrac{dH}{dt} = (a_{11} - a_{12}P)H \\[3mm] \dfrac{dP}{dt} = (-a_{21} + a_{22}H)P \end{array}\right\} \qquad (1)$$

where H and P are functions of t, a_{ij} $(i, j = 1, 2)$'s are positive constants. The critical points of (1) are given by

$$\frac{dH}{dt} = 0; \qquad \frac{dP}{dt} = 0 \qquad (2)$$

i.e. $(a_{11} - a_{12}P)H = 0$

$(-a_{21} + a_{22}H)P = 0$

$$\Rightarrow \quad (0,0), \left(H_0 = \frac{a_{21}}{a_{22}}, P_0 = \frac{a_{11}}{a_{12}} \right) \qquad (3)$$

Let us choose not the simple critical point $(0,0)$ but the other one, namely, (H_0, P_0) given by (3) and study its role about the behaviour of (1). To do this, let us see what happens to (1) around (in the nbd of) (H_0, P_0) i.e. let us move a bit around (H_0, P_0). We can do so by putting

$$\left.\begin{array}{l} H = H_0 + h \\ P = P_0 + p \end{array}\right\} \qquad (4)$$

where (h, p) are variations of (H_0, P_0) so small that their squares (second order terms) and higher order terms can be neglected. We, thus, seek a variant of (1) as follows.

Putting (4) in (1), using (3) and simplifying, we set

$$\left.\begin{array}{l} \dfrac{dh}{dt} = -\dfrac{a_{12}a_{21}}{a_{22}}p \\[4mm] \dfrac{dp}{dt} = \dfrac{a_{11}a_{22}}{a_{12}}h \end{array}\right\} \qquad (5)$$

Obviously (5) is a linearized version of (1)

Dividing the first of (5) by the second one, we get

$$\frac{dh}{dp} = -\frac{a_{12}{}^2 a_{21}}{a_{22}{}^2 a_{11}}\frac{p}{h}$$

or, $a_{11}a_{22}{}^2 hdh + a_{21}a_{12}{}^2 pdp = 0$

Integrating,

$$a_{11}a_{22}{}^2 h^2 + a_{21}a_{12}{}^2 p^2 = \text{constant} \qquad (6)$$

which represents a family of closed curves in the $(h-p)$ plane around (H_0, P_0).

Using (5), $\dfrac{d^2 h}{dt^2} = -\dfrac{a_{12}a_{21}}{a_{22}} \cdot \dfrac{a_{11}a_{22}}{a_{12}}h$

or, $\dfrac{d^2 h}{dt^2} + a_{11}a_{21}h = 0 \qquad (7)$

And a similar equation for p.

Solving (7), $h = A\cos\left\{\left(\sqrt{a_{11}a_{21}}\right)t + \varepsilon\right\} \qquad (8)$

Similarly, we get the value of p.

Thus the approximate values of H and P are obtained in terms of t.

Remark

Here is a method enabling us to determine in approximately quantitative terms, the values of H and P. This way of linearization is also referred to as perturbation. The stability or otherwise will be taken up in a separate chapter.

7.7 Some glimpses of nonlinear mechanics

Here we again go back to some situations of nonlinearities in dynamics or widely called, nonlinear mechanics, with the purpose of both understanding in the light of what we have learnt as nonlinear differential equations and their behaviour, too.

Our starting point, here again, is the energy which we know to be dissipative if there be something like friction; but, we can ignore it if this happens to be slow over fairly short periods of time. We fall back upon our time-honoured principle of conservation of energy, viz, the total of the kinetic energy and the potential energy is a constant. We speak of the system, in terms of physics, as a conservative system. We formulate this system, in the simplest terms, as

$$m\frac{d^2x}{dt^2} + F(x) = 0 \qquad (1)$$

which makes us recall the equation of motion of an oscillator like

$$m\frac{d^2x}{dt^2} + \mu^2 x = 0$$

or, with damping,

$$m\frac{d^2x}{dt^2} + k\frac{dx}{dt} + \mu^2 x = 0$$

In (1), we assume $F(x)$ to be analytic for all values of x and (1) is equivalent to the autonomous system

$$\left.\begin{array}{l} \dfrac{dx}{dt} = y \\[2ex] \dfrac{dy}{dt} = -\dfrac{F(x)}{m} \end{array}\right\} \qquad (2)$$

To obtain, as on earlier occasions, the paths of (2); dividing the second of (2) by first, we get

$$\frac{dy}{dx} = -\frac{F(x)}{my}$$ (3)

which we can write as

$$\text{`}my\,dy = -F(x)dx$$

Integrating, from (x,y) to (x_0,y_0) at $t = t_0$,

$$\frac{1}{2}my^2 - \frac{1}{2}my_0^2 = -\int_{x_0}^{x} F(x)dx$$

which we express as

$$\frac{1}{2}my^2 + \int_0^x F(x)dx = \frac{1}{2}my_0^2 + \int_0^{x_0} F(x)dx$$ (4)

Now, $\dfrac{1}{2}my^2 = \dfrac{1}{2}m\left(\dfrac{dx}{dt}\right)^2$ (5)

is the kinetic energy of the system and let

$$V(x) = \int_0^x F(x)dx$$ (6)

be its potential energy so that (4) is nothing but the statement of the law of conservation of total energy E in terms of symbols, viz., i.e.

$$\frac{1}{2}my^2 + V(x) = E = \frac{1}{2}my_0^2 + V_0^2(x)$$ (7)

If we now assign to E, a constant value, we can obtain from (7), the equation of paths of constant energy in the phase. The critical parts of the system (3) are $(x_r,0)$ where x_r's are the roots of $F(x)=0$.

Let us now try to have the sketch of the paths. One can say for the differential equation (3) that the paths intersect the x-axis at right angles and have horizontal tangents along the lines $x = x_r$. Further, from (7), we can find that the paths are symmetrical with respect to the x-axis. Now we make use of (7) to get the paths which are given by

$$y = \pm \sqrt{\frac{2}{m}\{E - V(x)\}} \qquad (8)$$

To have the paths, let us have the plane, x–z with z axis with same vertical line as the y axis of the phase plane. We draw the graph of $z = V(x)$ and few other horizontal lines $z = E$ in the x–z plane. The two planes x–z and x–y are shown in Fig. 7.2.

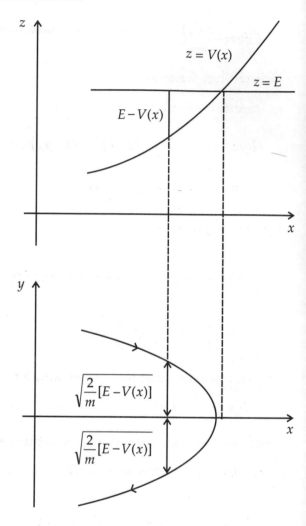

Fig. 7.2

Remark

One can work out as an excellent exercise to use the graph in order to show that, if the potential energy function given by

$$V(x) = -\int_0^x F(x)\,dx,$$

has

(a)   a relative minimum at $x = x_r$, then the critical point $(x_r, 0)$ is a centre and is stable.

(b)   a relative maximum at $x = x_r$ then the critical point $(x_r, 0)$ is a saddle point and is unstable.

(c)   a horizontal inflection point at $x = x_r$, then the point $(x_r, 0)$ is of a degenerate type called a cusp which is unstable.

Exercise

1. Determine the nature of the critical point(s) of the nonlinear systems

   (i) $\dfrac{dx}{dt} = x + 4y - x^3$

   $\dfrac{dy}{dt} = 6x - y + 2xy$

   (ii) $\dfrac{dx}{dt} = 8x - y^3$

   $\dfrac{dy}{dt} = -6y + 6x^2$

   (iii) $\dfrac{dx}{dt} = -x + y + 2x^4 - y^6$

   $\dfrac{dy}{dt} = x - 3y + 11y^4$

2. Investigate the stability of the point $(0,0)$ for the system

   $\dfrac{d^2x}{dt^2} + \dfrac{dx}{dt} + b \, \sin x = 0$

3. Investigate the behaviour of the system

   $\dfrac{dx}{dt} = \sin x - 4y$

   $\dfrac{dy}{dt} = \sin 2x - 5y$

4. Determine the behaviour of

   (i) $\dfrac{dx}{dt} = y(x^2 + 1)$

   $\dfrac{dy}{dt} = 2xy^2$

   (ii) $\dfrac{dx}{dt} = 2xy + x^3$

   $\dfrac{dy}{dt} = -x^2 + y^5$

(iii) $\dfrac{dx}{dt} = -2x + 3y + xy$

$\dfrac{dy}{dt} = -x + y - 2xy^2$

5. Determine the critical point(s) of

$\dfrac{dx}{dt} = y\left(1 + x - y^2\right)$

$\dfrac{dy}{dt} = x\left(1 + y - x^2\right)$

How do you characterise the linearization for a neighbourhood of these points?

6. For the system

$\dfrac{dx}{dt} = -x + y^2$

$\dfrac{dy}{dt} = -y^2 + x^2$

show that of the two critical points, one is a saddle. What is the eigen value for the other critical point? Can this be called degenerate? Draw the phase portrait.

7. Determine the nature of critical points of

$\dfrac{dx}{dt} = -y + x\left(x^2 + y^2\right)\sin\sqrt{x^2 + y^2}$

$\dfrac{dy}{dt} = x + y\left(x^2 + y^2\right)\sin\sqrt{x^2 + y^2}$

How can you have the linear variant at $(0,0)$? Can it have another value?

8. If the Lotka-Volterra system assumes the form

$\dfrac{dx}{dt} = 0.5x - xy$

$\dfrac{dy}{dt} = -2y + xy$ for $xy > 0$

find the critical point(s) and determine their nature. Sketch the family of solution curves in the first quadrant of the x-y plane.

9. Discuss the behaviour of the system

$$\frac{dx}{dt} = -2x + 3y + xy$$

$$\frac{dy}{dt} = -x + y + 2xy^2$$

10. Investigate for stability the critical point $(x = 0, y = 0)$ of the system

$$\frac{dx}{dt} = -x + y + 2xy^4 - y^6$$

$$\frac{dy}{dt} = x - 3y + 11y^4$$

11. Investigate the critical point $(0, 0)$ of the nonlinear system

$$\frac{dx}{dt} = x + 4y - x^2$$

$$\frac{dy}{dt} = 6x - y + 2xy$$

What kind of qualitative information can you get from the slope of the trajectories of the system?

12. What are the qualitative diagrams of the systems

(i) $$\frac{dx}{dt} = 2xy$$

$$\frac{dy}{dt} = 3y^2 - x^2$$

(ii) $$\frac{dx}{dt} = x^2$$

$$\frac{dy}{dt} = 2y^2 - xy?$$

What are your observations about the behaviour of each orbit system?

stability aspects : Liapunov's direct method

We have already given an inkling how the Russian mathematician Liapunov made an attempt for a method to establish the stability or otherwise, of a nonlinear system. Liapunov's function, the construction of which is the principal tenet of his method, has to be dealt with in greater depth and this is what is being sought in this chapter.

8.1 Liapunov's direct (second) method : A resumé

The motivation to this method, as we may recall, is the principle of energy in physical processes and this happened to be the crux of Liapunov's method of ascertaining the stability or otherwise of a nonlinear system. We have an intuitive feel that if the total energy of a physical system or strictly speaking, if its potential energy has a relative minimum, at a certain equilibrium point, then this equilibrium point is stable. This prompted Liapunov to generalize the idea of his direct method for studying stability in the wider context of mathematically nonlinear but autonomous systems.

$C = [x(t), y(t)]$ which is within C_2 for $t = t_0$. Then $V(t_0) < m$ and since $\dfrac{dV}{dt}$ is negative semi-definite, we find

$$\frac{dV}{dt} \leq 0 \qquad\qquad (7)$$

$\Rightarrow V(t) \leq V(t_0) < m$ for all $t > t_0$. Thus the path C cannot reach the circle C_1 for any $t > t_0$ and hence, the critical point is stable.

In order to show that the critical point is asymptotically stable, we need to establish that $V(t) \to 0$, as $t \to \infty$, of course, satisfying the additional given condition, in the statement of the theme.

Since $V(x, y)$ is positive definite, we can say that the path C approaches the critical point $(0, 0)$. Since $\dfrac{dV}{dt} < 0$, $V(t)$ is a decreasing function; since $V(t)$ is bounded below, $V(t) \to l$ as $t \to \infty$. What we simply need to show, now is that $l = 0$. Let us assert that $l > 0$. Let us choose a positive number $\bar{r} < r$ such that $V(x, y) < l$ whenever (x, y) is inside the circle the circle C_3 with radius $\bar{r}$; since $\dfrac{dV}{dt}$ is continuous and negative definite, it attains a negative maximum, say $-k$ in the annular region bounded by C_1 and C_3 and also on them. The whole of the path C for $t \geq t_0$ is contained by this region. Therefore

$$V(t) = V(t_0) + \int_{t_0}^{t} \frac{dV}{dt}\, dt \qquad\qquad (8)$$

which gives rise to

$$V(t) \leq V(t_0) - k(t - t_0) \qquad\qquad (9)$$

for all $t \geq t_0$.

But the R.H.S. of (9) $\to -\infty$ as $t \to \infty$, so that $V(t) \to -\infty$ as $t \to \infty$ which contradicts the assumption that $V(t) \geq 0$ and so, $l = 0$.

Remarks

1.   One must have realized by now that one of the vital purposes and importantly so, of the study of nonlinear systems is to look for a criterion or norm to guarantee stability. We did start off with some definitions of stability and asymptotic stability of an equilibrium part of the system

$$\frac{dx}{dt} = f(x) \tag{10}$$

where vector (arrows dropped) notations are applied.

We have just used the Liapunov's criteria to deal with stability. We now know that Liapunov's function emerges from Liapunov's stability theorem. Let us now look at it in a different way without losing its essence.

Let $V : U \to R$ be a differentiable function defined in a nbd $U \subset W$ of $\bar{x}$, and a sink for which, as we recall, there should be a norm on R^n such that $|x(t) - \bar{x}|$ decreases for solutions $x(t)$ near $\bar{x}$. What Liapunov did was to look for other functions that would be of use, in lieu of the norms for stability. Let $\dfrac{dV}{dt} : U \to R$ be the function defined by

$$\frac{dV(x)}{dt} = DV(x)(f(x))$$

where the right hand side is simply the operator $DV(x)$ applied to the vector $f(x)$. Then, by the normal chain rule on differentiation, we can write

$$\frac{dV(x)}{dt} = \frac{d}{dt} V(\phi_t(x))\big|_{t=0}$$

where $\phi_t(x)$ is the solution of (10)

Obviously, if $\dfrac{dV(x)}{dt}$ is negative, then V decreases along with the solution of (1) through x. With these preliminaries, we can now state Liapunov's stability theorem in another form :

Theorem : Let $\bar{x}\,\varepsilon\,W$ be an equilibrium point of

$$\frac{dx}{dt} = f(x)$$

Let $V:U \to R$ be a continuous function on a nbd $U \subset W$ of x differentiable on $U - \bar{x}$ such that

(a) $V(x)=0$ and $V(x)>0$ if $x \neq \bar{x}$

(b) $V(x) \leq 0$ in $U - \bar{x}$, then x is stable.

Furthermore, if also

(c) $V(x)<0$ in $U - \bar{x}$, then $\bar{x}$ is asymptotically stable.

We hardly need to reiterate that V satisfying (a) and (b) is the Liapunov function for $\bar{x}$. We often say that V is a strict Liapunov function if (c) is satisfied.

2.   The surface $V(x)=c$ for some $c>0$ is called a *Liapunov surface or a level surface*. This notion of Liapunov surfaces makes the Liapunov's stability theorem plausible. By increasing values of c, we can have a variety of Liapunov surfaces. What does then $\dfrac{dV}{dt} \leq 0$ mean? These inequalities imply that when a trajectory crosses a Liapunov surface $V(x)=c$, it gets into the set $\Omega_c =\{x\,\varepsilon\,R^n \,|V(x) \leq c\}$ and cannot come out again; when $\dfrac{dV}{dt}<0$, the trajectory keeps on moving from one Liapunov surface to an *inner* Liapunov surface (for a smaller value of c). As c goes on decreasing, the Liapunov surface $V(x)=c$ coincides with the origin, meaning thereby that the trajectory approaches the origin, with increasing time. But if $\dfrac{dV}{dt}<0$, nothing can be said whether the origin is being approached but that the origin is stable can be

asserted, for any trajectory cán well be within any nbd, by taking the initial state $x(0)$ to be also with the Liapunov surface lying with in the nbd.

3.   There can be another version of Liapunov theorem in the light of the terminology on positive or negative definite or semi-definite. The stationary point is stable if there is a continuously differentiable positive function $V(x)$ so that $\dfrac{dV(x)}{dt}$ is negative-definite. Liapunov's theorem can be applied without being able to solve the set of differential equations $\dfrac{dx}{dt} = f(x)$. With all the above remarks, let us now proceed to work out few examples to show that we can find Liapunov's function without there being any standard method to do so; of course, we have shown earlier one way to do so.

8.2 Illustrative examples

Example 1

Investigate the stability of the following system using Liapunov criteria

$$\dot{x} = y - x\left(x^2 + y^2\right)$$
$$\dot{y} = -x - y\left(x^2 + y^2\right)$$

Solution

Let $V = x^2 + y^2$, a positive definite function and $\dot{V} = -2(x^2 + y^2)^2$ which is negative definite and so the zero solution is asymptotically stable.

Example 2

Investigate the behaviour of the zero solution of

$$\dot{x} = (x - 2y)\left(1 - x^2 - 3y^2\right)$$
$$\dot{y} = -(y + x)\left(1 - x^2 - 3y^2\right)$$

Solution

Let us choose a function $V = x^2 + 2y^2$

$$\frac{dV}{dt} = \frac{\partial V}{\partial x}\dot{x} + \frac{\partial V}{\partial y}\dot{y}$$

$$= -2x(x-2y)(1-x^2-3y^2)-4y(y+x)(1-x^2-3y^2)$$

$$= -2(1-x^2-3y^2)(x^2+2y^2) \le 0$$

for small x, y's and also within $x^2 + 3y^2 \le 1$

The zero solution $x = 0, y = 0$ is stable according to Liapunov theorem.

Example 3

Investigate the behaviour of

$$\dot{x} = -5y - 2x^3$$
$$\dot{y} = 5x - 3y^2$$

Solution

Let us choose $V = x^2 + y^2$

We find that $\frac{dV}{dt} = 2x(-5y-2x^3)+2y(5x-3y^2)$

$$= -(4x^3+6y^3) < 0$$

i.e. V is negative definite

$$\frac{dV}{dt} = 0 \text{ at } x=y=0$$

$\therefore$ $(0,0)$ is asymptotically stable.

Example 4

Discuss the behaviour of $\ddot{x} + x^2\dot{x} + x^3 = 0$

Solution

This equation is equivalent to

$$\left.\begin{array}{l} \dot{x} = y \\ \dot{y} = -x^3 - x^2 y \end{array}\right\}$$

Let us take the Liapunov function

$$V(x,y) = \frac{1}{2}y^2 + \frac{1}{4}x^4$$

$$\therefore \quad \frac{dV}{dt} = y\dot{y} + x^3\dot{x}$$

$$= -x^3 y - x^2 y^2 + x^3\dot{y} = -x^2 y^2 < 0$$

$\frac{dV}{dt}$ vanishes only on the coordinate axes. Also, there is no solution other than the zero solution that remains on the axes for all $t \geq 0$.

Let us see what happens to the slope given by

$$\frac{dy}{dx} = \frac{-x^3 - x^2 y}{y}$$

which has finite values at all points on the y-axis except at $(0,0)$. This implies that a part of the path does not lie on the axis. On the other hand, $\frac{dy}{dx} \to \infty$ as the x-axis is approached, which means that a part of the path does not lie on this axis. The set of coordinate axes does not contain the paths except the origin of coordinates. The point $(0,0)$ is, by Liapunov's theorem, asymptotically stable (It is to be noted that $V(x,y) \to \infty$ as (x,y) where $x^2 + y^2 \to \infty$).

Example 5

Discuss the behaviour of

$$\dot{x} = -x + y^2$$

$$\dot{y} = -y - xy$$

Solution

Let us choose the Liapunov function

$$V(x,y) = x^2 + y^2$$

$$\frac{dV}{dt} = 2x(-x + y^2) + 2y(-y - xy)$$

$$= -2x^2 + 2xy^2 - 2y^2 - 2xy^2$$

$$= -2(x^2 + y^2) = -2V$$

$$\therefore \quad \frac{dV}{dt} = -2V$$

Integrating,

$$V = V(0,0)e^{-2t}$$

∴ The critical point or the zero solution can be said to be (exponentially) asymptotically stable.

Example 6

Investigate the behaviour of

$$\dot{x} = -6y - \frac{1}{4}xy^2$$

$$\dot{y} = 4x - \frac{1}{6}y$$

Solution

Let $V(x,y) = 2x^2 + 3y^2$

$$\therefore \quad \frac{dV}{dt} = 4x\left(-6y - \frac{1}{4}xy^2\right) + 6y\left(4x - \frac{1}{6}y\right)$$

$$= -x^2 y^2 - y^2 = -y^2\left(1 + x^2\right)$$

$\dfrac{dV}{dt}$ is negative semi-definite and it vanishes on the x-axis.

$\therefore$ This is a stable critical point.

Example 7

Discuss the behaviour of

$$\dot{x} = -y + \alpha x^3$$
$$\dot{y} = x + \alpha y^3$$

Solution

Let $V(x,y) = x^2 + y^2$

$$\frac{dV}{dt} = 2x\left(-y + \alpha x^3\right) + 2y\left(x + \alpha y^3\right)$$

$$= 2\alpha\left(x^4 + y^4\right)$$

The critical point is asymptotically stable if $\alpha < 0$

Example 8

Discuss the behaviour of the well known van der Pol's equation

$$\ddot{x} + \varepsilon\left(x^2 - 1\right)\dot{x} + x = 0 \quad (\varepsilon < 0)$$

Solution

The given equation is equivalent to

$$\dot{x} = \frac{dx}{dt} = y - \varepsilon\left(\frac{x^3}{3} - x\right)$$

$$\dot{y} = \frac{dy}{dt} = -x$$

Let $V(x,y) = \frac{1}{2}(x^2 + y^2)$

$$\frac{dV}{dt} = x\dot{x} + y\dot{y} = -\varepsilon x^2\left(\frac{x^2}{3} - 1\right)$$

$$\therefore \quad \frac{dV}{dt} \leq 0 \text{ for } x^2 \leq 3(\varepsilon < 0)$$

i.e. $\frac{dV}{dt} \leq 0$ in $\Omega = \{(x,y)\varepsilon R^2 : -\sqrt{3} < x < \sqrt{3}\}$ i.e. in $x^2 + y^2 < 3$

Thus, in the circle $x^2 + y^2 = 3$

we have $V > 0$ and $\dot{V} < 0$ for $x^2 + y^2 \neq 0$

$\therefore$ This critical point $(0,0)$ is in the region of asymptotic stability.

8.3 A few problems and observations

I.   The last problem in the last exercise set can be shown to be revealing.

Assuming the Liapunov function $V(x,y)$ as

$$V(x,y) = \frac{1}{2}(x^2 + y^2)$$

one finds that, for the system $\dot{x} = y - xf(x,y)$, $\dot{y} = -x - yf(x,y)$

$$\frac{dV}{dt} = -(x^2 + y^2)f(x,y)$$

which shows the behaviour, if $f(x,y) \geq 0$ and $f(x,y) < 0$, of the critical point $(0,0)$ to be stable and unstable respectively.

This leads us to the simple fact, which we have seen earlier, that one cannot say in definite terms anything about the stability of a critical point by the first order approximation.

II.   Let us consider a different sort of system in R^3 given by

$$\frac{dx}{dt} = 2y(z-1)$$

$$\frac{dy}{dt} = -x(z-1)$$

$$\frac{dz}{dt} = -z^3$$

The z-axis $\left(=\left|(x,y,z)\right|x=y=0\right)$ consists entirely of equilibrium points. Let us investigate the origin for stability. Let us look for a Liapunov function for $(0,0,0)$ of the form $V(x,y,z)=ax^2+by^2+cz^2$ with $a,b,c>0$. For such a choice of $V(x,y,z)$, we have

$$\frac{dV}{dt} = 2(ax\dot{x}+by\dot{y}+cz\dot{z})$$

or, $\dfrac{1}{2}\dfrac{dV}{dt} = 2axy(z-1)-bxy(z-1)-cz^4$

If we wish $\dfrac{dV}{dt}\leq 0$ then we need to put $2a=b$, $c=1$ so that $x^2+2y^2+z^2$ is a possible Liapunov function and the origin is a stable critical (equilibrium) point. Further, this can be easily shown to be asymptotically stable if $V(x,y,z)$ be a strict Liapunov function. Here is an example which shows clearly that the choice of the Liapunov function, whatever be the space of reference, is an exercise on ingenuity. That it is basically a matter of trial and error is also shown in the next example.

III.   Let us consider the (first order) differential equation given by

$$\dot{x} = -g(x)$$

where $g(x)$ is locally Lipschitz on $(-a,a)$ and satisfies $g(0)=0$, $xg(x)>0$ $\forall$ $x \neq 0$ and $x \varepsilon (-a,a)$. If we wish the origin to be asymptotically stable, let us consider a form of Liapunov function given by

$$V(x) = \int_0^x g(y)\,dy$$

$V(x)$ is continuously differentiable over the domain $D = (-a,a)$, $V(0)=0$ and $V'(x)>0$ for all $x \neq 0$.

We cannot say as yet whether $V(x,y)$ is, indeed, a Liapunov function. To see whether this is so or not, let us have

$$\frac{dV}{dt} = \frac{\partial V}{\partial x}\dot{x} = \frac{\partial V}{\partial x}\left[-g(x)\right] = -g^2(x)<0 \quad \forall x \varepsilon D \quad \{0\}$$

Hence, by Liapunov's theorem, the origin is asymptotically stable.

IV.   An important problem in non-linear studies is to predict the way a system evolves, as time moves on. Even though the process of evolution is complex, we often formalize this through a definition. Let us define a trajectory by $x = \xi(t)$, $y = \eta(t)$. The stationary point (x_0, y_0) is globally asymptotically stable if all trajectories satisfy $\lim_{\xi \to \infty}\xi(t) = x_0$ and $\lim_{\eta \to \infty}\eta(t) = y_0$.

    Apparently, the concept in this definition is linked with the concept of asymptotic stability, as mentioned earlier.

The equation : $\dfrac{d^2x}{dt^2} + 3\dfrac{dx}{dt} + 2x = 0$

has the solution $x(t) = c_1 e^{-t} + c_2 e^{-2t}$

Also, $\dfrac{dx}{dt} = -c_1 e^{-t} - 2c_2 e^{-2t}$

Both $\left(x \text{ and } \dfrac{dx}{dt} \right) \to (0,0)$ as $t \to \infty$.

The origin is thus globally asymptotically stable for solution of the system.

In the light of this definition, we can cash in a part of Liapunov's criteria by saying that if $\dfrac{dV}{dt}$ is negative definite and V is positive definite, the critical point is globally asymptotically stable.

V.   In some cases, there are more natural Liapunov functions in mechanical or electrical systems. For the mechanical system, we go back to the equation of motion of a mass m attached to a spring given by

$$m \frac{d^2 x}{dt^2} + k \frac{dx}{dt} + \mu^2 x = 0$$

where $k \ge 0$ is a constant representing the viscosity of the medium through which the mass moves and μ, a are constants. This equation is equivalent to

$$\frac{dx}{dt} = y$$

$$\frac{dy}{dt} = -\frac{\mu^2}{m} x - \frac{k}{m} y$$

Its only critical point is $(0,0)$. The K.E. is $\dfrac{1}{2} m y^2$ and P.E. (the energy stored in the spring) is

$$\int_0^x \mu^2 x \, dx = \frac{1}{2} \mu^2 x^2$$

$\therefore$ Total energy is given by

$$E(x,y) = \frac{1}{2} m y^2 + \frac{1}{2} \mu^2 x^2$$

$$\therefore \quad \frac{dE}{dt} = \frac{\partial E}{\partial x}\frac{dx}{dt} + \frac{\partial E}{\partial y}\frac{dy}{dt}$$

$$= \mu^2 xy + my\left(-\frac{k}{m}y - \frac{\mu^2}{m}x\right)$$

$$= -\mu^2 y^2 \leq 0$$

$E(x,y)$ is the Liapunov function and the critical point $(0,0)$ is stable.

VI. There is a stricter use of terminology where we talk about stability or asymptotically stability from Liapunov's criteria. We ought to say that the stationary (critical equation) point is stable/asymptotically stable in the sense of Liapunov.

VII. When we deal with linearized versions of nonlinear systems, we should use the terms stability and *asymptotic stability* with regard to first approximation.

VIII. We have seen in an illustrative example earlier that the origin may be asymptotically stable. We ought to be interested then how far from the origin, the path can be and still converge to the origin, as $t \to \infty$. Thus how we come to the idea of the *region of attraction* (also known as the region of asymptotic stability, *domain of attraction*, basin) to which we return later. Let $\phi(t;x)$ be the solution of $\dot{x} = f(x)$ with a given initial state (at the time $t=0$). If $\phi(t;x)$ is defined for all $t \geq 0$ and $\lim_{t \to \infty} \phi(t,x) = 0$, then we are in a position to define the region of attraction as the set of all points x. We can hardly find out the exact region of attraction analytically but we get an estimate of the same using Liapunov function. But how? What we need to find out is the set contained in the region of attraction. From the Liapunov's theorem, we can have the Liapunov function that satisfies the conditions of asymptotic stability over a domain and if, in addition to this, we have every trajectory $\Omega_c = \{x \varepsilon R^n \,|\, V(x) \leq c\}$ to be bounded and contained in D, then every trajectory beginning in Ω_c remains in Ω_c and approaches the origin as $t \to \infty$.

Thus, Ω_c can be taken as the region of attraction. As already remarked, we shall return to these ideas later on with examples. A poser that is likely to arise is this: can we enlarge this region of attraction? If so, under what conditions? Say, in the space R^n? If for any initial state x, the trajectory $\phi(t;x)$ approaches the origin as $t \to \infty$, however large $\|x\|$ may be, and it there be, in addition, a trajectory for an asymptotically stable equilibrium at the origin, then the origin can be said to be globally asymptotically stable, a term which has already been encountered. Its formal definition is given by the theorem which follows, without the proof.

Theorem

Let $x = 0$ be an equilibrium point to $\dot{x} = f(x)$

Let $V : R^n \to R$ be a continuously differentiable function such that

$V(0) = 0$ and $V(x) > 0$, $\forall x \neq 0$

$\|x\| \to \infty$ as $V(x) \to \infty$

$V(x) < 0$, $\forall x \neq 0$.

Then $x = 0$ is globally asymptotically stable.

Remark

Global asymptotic stability can be established if we can have $x \in R^n$ included in the interior of a bounded set Ω_c; $V(x) = c$ is the level surface which requires that conditions of Liapunov's theorem should hold globally when $D = R^n$. But this does not suffice; we need to have more conditions to ensure that any point in R^n can be included in a bounded set. In fact, Ω_c is bounded for all values of $c > 0$ if $V(x) \to \infty$ as $\|x\|^2 \to \infty$ and the function is said to be *radially bounded*.

IX. A question that ought to come up in regard to Liapunov's theorem is this : Are the conditions of Liapunov's theorem only sufficient? The answer is yes. If the criteria to stability or otherwise using Liapunov's function, do not suffice, we cannot say in definite terms; we need to go in for further investigations using other techniques.

Exercise

1. Investigate the behaviour of

$$\dot{x} = -6y - \frac{1}{4}xy^2$$
$$\dot{y} = 4x - \frac{1}{6}y$$

2. Investigate the behaviour of

$$\dot{x} = -4y - x^3$$
$$\dot{y} = 3x - y^3$$

3. Investigate the behaviour of (to a first approximation)

$$\dot{x} = 2x + 8 \sin y$$
$$\dot{y} = 2 - e^x - 3y - \cos y$$

4. Investigate the behaviour of

$$\dot{x} = 3x + y$$
$$\dot{y} = -4y + x^3$$

5. Investigate the behaviour of

$$\dot{x} = -y + x\left(r^2 - x^2 - y^2\right)$$
$$\dot{y} = x + y\left(r^2 - x^2 - y^2\right)$$

6. Investigate the behaviour of

$$\dot{x} = -x + y^2$$
$$\dot{y} = y + x^2$$

7. Investigate the behaviour of

$$\dot{x} = -2xy$$
$$\dot{y} = x^2 - y^2$$

8. Investigate the stability of the critical point $(0,0)$ of the system

$$\dot{x} = y - x\,f(x,y)$$
$$\dot{y} = -x - y\,f(x,y)$$

where $f(x,y)$ can be expanded in a convergent power series and $f(0,0) = 0$

9. What is a possible form of Liapunov function of the system

$$\frac{dx}{dt} = -x + 2x^2 + y^2$$

$$\frac{dy}{dt} = -y + xy \quad ?$$

Can this be used to determine the behaviour of the critical point? Justify your answer.

10. Construct a Liapunov function of the form $\alpha x^2 + \beta y^2$.

(where α and β are constants for the system) for

$$\frac{dx}{dt} = -x - y - x^3$$

$$\frac{dy}{dt} = x - y - y^3$$

How do you proceed then to find out the behaviour of the critical point $(0,0)$ of the system?

11. How would you determine whether the system

$$\frac{dx}{dt} = -3x + x^3 + 2xy^2$$

$$\frac{dy}{dt} = -2x + \frac{2}{3}y^3$$

has its critical point $(0,0)$ stable or asymptotically stable or otherwise, by constructing its Liapunov's function in the form $Ax^2 + By^2$, A, B being constants?

12. A particle moves on the straight line R under the influence of a Newtonian force depending only upon the position of the particle. If the force is always directed towards $0 \in R$ and vanishes at 0, is 0, in stable equilibrium?

[Hint : Take the system $\begin{cases} \dot{x} = y \\ \dot{y} = -g(x) \end{cases}$; construct the energy function $K \cdot E + P \cdot E$].

13. Find a Liapunov function for the equilibrium $(0,0)$ of

$$\frac{dx}{dt} = -2x - y^2$$

$$\frac{dy}{dt} = -x - x^2$$

14. If $V(x,y) = ax^{2m} + by^{2m}$ is taken as the Liapunov function of the system

$$\frac{dx}{dt} = -2xy$$

$$\frac{dy}{dt} = x^2 - y^3$$

what can be possible values of a, b, m, n (each > 0) so as to have the appropriate form $V(x,y)$?

15. Investigate the zero-solution of the system

$$\frac{dx}{dt} = -(x - 2y)(1 - x^2 - 3y^2)$$

$$\frac{dy}{dt} = -(x + y)(1 - x^2 - 3y^2)$$

for stability or otherwise.

16. Investigate the zero-solution of the autonomous system.

$$\frac{dx}{dt} = x^2 + y$$

$$\frac{dy}{dt} = y^2 + x$$

17. What is the Liapunov's function for the system

$$\frac{dx}{dt} = -5y - 2x^3$$

$$\frac{dy}{dt} = 5x - 3y^3 ?$$

What can you say about behaviour of the zero solution of the system?

18. How do you construct the Liapunov function of the equation

$$\frac{d^2x}{dt^2} + x^2 \frac{dx}{dt} + x^3 = 0 ?$$

What can you say about them ?

19. What is Liapunov's function for the system

$$\dot{x} = y - \varepsilon \left(\frac{x^3}{3} - x \right)$$

$$\dot{y} = -x ?$$

What can you conclude about the behaviour?

20. Discuss the behaviour of the critical point of the system

$$\frac{dx}{dt} = x^2 + y$$

$$\frac{dy}{dt} = y^2 + x$$

by constructing Liapunov function.

21. How do you make use of Liapunov's theorem to investigate the behaviour of the system

$$\frac{dx}{dt} = -(x - 2y)(1 - x^2 - 3y^2)$$

$$\frac{dy}{dt} = -(y + x)(1 - x^2 - 3y^2)?$$

22. How do you make use of Liapunov's theorem to investigate the behaviour of the system

$$\frac{dx}{dt} = -y + x(r^2 - x^2 - y^2)$$

$$\frac{dy}{dt} = x + y(r^2 - x^2 - y^2)?$$

23. How do you construct the Liapunov's function of the system for the pendulum given by

$$\frac{dx}{dt} = y$$

$$\frac{dy}{dt} = -a \sin x ?$$

What is the sign of the derivative of the Liapunov function?

24. Investigate the stability of the following system using a Liapunov function.

$$\frac{dx}{dt} = y - x(x^2 + y^2)$$

$$\frac{dy}{dt} = -x - y(x^2 + y^2)$$

25. What is the Liapunov function $V(x,y,t)$ for the function?

    How do you obtain $\dfrac{dV}{dt}$?

    Under what conditions can this be negative definite or semi-definite?

    (Hint: If $x<1$ and $y<1$ show that $\dfrac{dV}{dt}<0$)

26. Investigate for stability of the zero solution of the system

    $$\frac{dx}{dt} = -\frac{1}{2}x - \frac{1}{2}xy^2$$

    $$\frac{dy}{dt} = -\frac{3}{4}y + 3xz^3$$

    $$\frac{dz}{dt} = -\frac{2}{3}z - 2xyz^2$$

manifolds : introduction and applications in nonlinearity studies

9

In the Preamble and elsewhere, earlier, we have mentioned Poincare's name for introducing novel qualitative ways of studying nonlinear systems. It was through such methods that Poincare could make a dent on his study on the stability of the solar system. The essence of his celebrated work *Analysis Situs*, as he called it, was topological and one may say that there was a topological undercurrent through his work between 1892 and 1902. He made a conjecture of which topologists call 'manifolds', with which we begin this chapter and with some relevant implications in some selected areas of topology.

9.1 Manifolds

Manifolds are said to be very basic to occur in all kinds of situations. The immediate example one can cite is about the ordinary space of Euclidean geometry as a manifold. We have referred to motions of a pendulum several times by now. How can we mathematize the motion of a pendulum that is fixed at a pivot and free to move only in a vertical plane? If the motion of the bob is for a small distance, we can describe its position, by calling it positive or negative, according to its motion to the right or left i.e. we can do so by representing it as a line, as shown in Fig. 9.1(a) and 9.1(b).

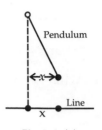

Fig 9.1 (a)

If we think of large motions of the bob to the right, well above the top, and then also to the left, we can describe its motion by a circle, as shown in Fig. 9.2.

Both line and circle occupy spaces which locally have one degree of freedom and so line and circle are manifolds (one dimensional manifold). Thus, a single pendulum in the plane can be described by one-dimensional fold and a pendulum in space requires a two-dimensional manifold (2-manifold), the sphere. If we are to model mathematically two pendulums as their respective circles, we get a different type 2-manifold, called the torus. In general, an n-manifold is a space that locally has n degrees of freedom. The n-dimensional manifold is a set that is locally similar to Euclidean space R^n ; 1-manifold is locally a curve. Each point of a manifold must have a neighbourhood (nbd) around itself that looks like R^n .

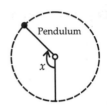

Fig 9.1 (b)

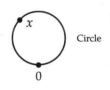

Fig 9.2

Remark

It may appear that we are no longer concerned with stability of equilibrium points of autonomous systems. Certainly, in no way, we are unconcerned. We are all aware of the limitations of our methods to identify stability or otherwise; indeed, don't we know that linearization of a nonlinear system is in no way applicable if the Jacobian matrix (computed at the equilibrium point) has zero real parts and no eigen values with positive real parts? Let us now look for ways if concepts on manifolds can provide such methods. In what follows, we shall work on manifolds preceded by formal definitions.

9.2 Definition

We consider, as before, the autonomous system given by

$$\dot{x} = f(x) \tag{1}$$

where $f : D \to R^n$ is continuously differentiable and $D \subset R^n$ is, evidently, the domain containing the origin $x = 0$. Let this origin be the equilibrium point of (1).

A k-dimensional manifold in R^n $(1 \le k < n)$ is a solution of the equation

$$\xi(x) = 0 \tag{2}$$

where $\xi : R^n \to R^{n-k}$ is sufficiently smooth i.e. continuously differentiable without any limit on the number of times.

For example, as mentioned earlier, the unit circle

$$\left\{ x \varepsilon R^2 \,\middle|\, x_1^2 + x_2^2 = 1 \right\}$$

is a one-dimensional manifold in R^2 and the unit sphere

$$\left\{ x \varepsilon R^n \,\middle|\, \sum_{i=1}^{n} x_1^2 = 1 \right\}$$

is $(n-1)$ dimensional manifold in R^n.

9.3 Invariant and centre manifolds

If, in particular, $\xi(x(0))=0=\xi(x(t))=0 \,\forall\, t(0,t_1)\subset R$ with $(0,t_1)$ as any time interval of definition of the solution $x(t)$, then the manifold $\{\xi(x)=0\}$ can be called an *invariant manifold*, (note, the analogy with an invariant set).

As in definition 9.2, we take $\dot{x}=f(x)$ (1)

With these definitions, let us go back to the process of linearization of (1) so as to identify where it is likely to become applicable and then how to get it sorted out by the notion of an invariant manifold and a centre manifold.

We can write the above (1) as

$$\dot{x}=Ax+\left\{f(x)-\frac{\partial f(0)}{\partial x}x\right\}=Ax+\bar{f}(x) \tag{2}$$

where $A=\left.\frac{\partial f}{\partial x}(x)\right|_{x=0}$;

$$\bar{f}(x)=f(x)-\frac{\partial f(0)}{\partial x}x \tag{3}$$

is thus amenable to differentiation twice, and

$$f(0)=0, \quad \frac{\partial f(0)}{\partial x}=0 \tag{4}$$

In keeping with what we have mentioned earlier, linearization cannot lead us anywhere, in regard to stability or otherwise, if we assume that A has k eigen values with no real points $m=n-k$ and eigen values with negative real points. Let there be a transformation T that transforms A into a block diagonal matrix such that

$$TAT^{-1}=\begin{bmatrix} A_1 & 0 \\ 0 & A_2 \end{bmatrix}$$

where all eigen values of A_1 have no real parts and all eigen values of A_2 have negative real parts, so that A_1 and A_2, are $k \times k$ and $m \times m$ matrices respectively.

Let us have $\begin{bmatrix} y \\ z \end{bmatrix} = Tx$; $y \varepsilon R^n$; $z \varepsilon R^m$

These make (1) equivalent to

$$\ddot{y} = A_1 y + g_1(y, z) \tag{5}$$

$$\ddot{z} = A_2 z + g_2(y, z) \tag{6}$$

where g_1 and g_2 have properties, same as those of f; apart from being continuously differentiable twice, we have

$$\left. \begin{array}{l} g_1(0,0) = 0, \ \dfrac{\partial g_1(0,0)}{\partial y} = 0, \ \dfrac{\partial g_1(0,0)}{\partial z} = 0 \\[3mm] g_2(0,0) = 0, \ \dfrac{\partial g_2(0,0)}{\partial y} = 0, \ \dfrac{\partial g_2(0,0)}{\partial z} = 0 \end{array} \right\} \tag{7}$$

Let $z = h(y)$ be an invariant manifold of (5) and (6) and let h be smooth. If

$$h(0) = 0, \ \frac{\partial h(0)}{\partial y} = 0$$

then $z = h(y)$ is said to be a *centre manifold*. On the basis of the above, we state, without proof, a theorem on the existence of a centre manifold.

Theorem 1

Let g_1 and g_2 be two continuously differentiable functions satisfying (7); let the eigen values of A_1 given by (5), have zero real parts and of A_2 given by (6), have negative real parts. Then there exists a constant $\varepsilon > 0$ and continuously differentiable function $h(y)$, defined for all $\|y\| < \varepsilon$, such that $z = h(y)$ is a centre manifold of (5) and (6).

Deduction

The above theorem enables one to deduce some forms of what are called 'reduced systems'. Given the initial state of the system (5) and (6), (taken together) the solution $\{y(t), z(t)\}$ stays in the manifold for all $t \geq 0$ i.e. $z(t) = \{h(y(t))\}$. The reduced system is the k th order differential equation given by

$$\dot{y} = A_1 y + g_1 \{y, h(y)\} \tag{8}$$

If we now put $\begin{bmatrix} y \\ \omega \end{bmatrix} = \begin{bmatrix} y \\ z - h(y) \end{bmatrix}$

the system (5) and (6) assume some forms which involve partial derivatives of $h(y)$. We may take recourse to the well-known Hurwitz method to determine the stability properties of the origin from the last two forms of reduced systems.

This principle is taken care of by the following statement (with no proof) as:

Theorem 2

If the origin $y = 0$ of the reduced system (8) is asymptotically stable (or unstable), the origin of the original system, given by (5) and (6), is accordingly, asymptotically stable (or unstable), assuming, of course, the conditions stated earlier.

Remarks

1.   With the same conditions, one can establish about the necessary and sufficient conditions on asymptotic stability with regard to (5) and (6) *vis a vis* those of (8)

2.   In regard to stability, we have to go in for having a continuously differentiable Liapunov function $V(y)$ such that

$$\frac{\partial V}{\partial y}\Big[A_1 y + g\big(y, h(y)\big)\Big] \le 0$$

in some nbd of $y = 0$, if the origin $y = 0$ of (5) and (6) is stable.

9.4 Stable and unstable manifolds

We know of a saddle fixed point to be unstable if initial values in its nbd move away. The set of initial values that moves towards the saddle (we often say, converges to the saddle) is called the *stable manifold* of the saddle.

For example, let

$$\dot{x} = Ax$$

with $A = \begin{pmatrix} 2 & 0 \\ 0 & \frac{1}{2} \end{pmatrix}$ and $x = \begin{pmatrix} x \\ y \end{pmatrix}$

The eigen value is 2, having the eigen vector $\begin{pmatrix} 1 \\ 0 \end{pmatrix}$ and the other eigen value is $\frac{1}{2}$ with the eigen vector $\begin{pmatrix} 0 \\ 1 \end{pmatrix}$. The latter direction, the x-axis, is in the direction of 0 and so, the stable manifold of 0. The x-axis moving away is the unstable manifold of 0; what happens if there be the inverse $f^{-1}(x,y) = \Big(\frac{1}{2}x, 2y\Big)$?

Definition

Let f be a smooth one to one map on R^1 and let p be a saddle fixed point (or periodic saddle point) for f. The stable manifold of p is the set of points x such that if $|f(x) - f(p)| \to 0$ as $x \to \infty$. The unstable manifold of p is thus the set of points x such that $|f^{-1}(x) - f^{-1}(p)| \to 0$ as $x \to \infty$.

Remark

We wish to make use of motions of manifolds for study of behaviour of fixed points, periodic points and periodic orbits. It would be convenient if we introduce the analogous and allied items of stable and unstable sub-spaces and corresponding spanning as well.

9.5 Stable and unstable sub-spaces : Motivation

We take an example of an uncoupled linear system in R^3 given by

$$\left. \begin{array}{l} \dot{x} = x \\ \dot{y} = y \\ \dot{z} = z \end{array} \right\} \tag{1}$$

The general solutions of (1) are given by

$$\left. \begin{array}{l} x(t) = c_1 e^t \\ y(t) = c_2 e^t \\ z(t) = c_3 e^t \end{array} \right\} \tag{2}$$

Its phase portrait is shown in Fig. 9.3.

The x-y plane is referred to as the unstable sub-spaces of the system (1) and z axis, called the stable sub-space(s) of the system (1)

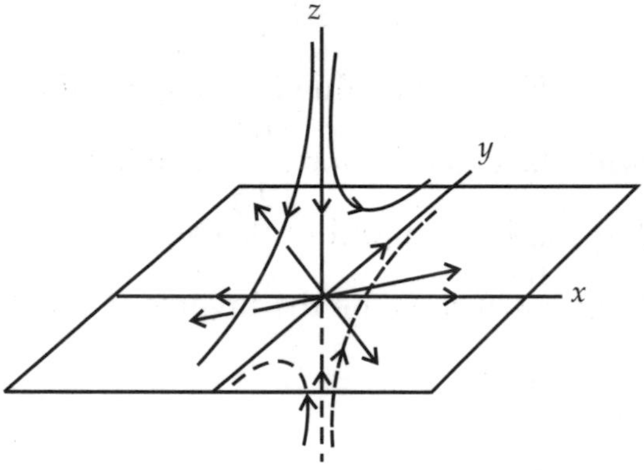

Let us now consider an uncoupled line or system given by

Fig 9.3

$$\dot{x} = Ax \tag{3}$$

where square matrix A has real and distinct eigen values. We can solve (3), using a theorem of linear algebra. This theorem essentially says that if there be a linear transformation $T : R^n \to R$, represented by the $n \times n$ matrix A with respect to the standard bases $\{e_1, e_2, \cdots\cdots, e_n\}$ for R^n, then with respect to any basis of eigen vectors $\{v_1, v_2, \cdots\cdots, v_n\}$, T is represented by the diagonal matrix of eigen values,

$\text{diag}\{\lambda_1, \lambda_2, \cdots\cdots, \lambda_n\}$, $\lambda_1, \lambda_2, \cdots, \lambda_n$ being the related distinct eigen values of the $n \times n$ matrix A. For its proof, see any book on linear algebra. Let us now define a linear transformation of coordinates

$$y = P^{-1}x$$

where P^{-1} is the invertible matrix. Then

$$x = Py$$

$$\dot{y} = P^{-1}\dot{x} = P^{-1}Ax = P^{-1}APy$$

$$\therefore \dot{y} = \text{diag}[\lambda_1, \lambda_2, \cdots, \lambda_n]y$$

$$\therefore y = \text{diag}[e^{\lambda_1 t}, e^{\lambda_2 t}, \cdots, e^{\lambda_n t}]y(0)$$

$$\because y(0) = P^{-1}x(0) \text{ and } x(t) = Py(t), \text{ then}$$

$$\dot{x} = Ax \tag{3}$$

has the solution

$$x(t) = PE(t)P^{-1}x(0) \tag{4}$$

where $E(t)$ is the diagonal matrix given by

$$E(t) = \text{diag}[e^{\lambda_1 t}, e^{\lambda_2 t}, \cdots, e^{\lambda_n t}]$$

Corollary

Hence, by the essence of the theorem, the solution of the linear system (3) is given by the function $x(t)$ defined by (4).

9.6 Illustrative example

Let us consider the linear system

$$\dot{x}_1 = -x_1 - 3x_2 \tag{1}$$

$$\dot{x}_2 = 2x_2 \tag{2}$$

Here $A = \begin{bmatrix} -1 & -3 \\ 0 & 2 \end{bmatrix}$

$\therefore$ The eigen values are $\lambda_1 = -1$, and $\lambda_2 = 2$

A pair of eigen vectors is given by

$$v_1 = \begin{bmatrix} 1 \\ 0 \end{bmatrix}, \quad v_2 = \begin{bmatrix} -1 \\ 1 \end{bmatrix}$$

The matrix P and its inverse are then given by

$$P = \begin{bmatrix} -1 & -1 \\ 0 & 1 \end{bmatrix} \text{ and } P^{-1} = \begin{bmatrix} 1 & 1 \\ 0 & 1 \end{bmatrix}$$

It can be verified that

$$P^{-1}AP = \begin{bmatrix} -1 & 0 \\ 0 & 2 \end{bmatrix};$$

hence under, $\bar{y} = P^{-1}\bar{x}$, we can write

$$\dot{y}_1 = -y_1$$

$$\dot{y}_2 = 2y_2$$

which has general solutions given by

$$y_1(t) = c_1 e^{-t}$$

$$y_2(t) = c_2 e^{2t}$$

Also, $\bar{x}(t) = P \begin{bmatrix} e^{-t} & 0 \\ 0 & e^{2t} \end{bmatrix} P^{-1}C$ with $C = x(0)$

$$\therefore \quad \left. \begin{array}{l} x_1(t) = c_1 e^{-t} + c_2 \left(e^{-t} - e^{2t} \right) \\ x_2(t) = c_2 e^{2t} \end{array} \right\} \tag{3}$$

The phase portraits of (3) can be sketched [See Fig. 9.4(a) and Fig. 9.4(b)]

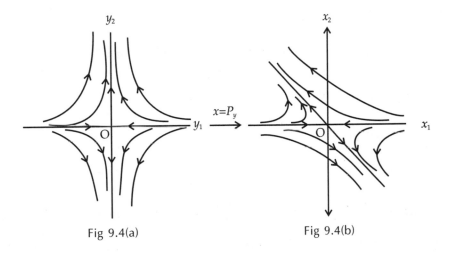

Fig 9.4(a)   Fig 9.4(b)

It is clear that the phase-portrait in x_1-x_2 plane can be obtained from the phase-portrait y_1-y_2 plane by the trajectory $x = Py$.

9.7 Forms of stable and unstable sub-spaces

Now we can state the following :

Let the $n \times n$ matrix A have k negative eigen values $\lambda_1, \lambda_2, \cdots, \lambda_k$ and $n-k$ positive eigen values $\lambda_{k+1}, \lambda_{k+2}, \cdots, \lambda_n$ and let them be distinct. Let $\{v_1, v_2, \cdots, v_n\}$ be corresponding eigen vectors. Then the stable and unstable sub-spaces of the linear system $\dot{x} = Ax$, E^s and E^p are the linear sub-spaces spanned by $\{v_1, v_2, \cdots, v_k\}$ and $\{v_{k+1}, v_{k+2}, \cdots, v_n\}$ respectively i.e.

$$E^s = \text{span}\{v_1, v_2, \cdots, v_k\}$$

$$E^n = \text{span}\{v_{k+1}, v_{k+2}, \cdots, v_n\}$$

If the matrix A has purely imaginary values, then there is also a centre sub-space of E^c of the linear system $\dot{x} = Ax$.

Let us seek to generalize these notions.

Let $w_j = u_j + iv_j$ be a generalized eigen vector of the (real) matrix A, corresponding to the eigen value $\lambda_j = a_j + ib_j$. In particular, if $b_j = 0$ then $v_j = 0$. Also, let $B = \{u_1, u_2, \cdots, u_k, u_{k+1}, \cdots, u_m, v_n\}$ be a basis of R^n (where $n = 2m - k$). Then we write

$$E^s = \text{span}\{\vec{u}_j, \vec{v}_j \,\big|\, a_j < 0\}$$

$$E^c = \text{span}\{\vec{u}_j, \vec{v}_j \,\big|\, a_j = 0\}$$

$$E^p = \text{span}\{\vec{u}_j, \vec{v}_j \,\big|\, a_j > 0\}$$

i.e. E^s, E^c and E^p are the sub-spaces of R^n spanned by the real and imaginary parts of generalized eigen vectors corresponding to eigen values λ_j with negative, zero and positive real parts respectively.

9.8 Illustrative example

Let a matrix A be given by

$$A = \begin{bmatrix} -2 & -1 & 0 \\ 1 & -2 & 0 \\ 0 & 0 & 3 \end{bmatrix} \text{ with } \dot{x} = Ax$$

This has the eigen vectors

$$w_j = u_j + iv_j = \begin{bmatrix} 0 \\ 1 \\ 0 \end{bmatrix} + i \begin{bmatrix} 1 \\ 0 \\ 0 \end{bmatrix} \text{ corresponding the } \lambda_1 = -2 + i \text{, and}$$

$$u_2 = \begin{bmatrix} 0 \\ 0 \\ 1 \end{bmatrix} \text{ corresponding to } \lambda_2 = 3$$

The stable sub-space E^s of (1) is the x_1-x_2 plane and the unstable sub-space E^u of (1) is the x_3-axis. The phase portrait for the system is shown in Fig. 9.5.

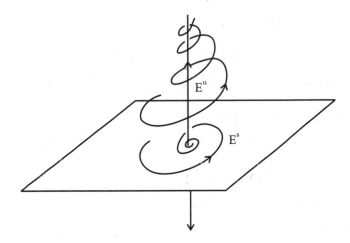

Fig. 9.5 : Stable and unstable sub-spaces of E^s and E^u.

Remarks

1. The above ideas on stable and unstable sub-spaces for the fixed point are used for defining *local stable manifold* for P in the nbd U^j, as follows, by the following set :

    $W^s(P_1U^j,f) = \{Q \in U^1; f^j(Q) \in U^j\}$ for $j>0$ and $\operatorname{div}(f^j(A),B) \to 0$ as $j \to +\infty$

    given a (hyperbolic) fixed point P for a C^k map f and given a nbd $U^j \subset U$ of P.

    In order to define the unstable manifold, we need to define what is called the past history of a point Q to be a sequence of points $\{Q_{-j}\}_{j=0}^{\infty}$ such that $Q_0 = Q$ and $f(Q_{-j-1}) = Q_{-j}$ for $j \geq 0$. The local *unstable manifold* for P is V^j is said to be the set :

    $W^u\{P, U^j, f\} = \{Q \in U^j : \exists \text{ some choice of the past history of } Q\{Q_{-j}\}_{j=0}^{q} \subset U^j\}$ such that $d(Q_{-j}, P) \to \infty$ as $j \to \infty$.

2.   Having described local stable and unstable manifolds, the global unstable manifold is given by

$$W^u(P, f) = \underset{j \geq 0}{U} f^j W^u(P, U^j, f)$$

and if f is invertible, then the (global) stable manifold is obtained by

$$W^s(P, f) = \underset{j \geq 0}{U} f^j W^s(P, U^s, f)$$

3.   There is the Stable Manifold Theorem which, now essentially, tells us how to represent local stable and unstable manifolds; these manifolds are C^k embedded manifolds represented through the graph of a map from a disk in one of the subspaces to the other subspaces. The Hartman-Grobman theorem gives an indication about the disks, without being able to tell us whether they are differentiable or not. The Stable Manifold theorem says that such manifolds are Lipschitz, which Hartman-Grobman does not. This theorem essentially provides information about points on the stable and unstable manifolds.

4.   In keeping with the requirements of Stable Manifold Theorem, we represent a closed disk in one of the subspaces; thus for any Banach space, ε and $\delta > 0$, the closed disk in ξ around the origin of radius δ is represented by $\varepsilon(\delta) = \{x \in \varepsilon : |x| \leq \delta\}$.

5.   It is quite natural to presume, after having been initiated to centre manifold, as to whether there can be the so-called centre-stable and centre-unstable manifolds. The answer is categorically yes. One can advance a statement of the Centre Manifold Theorem on the lines of Stability Manifold theorem, which we refrain from doing so once again because of its being too involved.

6.   The Centre Manifold is in no way unique. We show this after Anosov with the help of an example. Let us consider the system

$$\dot{x} = x^2$$
$$\dot{y} = -y$$

One can show the origin to be non-hyperbolic fixed point with eigen values –1 and 0; y-axis can be shown to be a stable manifold of the origin. To find out centre manifold(s), let us consider that $\dfrac{dy}{dx} = \dfrac{-y}{x^2}$ so that $y = ce^{\frac{1}{x}}$ is a solution whatever be c. Thus, for any value of cc, the graph of the following function gives a centre manifold

$$U(x,c) \;= 0 \text{ for } x \geq 0$$

$$= ce^x \text{ for } x < 0$$

When $x < 0$, also $U(x,c) \to 0$ as $x \to 0$. Thus $U(x,c)$ is continuous at $x = 0$. One can also show that $U(x,c) : c \to c^\infty$ when $x \to \infty$. For any c, the graph of $U(x,c)$ is tangent to the x-axis at $x = 0$ and is invariant, as well. Therefore, for any value of c, this graph is a centre manifold which is in no way unique.

9.9 A new look at stability: Structural stability *vis a vis* topological equivalence

In the qualitative study of nonlinear systems, stability hardly ceases to be matter of concern. Let us now look at it afresh in the wider context of manifolds. This enables us to go in for a new aspect of stability. We have already made use of linearization and/or perturbation of systems and corresponding responses to such small disturbances in the nbd of the system. Specifically speaking, let us consider the n-dimensional system.

$$\dot{x} = f(x) \tag{1}$$

Let $\mathfrak{J}$ be the set of vector functions $s(x) \in \mathfrak{J}$ which are taken to be uniformly bounded along with their continuous derivatives. This implies that for some number $M > 0$,

$$s(x) < M, \quad \left| \frac{\partial s(x)}{\partial x_i} \right| < M$$

for all $s \in \mathfrak{S}$, $x \in R^n$, and $i = 1, 3, \cdots, n$. If $\exists$ a value for ε, of course, for all s, such that the phase portraits of all the systems

$$\dot{x} = f(x), \ \dot{x} = f(x) + \varepsilon \, s(x) \tag{2}$$

are *similar* in a certain sense, which we should define, the system can be said to be *structurally stable*. The mathematical connotation of the term 'similar' is 'topological equivalence' in that there should exist a homoeomorphism (i.e. a continuously invertible mapping) with such a pairing off of portraits so that the pattern of direction is preserved by the given system. One may even think aloud if a single $s(x)$ will bring about unstable equilibrium points or not. One can take simple examples to explore if the systems are structurally stable or otherwise.

Let us consider the system $\dot{x} = x$.

Let us consider a related (perturbed) system given by

$$\dot{x} = x + \varepsilon \, s(x) \tag{3}$$

where, as mentioned earlier, s's are continuously differentiable and $\exists$ a value of M such that $|s(x)| < M$, for all x and for all s.

The unperturbed system

$$\dot{x} = x$$

has a single unstable equilibrium point at $x = 0$. The perturbed system has the equilibrium points given by

$$x + \varepsilon \, s(x) = 0 \tag{4}$$

Let us choose ε such that $\varepsilon < \dfrac{1}{2M}$. Then

$\left| \varepsilon\, s(x) \right| < \varepsilon\, M < \dfrac{1}{2}$. Then

$\left| \varepsilon\, s(x) \right| < \varepsilon\, M < \dfrac{1}{2}$ for all x

so that

$$f'(x) = 1 + \varepsilon\, s'(x) > \frac{1}{2}$$

for all x.

The equation (4) has one solution, for the relevant graph of $X(x)$ intersects the x-axis at exactly one point.

Since $\left| s(x) \right| < M$ for all, we get from (4) that this solution approaches the origin at $x = 0$. The perturbed equilibrium point, thus, approaches the unperturbed one. Since M is the same for all the $s(x)$, the said ε will suffice for all and the first condition of the definition of structural stability is fulfilled. Now, linearizing (4), we have

$$\dot{x} = \left\{ 1 + \varepsilon\, s'(x_s) \right\} x$$

where x_s is the new equilibrium point. By using the same value of ε, as earlier, the coefficient can be made positive and the new system is, therefore, also unstable.

The system is thus structurally stable, at least in respect of some properties being satisfied because of small perturbations.

Let us consider another example $\dot{x} = x^2$

The equilibrium point (single) at $x = 0$ is unstable. Let us perturb the system by $\varepsilon s(x)$ where $s(x) = -1$ so that $\dot{x} = x^2 - \varepsilon$ which has two equilibrium points $x = \varepsilon^{1/2},\ -\varepsilon^{1/2}$. But here we cannot make use of one dimensional homoeomorphism in this situation. Thus the system is structurally stable.

Remark

Having dwelt on manifolds, we need to have posers like : How are they linked with the study of qualitative studies of nonlinear systems? How can we have some inkling of cornerstones of such systems from different points of view? To provide possible answers, we need to go back to what we call the phase space : indeed, a total metric space can be called the phase space which is usually chosen to be either R^n or $R^{n-k}X, T^k$ where k is a k-dimensional manifold.

We have already come across $\omega -$, and $\alpha -$ limit points and that an equilibrium state has unique $\alpha -$ and $\omega -$ limit sets. If Ω_L and A_L represent the sets of $\omega -$ and $\alpha -$ limiting points then, after Poincare and Bendixson, we can say $\Omega(A_L)$ to be one of topological types which include equilibrium states, periodic trajectories or often, cycles composed of equilibrium states, and the linked trajectories which tend to these equilibrium states as $t \to +\infty$. How can these trajectories partition the structure of the phase space so as to determine the system? Obviously, we need to look for a kind of qualitative partitioning; we use the term 'topological' in lieu of 'qualitative'. We have already made use of the terms 'topological types'. We need to find necessarily phase portraits. A question that readily comes up is this : when can two phase portraits be similar? Or qualitatively speaking, when can they be called 'topologically equivalent'? Hence, we require a definition.

9.10 Definition

Two systems are said to be topologically equivalent if there exists a homoeomorphism of the phase spaces which map trajectories of one system into trajectories of the second.

Two trajectories L_1 and L_2 are said to be topologically equivalent, if for a given $\epsilon > 0$, there exist homoeomorphisms $h_1, h_2, \cdots, h_{m(t)}$ satisfying $(h_k, 1) < \varepsilon$ such that

$$L_2 = h_{m(t)} \cdots \cdots h_1 \, L_1$$

where $k = 1, 2, \cdots, m(t)$ and I is the identity homoeomorphism. With this idea of topological equivalence, let us make few alternative versions of descriptions of structural stability of a system.

9.11 Structural stability : Some admissible descriptions

1. The system $\dot{x} = f(x)$ is called structurally stable if there exists an $\varepsilon > 0$ such that if $|\overline{f} - f| < \varepsilon$, then f and $\overline{f}$ are topologically equivalent.

2. The equilibrium state 0. $x = 0$ of an x-dimensional system of differential equation in R^n, given by

    $$\dot{x} = f(x), f(x) \in C^k, k \leq 1$$

    is called structurally stable if the roots $(\lambda, \cdots \cdots \lambda_n)$ of the characteristic equation

    $$\det\left(\frac{\partial f_{(0)}}{\partial x} - \lambda I\right) = 0$$

    do not lie on the imaginary axis.

3. In sum, given the system $\dot{x} = f(x)$ with $f \in C^{(1)}(E)$ where E is an open subset of R^n, we can study the qualitative behaviour of the given system, as we change the function of the vector field f of the system. If the qualitative behaviour remains the same for all nearby vector fields, the given system i.e. the vector field f, can be taken to be structurally stable.

Remark

In simple but symbolic terms, alternatively speaking, a system $\dot{x} = f(x)$ is said to be structurally stable if its phase-portrait is topologically equivalent to the portrait of $\dot{x} = f(x) + \delta f(x)$ where δf is an arbitrary smooth function which is sufficiently small $\left(\text{i.e. } \|\max \delta f(x)\| \varepsilon \ \forall \ x \in R^{n}\right)$.

Exercise

1. Show that the matrix

$$A = \begin{bmatrix} 0 & 1 & 0 \\ 1 & 0 & 0 \\ 0 & 0 & 2 \end{bmatrix}$$ shows the centre sub-spaces and unstable sub-spaces.

2. Sketch the centre sub-spaces portrait of the linear system with $A = \begin{bmatrix} 0 & 0 \\ 1 & 0 \end{bmatrix}$

3. What is the critical point of the $\quad \dot{x} = -2x + \dfrac{3}{2}y \, ;$

$$y = -5x + \frac{11}{2}y \, ?$$

What are the eigen values? What are the corresponding eigen vectors? What is the stable manifold? Does it have any unstable manifold? If so, what is that?

4. Discuss the stability/instability of manifolds, if any, of the system $\quad \dot{x} = \dfrac{1}{2}x \, ;$

$$\dot{y} = 2y - 7x^2$$

5. What are possible sketches of centre sub-spaces, unstable sub-spaces of the linear system with

$$A = \begin{bmatrix} 0 & -1 & 0 \\ 1 & 0 & 0 \\ 0 & 0 & 2 \end{bmatrix}$$

periodicity : orbits, limit cycles, Poincare map

10

The term 'period' is in no way, ordinarily, unknown. Its adjectival use such as 'periodic function' is also familiar; $\sin x$, $\cos x$ etc. are periodic functions with period 2π. How do these then fit in the context of qualitative approach to nonlinear differential equations? Does it find any adjectival use there? Can we conceive of 'periodic orbits'? Nonlinear equations have related linearized versions; a simple example brings out a harmonic equation having a periodic solution and undoubtedly, representing a closed curve. How is it related to the behaviour of critical points of one kind or the other? These are queries that do crop up when we discuss solutions *vis a vis* their trajectories in the setting on nonlinearity. The purpose of this chapter is to dwell on some specifics relating to periodicity and also, what they lead up to.

10.1 Periodic solutions, periodic orbits, periodic points

We know that the critical point (equilibrium solutions) of the system

$$\left.\begin{array}{l} \dot{x} = y \\ \dot{y} = -x \end{array}\right\}$$

which can correspond to a variety of nonlinear systems is a centre (vortex point) and is stable. The solution is periodic and the orbits are circles with the critical point $(0,0)$ as its centre. In the case of autonomous equations (system), the periodic solutions correspond to closed orbits in phase-spaces, i.e. a periodic solution

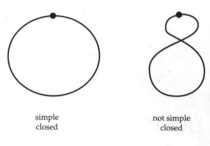

simple closed

not simple closed

Fig. 10.1

corresponds to a simple closed orbit. Let us seek to establish this. An orbit defined by $x = \xi(t), y = \eta(t)$ cannot cross itself but it can come back to its starting point and then, start on. We can thus have,

$$\xi(T) = \xi(0), \quad \eta(T) = \eta(0), \quad T > 0 \tag{1}$$

A non-constant orbit with this property is said to be a closed curve and further, if it does not cross itself, it is called a simple closed curve, as shown in Fig. 10.1

It is because of (1) and uniqueness, that one can write

$$\xi(T + t) = \xi(t), \quad \eta(T + t) = \eta(t) \tag{2}$$

which is true because orbits defined by

$$x = \xi(T + t), \ y = \eta(T + t); \quad x = \xi(t), \ y = \eta(t)$$

i.e. (1) and (2) both pass through the same point when $t = 0$. We can say that the functions ξ and η, as in (2), have the period T. On the otherhand, if we put $t = 0$ in (2), we get back (1). This establishes what we have sought to do. We can do this otherwise, formally. For a periodic solution, after a time T; $x = \varphi(t)$ should have the same value in R^n so that the periodic solution produces a closed orbit or cycle in phase space.

The converse is also true. For this, let us consider a closed orbit C in phase space and a point $x_0 \in C$. The solution of $\dot{x} = f(x)$, say, $\varphi(t)$ starts at $t = 0$ in x_0 and traces out an orbit C. Since the solution is unique, C cannot contain a critical point. So

$|f(x)| \geq a > 0$ for $x \in C$

$\Rightarrow |\dot{x}| \geq a > 0$, so that at a time $t = T$, the path returns to x_0.

Let us now prove that $\varphi(t+T) = \varphi(t) \quad \forall t \in R$.

Let $t = nT + t_1$, $n \in Z$, $0 < t_1 < T$

Since $\varphi(t)$ is the solution of $\dot{x} = f(x)$ in the domain $D \subset R^n$ then $\varphi(t - t_0)$, t_0 being a constant, is also a solution. If $\varphi(t_1) = x_1$, then $\varphi(t - nT)$ is also a solution with

$$\varphi(t_1 + nT) = x_1$$

$$\therefore \quad \varphi(t_1) = \varphi(t_1 + nT)$$

Since t_1 can take any value in $(0, T)$, then $\varphi(t)$ is T-periodic.

It may be noted that periodic orbits are also closed orbits.

Let us now turn to points on orbits.

In an orbit, there may be a point or points where it may converge; may be $f(P_1) = P_2$ and $f(P_2) = P_1$ for points P_1 and P_2 on the orbit with f as the map on R. We say that P is a *periodic point* of *period k* if $f^k(P) = P$, where k is the smallest positive integer.

The orbit with initial point P (which occurs k times) is called a *periodic orbit of period k*. We say this as *period-k* point and *period-k orbit*. The question arises whether this definition is the same as that of (2). For this, it would be convenient to have the definition of what is called 'flow' of an autonomous differential equation. We define the *flow F* of an autonomous differential equation as the function of t and initial value x_0 representing the set of solutions. So $F(t, x_0)$ is the value at time t of the solution with initial value x_0. We can now define *periodic orbits* anew. If there exists a $T(>0)$ such that $F(t + T, v_0) = F(t, v_0)$ and v_0 is not in equilibrium, then the solution $F(t, v_0)$ is called a *periodic orbit* or *cycle*. The least such number T is called the *period* of the orbit. In (1) above, the solution $x^2 + y^2 - 1$ is a circle with radius unity i.e. if we write $F(t, v_0)$ as the circle

$|v_0|$ is its radius. Every initial condition lies as a circular periodic orbit of period 2π, except for the origin, which is an equilibrium or a critical point. In a physical system e.g. for the simple pendulum (with no damping) the solutions correspond to back and forth periodic motions of the pendulum.

A periodic point P is called Liapunov stable, provided given any $\varepsilon > 0$, there exists a $\delta > 0$ such that

$$\left| f^j(x) - f^j(p) \right| < \varepsilon \text{ for all } |x - p| < \delta \text{ and } j \geq 0$$

A periodic point P is called asymptotically stable (attracting) provided it is stable (in the sense of Liapunov) and there is a $\delta > 0$ such that $|x - p| < \delta$, then $\left| f^j(x) - f^j(p) \right| \to 0$ as $j \to \infty$

where $f : R^n \to R^n$, a linear map, is given by $f(x) = Ax$ with A as a $n \times n$ matrix.

Remarks

1. The last two definitions are often referred to, along with another important point, namely, a fixed point P of f if $f(P) = P$. We shall have later occasions to deal with them, particularly, in the context of the important Hartman–Grobman theorem.

2. What is important in regard to periodic orbits is to follow the trajectories in its neighbourhood as they move around the periodic orbit, or in other words, the flow in the nbd of a periodic orbit. Let us consider an example with the orbits given as functions of time. We have already done it earlier. Let the system be

$$\frac{dx}{dt} = -y + x\left(1 - x^2 - y^2\right)$$

$$\frac{dy}{dt} = x + y\left(1 - x^2 - y^2\right)$$

In polar coordinates $(x = r\cos\theta, y = r\sin\theta)$ this set gives

$$\frac{dr}{dt} = r(1-r^2)$$

$$\frac{d\theta}{dt} = 1$$

If $\theta(0)=0$, then for the orbits, $\theta(2\pi)=2\pi$. Thus the solutions return to the $\theta = 0$ and 2π after a time of 2π. The map which takes r value at time 0 to the r value at time 2π really means the making of one circuit around the periodic orbit. This map is called the *first return map* or Poincare map to which we shall return later on.

10.2 Some notions relating to orbits

1. Orbital derivative

Let $F:R^n \to R$ and $x:R \to R$ (F is differentiable and x, a vector function)

Then $L_t F = \dfrac{\partial F}{\partial x}\dot{x} = \dfrac{\partial F}{\partial x_1}\dot{x}_1 + \cdots + \dfrac{\partial F}{\partial x_n}\dot{x}_n$

where $x_1, x_2, \ldots x_n$ are the components of x and L_t is called the *orbital derivative*.

2. Integral manifold

For the equation $\dot{x} = f(x), x \in D \subset R^n$, the function $F(x)$ is called the first integral of the equation $\dot{x} = f(x)$ in D if $L, F = 0$ in D.

Thus, it follows that the first integral $F(x)$ is constant along a set.

Conversely, taking $F(x) = $ constant, let us consider level sets of the function $F(x)$ given by the equation. Such a level set defined by $F(x)=c$ which consists of a family of orbits is called an *integral manifold*.

3. Floquet's theorem

Statement : Let us now consider the non-homogeneous linear dynamical system

$$\frac{dX}{dt} = \rho(t) \cdot X \tag{1}$$

where $t \in R$ and $\rho(t)$ is a continuous T-periodic $(n \times n)$ matrix. Then for the system (1), each fundamental matrix $\varphi(t)$ of this equation can be written as the product of two $(n \times n)$ matrices i.e.

$$\varphi(t) = \rho(t) \cdot e^{\beta t} \tag{2}$$

where $\rho(t)$ is a T-periodic $(n \times n)$ matrix and β is a constant $(n \times n)$ matrix.

Proof : Since $\varphi(t)$ is the fundamental matrix, it is composed of n-independent solutions of the given equation.

We now see that if $\varphi(t+T)$ is a fundamental matrix or not. For this, we put $z = t + T$

Then $\dfrac{dX}{dz} = \dfrac{dX}{dt} \cdot \dfrac{dt}{dz} = \rho(t) \cdot X \cdot 1$ since $\dfrac{dz}{dt} = 1$

$$= \rho(z - T) \cdot X \tag{3}$$

$\therefore$ $\varphi(z)$ is also a fundamental matrix.

The fundamental matrices $\varphi(t)$ and $\varphi(z)$ i.e. $\varphi(t+T)$ are linearly dependent. So there must exist a non-singular $(n \times n)$ matrix c such that

$$\varphi(t+T) = c\, \varphi(t) \tag{4}$$

$\therefore$ $\exists$ a matrix β such that

$$c = e^{\beta T} \tag{5}$$

We now put $\quad \varphi(t) \cdot e^{-\beta t} = \rho(t) \tag{6}$

Then $\qquad\qquad \rho(t+T)=\varphi(t+T)\cdot e^{-\beta(t+T)}$

Then $\qquad\qquad\qquad = \varphi(t)\cdot e^{-\beta t}\cdot e^{-\beta T}$ [using (4)]

$\qquad\qquad\qquad\qquad = \varphi(t)\cdot e^{-\beta t}$ [using (5)]

$\qquad\qquad\qquad\qquad = \rho(t)$ [using (6)]

$\therefore$ $\rho(t)$ is T-periodic.

Hence the proof.

4. Floquet's exponent

The eigen values ρ of c are called the characteristic multipliers. Each complex number λ such that

$$\rho = e^{\lambda T}$$

is called the characteristic exponent or Floquet's exponent.

From Floquet's theorem, it follows that the solutions of

$$\frac{dX}{dt} = P(t)\cdot X$$

consist of products of polynomials in t, $\exp(\lambda T)$ and T periodic terms.

Let $\dot{X} = P(t)\cdot X$ be transformed by

$\qquad X = \rho(t)\cdot Y$

Therefore, we get $\dot{\rho}\,Y + \rho\,\dot{Y} = P(t)\cdot \rho\,Y$

$\qquad$ or, $\dot{Y} = \rho^{-1}(P\rho - \dot{\rho})Y$ $\qquad\qquad\qquad\qquad\qquad$ (7)

Differentiating

$\qquad \rho(t) = \Phi(t)e^{-\beta t}$

we get $\dot{\rho} = \dot{\Phi}e^{-\beta t} + \Phi e^{-\beta t}\cdot(-\beta)$

$\qquad$ or, $\rho = P(t)\cdot \Phi(t)\cdot e^{-\beta t} + \Phi(t)\cdot e^{-\beta t}(-\beta)$

$[\because \ \dot{\Phi} = P(t) \cdot \Phi$ because Φ is a fundamental matrix$]$

or, $\dot{\rho} = P\rho - \rho\beta$ $\hspace{4cm}$ (8)

and so we get from (7) and (8),

$$\dot{Y} = \beta Y \hspace{4cm} (9)$$

Thus, the transformation

$$X = \rho(t)Y$$

carries the equation $\dot{X} = P(t) \cdot X$ into an equation with constant coefficients, the solution of which are vector polynomials in t, multiplied by $e^{\lambda t}$.

Remark and exercise

The Floquet theorem is fundamentally important as a provider of a vital result, by periodic equations. It is precisely the enabling mechanism to write the fundamental matrix of the relevant equation as the product of T-periodic matrix and a (generally) a non-periodic matrix. A simple statement of Floquet's theorem can be set forth as :

If $\dot{x} = A(t): x \neq 1, \cdots$ $\hspace{4cm}$ (10)

be the equation with $A(t)$ being continuous T-periodic $n \times n$ matrix, then each fundamental matrix $\Phi(t)$ of (10) can be written as the product of the $n \times n$ matrices i.e. $\Phi(t) = P(t)e^{\beta t}$ with $P(t)$ being T-periodic and β a constant $n \times n$ matrix. [Hint : Please show first that $\Phi(t)$ is composed of independent solutions and then make use of the fact that the fundamental matrices $\Phi(t)$ and $\Phi(T) = \Phi(t+T)$ are linearly dependent which means that $\exists$ a nonsingular $n \times n$ matrix such that $\Phi(t+T) = \Phi(t)c \Rightarrow \exists$ a constant matrix β such that $c = e^{\beta t}$. Then proceed to prove that $\Phi(t)\exp(-\beta t)$ is T-periodic i.e. $\rho(t+T) = \rho(t)$ and to do this, put $\Phi(t)e^{-\beta t} = \rho(t)$.]

Can we use, now, a transformation $x = \rho(t)y$ which makes the equation $\dot{x} = A(t)x$

assume the form of an equation, with constant coefficients, the solution of which are vector-polynomials in t multiplied with $\exp(T)$ where $\rho = e^{\lambda T}$, λ being the Floquet number? [Hint : Put $x = \rho(t)y$ and proceed, as shown a bit earlier]

What can be said about existence of T-periodic solutions of $\dot{x} = A(t)x$?

What should be the necessary and sufficient condition for asymptotic stability of trivial solutions of $\dot{x} = A(t)x$? How do they depend on the characteristic (Floquet) exponents? What can be said about such conditions for stability of the solution?

In this context, a remark should be that there does not exist a general method to calculate the matrix $\rho(t)$, Floquet number etc.

10.3 Some pre-requisites on curves

We have already stated what we mean by a curve defined by

$$x = \xi(t), \ y = \eta(t) \text{ for } 0 \leq t \leq T$$

with ξ and η being continuous. We also know if the endpoint coincides with the starting point, the curve becomes a closed curve i.e. if $\xi(0) = \xi(T)$; $\eta(0) = \eta(T)$. If $\xi(t_1) = \xi(t_2)$, $\eta(t_1) = \eta(t_2)$, $0 \leq t_1 \leq T$ are true only when $t_1 = t_2$; the curve is *simple* which, otherwise, means that the curve does not intersect itself. With these, let us describe (a) a Jordan curve (b) connected set (region) (c) domain, although some of these are intuitively clear.

(a)   **Jordan curve** : A Jordan curve is basically a continuous one-to-one image of a circle. A simple closed curve is a Jordan curve. How can we conceive of a Jordan curve in terms of the parameter 't'? This interval (say, of time) $0 \leq t \leq T$ can be thought of as an entity wrapped around a circle of circumference T. Marie Ennemond Camille Jordan, the French mathematician, proposed the well-known *The Jordan Curve Theorem* in 1887. We shall state this, after describing what a domain is all about.

(b)   **Connected Set** : An open set S is said to be connected if every pair of points on S can be joined by a simple curve that lies wholly in S.

(c)   **Domain** : An open connected set is called a domain and is usually denoted by D.

Jordan Curve theorem : A simple closed curve splits the plane R^2 in two parts or strictly speaking, domains : an interior domain (which is bounded) and an exterior domain.

Remarks

1. Although formulated by Jordan, this theorem could be proved by the American mathematician Oswald Veblen in 1095. This is also called Jordan separation theorem.

2. It follows that whenever a Jordan curve lies in the domain D, the interior of the curve lies also in D. We call such a domain D to be simply connected. Obviously D has no gaps (or holes) and a multiply-connected domain has holes.

3. Jordan separation theorem thus divides R^2 in two parts, the interior and exterior, of closed orbits.

4. It is to be noted that such statements have to depend on the topology of the plane.

5. With the foregoing descriptions, let us now proceed to consider the criteria for periodic solutions of autonomous systems. The first criterion is due to the Swedish mathematician Ivan Bendixson in 1901.

6. No criteria, nothing of its kind, can be of use, unless we state (without proof) the concerned theorem of Henri Poincare :

Let $(f,g) \in C^{(0)}$ in a simply connected domain D and let C be a simple closed trajectory of $\dot{x} = f(x,y)$, $\dot{y} = g(x,y)$ lying in D.

Then there is at least one critical point inside or on C.

The 'simple closed trajectory' is nothing but a Jordan curve.

If $(f,g) \in C^{(1)}$, there can be no critical point on C, which means that there is a critical point inside C.

10.4 Bendixson criterion
(on the existence of periodic solution of autonomous systems.)

Statement : Let the autonomous system be

$$\left. \begin{array}{l} \dot{x} = f(x,y) \\ \dot{y} = g(x,y) \end{array} \right\} \tag{1}$$

in a domain $D \subset R^2$. Assuming that the domain D is simply connected, and both f and g are continuously differentiable in D, the above set of equations can have only periodic solutions if $\vec{\nabla} \cdot (f,g)$ changes sign in D or if $\vec{\nabla} \cdot (f,g) = 0$ in D.

We can establish this as follows :

Suppose we have a closed orbit C in D corresponding to the solution of the given equation and let G be the interior of C. Applying Green's theorem, we get,

$$\iint_D \vec{\nabla} \cdot (f,g) dv = \int_C (f\,dy - g\,dx)$$

$$= \int_C \left(f\frac{dy}{dt} - g\frac{dx}{dt} \right) dt$$

$$\therefore \iint_D \vec{\nabla} \cdot (f,g) dv = 0,$$

since the integrand to the RHS being zero, as the closed orbit C corresponds to the solution of (1). So the integral vanishes and this means that $\vec{\nabla} \cdot (f,g)$ cannot have a definite sign i.e. $\vec{\nabla} \cdot (f,g)$ must change its sign.

10.5 Illustrative examples

Example 1

How do you apply Bendixson criterion for the non-linear oscillator with a non-linear damping $\ddot{x}+p(x)\dot{x}+q(x)=0$ to show that it has no periodic solution, where $p(x)$ and $q(x)$ are smooth functions and $p(x)>0$, $x \in R$?

Solution : This equation is equivalent to the system

$$\dot{x}=y$$

$$\dot{y}=-q(x)-p(x)y$$

$$\frac{\partial f}{\partial x}+\frac{\partial g}{\partial y}=0-p(x)\cdot 1=-p(x)<0 \quad \text{since } p(x)>0, \text{ as given}$$

$\therefore$ Divergence of the vector function

i.e. $\dfrac{\partial f}{\partial x}+\dfrac{\partial g}{\partial y}=-p(x)<0$ is negative (definite)

$\therefore$ By Bendixson criterion, the given system has no periodic solution.

Remarks

1. Thus we have an isolated periodic solution of an autonomous system represented on the phase plane by a closed path. It is called *limit cycle* to which we shall come back in greater details.

2. We shall next consider another version of Bendixson's criterion, improved upon by the French mathematician Henri Dulac in 1933.

Example 2

Investigate the behaviour of the equation

$$\ddot{x}+\varepsilon\left(x^{2}+\dot{x}^{2}-1\right)\dot{x}+x^{3}=0$$

Solution : The given equation can be written as

$$\ddot{x}+\varepsilon f(x,\dot{x})\dot{x}+g(x)=0$$

where $f(x,\dot{x})=x^2+\dot{x}^2-1$

$$g(x)=x^3$$

Let us put $\dot{x}=y$ then $f(x,y)=x^2+y^2-1$

Now let $G(x)=\int_0^x g(x)dx=\frac{1}{4}x^4$

We consider the contour $\xi:\frac{1}{2}y^2+G(x)=c$

i.e. $\xi:\frac{1}{2}y^2+\frac{1}{4}x^4=c$

The periodic solution located lies between two such contours, one inside and the other outside the curve $f(x,y)=0$ i.e. $x^2+y^2=1$ and is most closely fixed by finding the smallest contour lying outside this circle and the largest lying inside. We require respectively minimum/maximum of x^2+y^2 subject to $\frac{x^4}{4}+\frac{y^2}{2}=c$, c being chosen so that minimum/maximum is equal to 1.

10.6 Bendixson—Dulac theorem

Statement : Let $(f,g)\in C^{(1)}$ in a simply connected domain D and let R be a $C^{(1)}$ function such that $(Rf)_x+(Rg)_y\neq0$, $(x,y)\in D$

Then the system

$$\dot{x}=f(x,y)\left.\right\}$$
$$\dot{y}=g(x,y)\left.\right\}$$

has no closed curve trajectory in D.

Proof : The system is given by

$$\left.\begin{array}{c} \dot{x} = f(x,y) \\ \dot{y} = g(x,y) \end{array}\right\} \tag{1}$$

Now $\displaystyle\int_C R(g\,dx - f\,dy) = \int_0^T R\left(g\frac{dx}{dt} - f\frac{dy}{dt}\right)dt$

$$= 0 \text{ by } (1)$$

Using Green's theorem

$$\iint_G \left\{(Rf)_x + (Rg)_y\right\}dx\,dy = 0$$

where G is the interior domain of C. The integrand being not zero; it must be either positive or negative throughout D which is simply connected. The integrand is thus non-zero, which is a contradiction. Therefore, C of (1) is not a closed path.

Illustration

We consider the non-linear system (of competitive populations)

$$\dot{N}_1 = N_1(r_1 - a_1N_1 - a_2N_2)$$

$$\dot{N}_2 = N_2(r_2 - b_1N_1 - b_2N_2)$$

Let us assume only that $a_1b_2 \geq 0$ and that both a_1 and b_2 are both zero.

Let us choose $R = \dfrac{1}{N_1N_2}$

Here $Rf = \dfrac{r_1}{N_2} - \dfrac{a_1N_1}{N_2} - a_2$

$\qquad Rg = \dfrac{r_2}{N_1} - b_1 - \dfrac{b_2N_2}{N_1}$

$(Rf)_{N_1} + (Rg)_{N_2} \neq 0$ and hence, there is no closed orbit in this region.

10.7 Existence of periodic orbits : Poincare–Bendixson theorem

With the above spadework, the task now is to state something about the existence of periodic orbits or periodic solutions of a general class of nonlinear systems. This is precisely given by the famous *Poincare–Bendixson Theorem*, which is stated as follows :

Let $(f,g) \in C^{(1)}$ in a domain D and let Λ be a trajectory of $\dot{x} = f(x,y)$ and $\dot{y} = g(x,y)$ for $t \geq 0$. Let Λ be contained in a bounded closed subset of D that has no critical points. Then Λ^+ is an orbit of the differential equation and is a Jordan curve.

Before we say something about the proof, it should be mentioned that there are some versions of the statement of this theorem. First, we note that if Λ itself is a Jordan curve, then $\Lambda = \Lambda^+$; but Λ being, not in general, a closed curve, it keeps on spiralling towards the closed orbit Λ^+. We get, in either case, a periodic trajectory. This takes us to, Λ^+ being the limit cycle, a periodic orbit around which other trajectories spiral and tend to move towards it. Its proof is involved and so we keep it in the appendix I. We shall, of course, see how to apply it after considering limit cycles.

10.7 Periodic orbits—Limit cycles

It is a matter of history that towards the end of the 19th century, Henri Poincare grappled with periodic solutions of ordinary differential equations. He was, in particular, looking for periodic solution(s) of a non-linear differential equation. His aim had been to reduce such a study to that of a map on itself. Can the existence of a periodic solution of a non-linear differential equation be associated with that of a fixed point on the map? This led him to the concept of a limit cycle which we precisely dwell on in this chapter along with other allied aspects.

Prelude to limit cycle

We begin, as before, with $x(t)$, $y(t)$ as solution of the system

$$\frac{dx}{dt} = P(x, y)$$

$$\frac{dy}{dt} = Q(x, y)$$

As we know, we can make the system to have the non-initial periodic solution if

$$x(t) = x(t + T)$$
$$y(t) = y(t + T)$$

for some $T > 0$. Also, if the curve corresponding to the solution is closed, then for some T

$$x(T) = 0, \; y(T) = y(0)$$

If we take the circle, say Γ as

$\{z \in C : |z| = 1\} = \{e^{2\pi i x}; x \in R\}$, then we can write the map as $f : \Gamma \to \Gamma$ or $z \to f(z)$

Let us say a bit more about f. We assume that (a) f is differentiable with continuous derivatives (b) f has an inverse f^{-1}, which is differentiable with continuous derivatives. We call such a f to be a diffeomorphism. We can now define anew formally the *orbit* of a point $P \in \Gamma$, denoted by $O(P)$, as

$$\{\ldots\ldots, f^{-1}(P), P, f^{1}(P), \ldots\ldots\} = \{f^{n}(P) : n \in R\}$$

We are now in a position to say that the image of a periodic solution in the phase portrait is a closed trajectory which can be called a periodic orbit or a closed orbit.

It is easy to recollect that the system

$$\dot{x} = y$$
$$\dot{y} = -x$$

has a periodic solution corresponding to closed curves around a centre (vortex point). Let us see what happens to a non-linear system built on this example. Let this be given by

$$\dot{x} = y + x\left(1 - x^2 - y^2\right)$$
$$\dot{y} = -x + y\left(1 - x^2 - y^2\right)$$

To deal with this, without solving, we use polar coordinates and put

$$x = r\cos\theta, \quad y = r\sin\theta$$
$$r^2 = x^2 + y^2, \quad x\dot{y} - y\dot{x} = r^2\dot{\theta}$$
$$r\dot{r} = x\dot{x} + y\dot{y}$$

Then the system reduces to

$$\dot{r} = r\left(1 - r^2\right), \quad \dot{\theta} = -1$$

The general solution is given by

$$r = \frac{1}{\left(1 + ce^{-2t}\right)^{\frac{1}{2}}}, \quad \theta = -(t - t_0) \text{ with } t_0 = 0,$$

$$x = \frac{\cos t}{\left(1 + ce^{-2t}\right)^{\frac{1}{2}}}, \quad y = \frac{\sin t}{\left(1 + ce^{-2t}\right)^{\frac{1}{2}}}$$

If $c > 0$, the solution is a spiral in the phase plane, starting inside the circle and tending to the circle as a limit as t changes from $-\infty$ to $+\infty$.

If $c < 0$, the spiral approaches the circle from outside. The circle is the limit cycle. Thus, in the non-linear system, we have some closed curves as limiting sets for the trajectory corresponding to a solution as $t = \pm\infty$. Such closed curves are known as *limit cycles*. Whatever be the initial conditions towards which solutions tend as $t \to \pm\infty$, the limit cycles are stable closed curves and they are either isolated periodic solution or asymptotic limits of solutions, as shown in Fig. 10.2.

Let us consider another well known non-linear system given by the van der Pol's equation, viz.

$$\dot{x} = y$$

$$\dot{y} = -x + \varepsilon\left(1 - x^2\right)y$$

These give $\dfrac{dy}{dx} = -\dfrac{x - \varepsilon\left(1 - x^2\right)y}{y}$

If $|x| \square\ 1$, then $\dot{x} = y$

$$\dot{y} = \left(\varepsilon y - x\right)$$

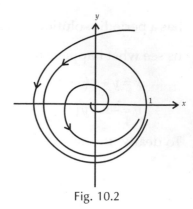

Fig. 10.2

which give rise to the characteristic equation having

complex roots with real positive parts and so, the critical point is an (unstable) spiral; if $|x| \square\ 1$, $\dfrac{1}{2}\dfrac{d}{dt}\left(\dot{x}^2 + \dot{y}^2\right)$ is negative which also implies a spiral, critical point tending to the origin as $t \to \infty$

Using polar coordinates, $r^2 = x^2 + y^2$

$$r\dot{r} = x\dot{x} + y\dot{y} = xy + y\left[-x + \varepsilon\left(1 - x^2\right)y\right]$$

or, $r\dot{r} = \varepsilon\left(1 - x^2\right)y^2$

or, $\dfrac{dr}{dt} = \dfrac{\varepsilon\left(1 - x^2\right)y^2}{r}$

If $y \neq 0$, then $\dfrac{\varepsilon y^2}{r} < 0$ and $\dfrac{dr}{dt}$ has the same sign as $\left(1 - x^2\right)$. If $|x| < 1$, then $\dfrac{dr}{dt} > 0$ and r increases with t. For small ε and $|x| \square\ 4$, any sketch in the xy plane gives an outward spiral while for $|x| \square\ 1$, and $\dfrac{dr}{dt} < 0$, the sketch shows an inward spiral. These two curves cannot meet except at a singular point $(0,0)$ and hence, each is asymptotic to a closed curve. This curve is the limit cycle we are looking for. Thus we find here an isolated periodic orbit, called a *limit cycle*. Since all the trajectories in the vicinity of the limit cycle tend to the limit cycle as $t \to \infty$, a limit cycle with this property is a *stable limit*

Fig. 10.3

cycle. On the other hand, we have all trajectories starting from points arbitrarily close to the limit cycle tending away from it as $t \to \infty$, as shown Fig.10.3.

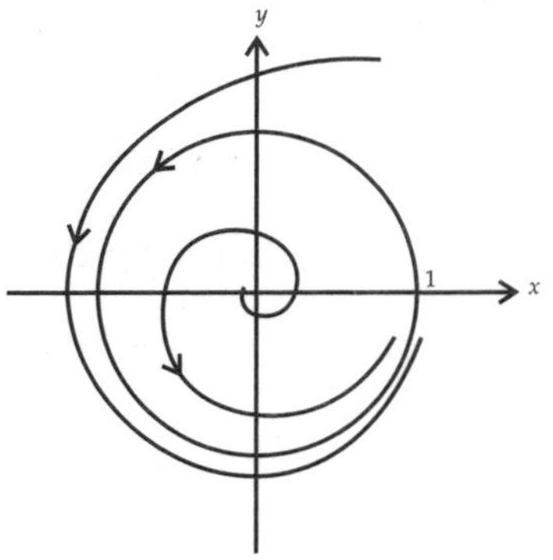

Remarks

1. A question that arises in this: How many limit cycles can an autonomous system of two equations have? The answer is not as yet definite. The system may have at most three limit cycles, under some conditions.

2. As an exercise, we can work out the conditions under which the trajectories around a vortex point are closed.

3. If these are trajectories of the system which spiral towards a limit cycle from inside and from outside, the cycle is called *arbitrary stable*. If, here, trajectories wind around a limit cycle while the inside circle unwinds, from it, it is *arbitrary semi-stable*. If the periodic solution is no longer a limit cycle, e.g. a sequence of concentric circles, we have the case what is called a *natural stability*.

4. For the non-linear system

    $$\ddot{x} - \left(2\mu - c\dot{x}^2\right)cx + ax = 0, \ a, \ c > 0$$

    if in the nbd of the origin $2\mu \Box cx^2$, the origin in the x-$\dot{x}$ plane can be shown to be an unstable spiral point, and if $cx^2 \Box 2\mu$ the origin is a stable spiral point; since the two spirals (one moving inward and the other, outward) cannot intersect, they are asymptotic to a closed curve i.e. a limit cycle and hence, the motion of the system is ultimately periodic.

5. In general, the above procedure does not lead to a limit cycle. We need a theorem that given the system, what are the sufficient conditions of existence of the limit

cycle? One of the few general theorems of this nature is the following (having the semblances of Poincare-Bendixson–Dulac theorem).

Let R be the bounded region of the phase plane together with its boundary; let us assume that R does not contain any critical point of the system.

$$\left.\begin{array}{l} \dfrac{dx}{dt} = F(x, y) \\[2mm] \dfrac{dy}{dt} = G(x, y) \end{array}\right\} \qquad (1)$$

If $C = [x(t), y(t)]$ be a path of (1) lying for some t_0 and remains in R for all $t \geq t_0$, then C is either itself a closed path or spirals towards a path as $t \to \infty$. The theorem gives us the criterion for non-closed paths of (1).

Let us use Bendixson criterion once again

Let us suppose, if in addition $\dfrac{\partial F}{\partial x} + \dfrac{\partial G}{\partial y}$ has the same sign throughout R then (1) has no closed path in the region R.

For establishing this, we write

$$\int_C \left[F(x, y)\,dy - G(x, y)\,dx\right] = \iint_R \left(\frac{\partial F}{\partial x} + \frac{\partial G}{\partial y}\right) dx\, dy$$

(the line integral is taken in anti–clock sense)

We now assume that C is a closed path of (1). Let $[x(t_0), y(t_0)]$ be an arbitrary solution; we find C in terms of the parameter t. Let T be the period of a solution. Then we can write $x = f(t)\ y = g(t)$.

$$\frac{df}{dt} = F[f(t), g(t)]$$

$$\frac{dg}{dt} = G[f(t), g(t)]$$

$$\therefore \int_c \left[F(x,y)dy - G(x,y)dx \right] = \int_0^T \left\{ F(f,g)\frac{dg}{dt} - G(f,g)\frac{df}{dt} \right\} dt$$

$$= \int_0^T \left\{ F[f,g]G[f,g] - G[f,g]F[f,g] \right\} dt$$

$$= 0$$

$$\therefore \iint_R \left(\frac{\partial F}{\partial x} + \frac{\partial G}{\partial y} \right) dx\, dy = 0$$

This double integral vanishes only when $\left(\dfrac{\partial F}{\partial x} + \dfrac{\partial G}{\partial y} \right)$ changes in sign which is a contradiction. Therefore C is not a path of (1) and hence (1) does not have any closed path.

10.8 Some applications

Example 1: Let $\quad \dfrac{dx}{dt} = 2x + y + x^3$

$$\frac{dy}{dt} = 3x - y + y^3$$

Here $\dfrac{\partial F}{\partial x} + \dfrac{\partial G}{\partial y} = 3(x^2 + y^2 + 1)$ which is positive throughout the whole x-y phase plane. Hence the system has no closed path.

Example 2 : van der Pol's equation and Lienard equation

Balthasov van der Pol, a Dutch applied mathematician and an engineer while investigating a certain type of electrical services circuit containing a nonlinear resistance, in 1924, came across the equation

$$\frac{d^2x}{dt^2} + \varepsilon(x^2 - 1)\frac{dx}{dt} + x = A\sin\omega t$$

where ε, ω, A are constants with $A > 0$. According to him, with $A = 0$, this nonlinear equation gives rise to a non-constant periodic solution. So it garners great attention in mathematical studies on periodic orbits. What we now seek to do is to consider a slightly more general set of equations, called the Lienard's equation.

$$\frac{d^2x}{dt^2} + f(x)\frac{dx}{dt} + g(x) = 0$$

10.9 Lienard theorem

Let $\dfrac{d^2x}{dt^2} + f(x)\dfrac{dx}{dt} + g(x) = 0$ \hfill (1)

where the functions $f(x)$ and $g(x)$ satisfy the following conditions :

(i)   both are continuous and have derivatives for all x

(ii) $g(x)$ is an odd function such that $g(x) > 0$, $x > 0$ and $f(x)$ is an even function.

(iii)   the odd function $F(x) = \int_0^x f(x)\, dx$ has exactly one positive at $x = a$, is negative for

$0 < x < a$ and is non-decreasing for $x > a$. Also $F(x) \to \infty$ as $x \to \infty$, then the

Lienard's equation

$$\frac{d^2x}{dt^2} + f(x)\frac{dx}{dt} + g(x) = 0 \tag{1}$$

has a unique closed path surrounding the origin in the phase plane and this path

is approached spirally by every other path as $t \to \infty$.

Proof

The system (1) is equivalent to

$$\frac{dx}{dt} = y \tag{2}$$

$$\frac{dy}{dt} = -g(x) - yf(x)$$

Because of condition (i), the existence and uniqueness of the equations hold.

From condition (ii) $g(0) = 0$ and $g(x) \neq 0$ for $x \neq 0$.

So the origin $(0,0)$ is the only critical point. Also, we know that any closed

path must be surrounding the origin.

Now $\dfrac{d^2x}{dt^2} + f(x)\dfrac{dx}{dt} = \dfrac{d}{dt}\left[\dfrac{dx}{dt} + \int_0^x f(x)\,dx\right]$

$$= \dfrac{d}{dt}\left[y + F(x)\right]$$

$$= \dfrac{dz}{dt} \quad \text{where } z = y + F(x)$$

∴ the equations (2) then become

$$\left.\begin{aligned}\dfrac{dx}{dt} &= z - F(x)\\[2mm]\dfrac{dz}{dt} &= -g(x)\end{aligned}\right\} \tag{3}$$

i.e. the $(x\text{-}z \text{ plane})$

Again, we find (a) the existence and the uniqueness to hold; (b) the origin is the only critical point and (c) any closed path must surround the origin. The one to one correspondence $(x, y) \square \ (x, z)$ between points of two planes, continuity both ways and therefore, correspondence to closed paths, configurations in two planes can be taken to be qualitatively similar.

Now, the differential equation of the paths in the $x\text{-}z$ plane is

$$\dfrac{dz}{dx} = \dfrac{-g(x)}{z - F(x)} \tag{4}$$

Let us analyse the path given by (4).

First, since $g(x)$ and $F(x)$ are odd, there is no change in equations (3) and (4) if x and z are replaced by $-x$ and $-z$. This means that any curve symmetric to a curve with respect to the origin is also a path. This enables us to get paths in the left half plane $(x < 0)$ if we know the paths in the right half plane $(x > 0)$, by just reflection through the origin.

Second, equation (1) shows that the paths become horizontal only when they cross the z-axis and become vertical as they cross the curve $z = F(x)$. If we look at the signs of the right hand side of equation (3), we find that the all paths are directed to the right. Above the curve $z = F(x)$ and to the left below, this curve (path) moves downwards or upwards according as

$(x > 0)$ or $(x < 0)$ (See Fig. 10.4).

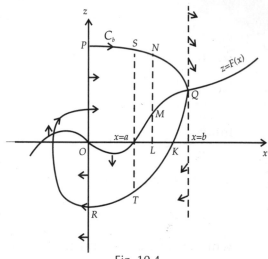

Fig. 10.4

From the above remarks, it follows that the curve $z = F(x)$, z-axis and the vertical line through any point Q on the right of the curve $z = F(x)$, can be crossed only in directions indicated by the arrows shown in the above figure. Let us choose the solution of (3) defining a path C through Q on the right of the curve $z = F(x)$ such that the point Q corresponds to the value at time $t = 0$; then as t increases to positive values, a point on C with co-ordinates $(x(t), y(t))$ moves down and to the left until it crosses the z-axis at a point R and as t decreases to negative values, a point on C, rises to the left until it crosses the z-axis at the point P. Let b be the abscissa of Q. Let us denote the path of C by C_b. The path being symmetric, the path C_b goes beyond P and R into the left plane and the path will be a closed one, if the distances OP and OR are equal. To show that there is a unique *closed path*, it would suffice to show that, there is a unique value of b when $OP = OR$. To prove that, let us introduce

$G(x) = \int_0^x g(x) dx$ and consider the function

$E(x,z) = \dfrac{1}{2}z^2 + G(x)$; in the x-z plane on the z-axis $G(x) = 0$; then $E(x,z) = \dfrac{1}{2}z^2$.

Now, $\dfrac{d\mathrm{E}}{dt}=g(x)\dfrac{dx}{dt}+z\dfrac{dz}{dt}$

$$=-\big[z-F(x)\big]\dfrac{dz}{dt}+z\,\dfrac{dz}{dt}$$

$$=F(x)\dfrac{dz}{dt}$$

$\therefore\qquad dE=F(x)\,dz$

Now let $\mathrm{I}(b)=\displaystyle\int_{PR} F\,dz$

Integrating $F\,dz$ along the path OC_b from P to R

$$\mathrm{I}(b)=\mathrm{E_R}-\mathrm{E_P}$$

$$=\dfrac{1}{2}\big(OR^2-OP^2\big)$$

which shows that there is a unique b such that $\mathrm{I}(b)=0$ i.e. $OP=OR$

If $b\le a$ then F and dz are both negative

$\therefore\qquad \mathrm{I}(b)>0$

The path cannot be closed.

Let us now suppose that $b>a$, as shown in the above figure, and split up $\mathrm{I}(b)$ in two parts $\mathrm{I}_1(b)$ and $\mathrm{I}_2(b)$.

i.e. $\qquad \mathrm{I}_1(b)=\displaystyle\int_{PS} F\,dz+\int_{TR} F\,dz$

$\qquad\quad \mathrm{I}_2(b)=\displaystyle\int_{ST} F\,dz$

so that $\quad \mathrm{I}(b)=\mathrm{I}_1(b)+\mathrm{I}_2(b)$

Since, F and dz are negative and path C_b is traversed from P to S and then, from T to R , it is clear that $\mathrm{I}_1(b)$ is greater than 0 i.e. $\mathrm{I}_1(b)>0$.

If, on the other hand, we go from S to T along C_b , we have $F>0$ but $dz<0$, so that $\mathrm{I}_2(b)<0$.

To show that $I(b)$ is a decreasing function of b by considering separately $I_1(b)$ and $I_2(b)$, let us use equation (1) from which we can write

$$F(x)\,dz = F(x)\frac{dz}{dx}\,dx$$

$$= -\frac{g(x)F(x)}{z - F(x)}\,dx$$

Now, increasing b means raising the arc PS and lowering the arc TR which, in turn, decreases the magnitude of $-\dfrac{g(x)F(x)}{z-F(x)}$ for a given x between 0 and a. Since the limits of integration of $I_1(b)$ are fixed, there is a decrease in $I_1(b)$. Furthermore, since $F(x) > 0$ and is non-decreasing to the right of a, we see that the increase in b gives rise to an increase in the number $-I_2(b)$ and hence, a decrease in $I_2(b)$.

$\therefore I(b) = I_1(b) + I_2(b)$ is a decreasing function for $b \geq a$.

Let us now proceed to show that $I_2(b) \to -\infty$ as $b \to \infty$.

If L, in the above figure, is fixed and k is on the right of L, then

$$I_2(b) = \int_{ST} F\,dz < \int_{NK} F\,dz \leq (-LM)(LN) \text{ and as } b \to \infty, LN \to \infty$$

$\therefore \ I_2(b) \to -\infty$ as $b \to \infty$.

Accordingly, $I(b)$ is a decreasing continuous function of b for $b \geq a$, $I(a) \geq 0$ and $I(b) \to -\infty$ as $b \to \infty$.

It, therefore, follows that $I(b) = 0$ for one and only $b = b_0$.

$\therefore$ There is one and only *one closed path* C_b.

Finally, we observe that $OR > OP$ for $b < b_0$.

Therefore, considering also the symmetry, we find that the paths inside C_b spiral out to C_{b_0}. Similarly for $OR < OP$, for $b > b_0$, paths outside C_b spiral into C_{b_0}.

10.10 Application

Let us apply the above theorem to van der Pol's equation given by

$$\frac{d^2x}{dt^2} + \mu(x^2 - 1)\frac{dx}{dt} + x = 0, \ \mu > 0$$

Here, $f(x) = \mu(x^2 - 1); \ f(-x) = \mu((-x)^2 - 1) = f(x)$

$$g(x) = x; \ g(-x) = -x = -g(x)$$

The condition (i) is satisfied.

The condition (ii) is also satisfied.

Now $F(x) = \mu\left(\dfrac{x^3}{3} - x\right)$

$$= \frac{1}{3}\mu x(x^2 - 3)$$

$F(-x) = -F(x)$ and $F(x)$ is an odd function.

$F(x)$ has a single positive 0 at $x = \sqrt{3}$, is negative for $0 < x < \sqrt{3}$. $F(x)$ is positive for $x > \sqrt{3}$ and $F(x) \to \infty$ as $x \to \infty$

$$F'(x) = \mu(x^2 - 1) \text{ which is positive for } x < 1.$$

$\therefore$ $F(x)$ is non-decreasing; in fact, it is increasing for $x > \sqrt{3}$.

All the conditions of the theorem for periodic solutions are satisfied.

$\therefore$ the van der Pol's equation is an unique closed path which is approached spirally by every other path.

Corollary

The Rayleigh's equation

$$a\ddot{x} + b(x^2 - 1)\dot{x} + cx = 0$$

is also transformed into van der Pol's equation by a suitable transformation.

Remark

An alternative statement of the Lienard theorem :

Consider the equation $\ddot{x} + f(x)\dot{x} + x = 0$

with $f(x)$ being Lipschitz continuous in R.

We assume that

(a) $F(x) = \int_0^x f(x)\,dx$ is an odd function.

(b) $F(x) \to \infty$ as $x \to \infty$

∃ a constant β such that for $\beta > 0$, for $x > \beta$ and $F(x) > 0$

i.e. monotonically increasing

(c)   ∃ a constant $\alpha > 0$ such that $0 < c < \alpha$, $F(x) < 0$

The above system has at least one periodic solution.

Moreover if $\alpha = \beta$, ∃ only one periodic solution (See

Fig. 10.5).

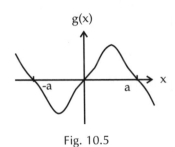

Fig. 10.5

10.11 Recalling Poincare–Bendixson theorem

As already observed, this continues to be, even today, a cardinal theorem on periodic paths. The proof of this theorem is pretty difficult but its usefulness is undeniably overwhelming. We plan to take up the proof in the appendix in the formal style. Its truth needs to permeate throughout whatever we do with periodic orbits or the like. Hence, even in passing, we mention below, in two distinct forms, by *imposing* or *relaxing* conditions, under which Poincare–Bendixson theorem holds. The normal parlance is to make use of two words, 'strong' and 'weak' forms and so, we do it as follows:

10.12(A) Poincare–Bendixson theorem of strong form

Let us consider the autonomous system

$$\left.\begin{array}{l} \dfrac{dx}{dt} = F(x,y) \\[2mm] \dfrac{dy}{dt} = G(x,y) \end{array}\right\}$$

(1)

where $F(x,y)$ and $G(x,y)$ are continuous along with the first order partial derivatives in a domain D of x-y plane. Let D_1 be a bounded domain of D and let us denote the region of the domain D_1 with its boundary. Let C^+ defined by $\{x = f(t), y = g(t); t \geq 0\}$ be a half path of (1) contained in R. Let $L(C^+)$ be the limit set which does not contain the critical point; either (a) the half path C^+ is itself a closed [in this case C^+ or $L(C^+)$ become identical] or ( ) $L(C^+)$ is a closed path which C^+ spirally goes from inside or outside [in case $L(C^+)$ becomes a limit cycle]. Thus, in either case, there exists a closed path of (1) in R. If the region does not contain the critical points of (1), then the limit $L(C^+)$ will contain no critical points of (1). Another modified statement of the theorem is stated below.

10.12(B) The Poincare–Bendixson theorem of weak form

Let us suppose that R contains a critical point of (1), contains a half of (1) and also contains a closed path. Let the equation (1) have the critical points but no other critical points within some

$$K \;: (x - x_0)^2 + (y - y_0)^2 = r^2$$

Then we can always find an annular region whose boundaries consist of two smaller circles :

$$(x - x_0)^2 + (y - y_0)^2 = r_1^2$$

$$(x - x_0)^2 + (y - y_0)^2 = r_2^2 \qquad \text{where } 0 < r_1 < r_2 < r$$

We can take this as a region R containing no singular points of (1); we can then show that the half path C^+ of (1) (say for $t \geq t_0$) is entirely contained in R, so that we can conclude that a closed path C^0 of (1) is also contained in R.

Example

$$\frac{dx}{dt} = -y + x\left(1 - x^2 - y^2\right)$$

$$\frac{dy}{dt} = x + y\left(1 - x^2 - y^2\right)$$

The annular region contains no points of the system. If the annular region contains the half path of the system, then we can apply Poincare Bendixson theorem of weak form.

On the circle $x^2 + y^2 = \dfrac{1}{4}$, $\dfrac{dr}{dt} < 0$, and $r = \sqrt{x^2 + y^2}$

and hence, r is decreasing, the radius vector points into R at every point outside the circle. Hence a path C entering at $t = t_0$ will remain in R for $t \geq t_0$ and this gives us the half path containing R.

$\therefore$ By Poincare –Bendixson theorem of weak form, R contains a closed path C.

10.13 Reconsidering Poincare map

Let us consider the system, treated earlier

$$\frac{dx}{dt} = -y + x\left(1 - x^2 - y^2\right)$$

$$\frac{dy}{dt} = x + y\left(1 - x^2 - y^2\right)$$

Introducing polar coordinates (r, θ) we have $x = r\cos\theta$, $y = r\sin\theta$

The system can be written in the polar coordinates (r, θ), as

$$\frac{dr}{dt}=r\left(1-r^2\right)$$

$$\frac{d\theta}{dt}=1$$

The solution is given by

$$r(t,r_0)=\left[1+\left(\frac{1}{r^2}-1\right)e^{-2t}\right]^{-\frac{1}{2}}$$

$$\theta(t,\theta_0)=t+\theta_0,$$

(r_0,θ_0) being the initial values of (r,θ)

Let Σ be the ray $\theta=\theta_0$ through the origin then Σ is perpendicular to the Γ and the trajectory through the point $(r_0,\theta_0)\in\Sigma\cap\Gamma$ at $t=0$ intersects ray $\theta=\theta_0$ and again, at $P=2\pi$ (See Fig. 10.6).

The Poincare map is given by

$$P(r_0)=\left[1+\left(\frac{1}{r_0^{\,2}}-1\right)e^{-2t}\right]^{-\frac{1}{2}}$$

$$\therefore P(1)=1$$

Also, we see that

$$P'(r_0)=e^{-4\pi}\cdot r_0^{-3}\left[1+\left(\frac{1}{r_0^{\,2}}-1\right)e^{-4\pi}\right]^{-\frac{3}{2}}$$

$$P'(1)=e^{-4\pi}<1$$

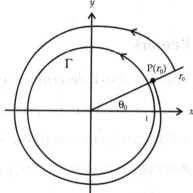

Fig. 10.6 : The Poincaré map for the system

This is an example of *Poincare map*. This is also called the *first return map*.

Poincare suggested to consider the first return map, associating to an initial point, on the line segment, the real point of intersection of its trajectory with the segment. Obviously, the profile of the Poincare map enables one to investigate the behaviour of the motion on a long term basis. To repeat, if we look at orbits with $\theta(0)=0$, the $\theta(2\pi)=2\pi$, the map P which takes the value r at $\dot{r}<0$ to the r at $t=2\pi$ includes the effect of making one complete path around the periodic orbit. P is nothing but the first return map or Poincare map, from the surface $\{\theta = 0, \bmod 2\pi\}$ to itself. It is clearly seen that $r = 1$ is an attracting orbit, since $\dot{r} > 0$ for $r < 0$ and $\dot{r} < 0$ for $r > 0$ we can now set forth the following definition in formal terms:

Definition: Let there be a periodic orbit Γ of period T with $P \in \Gamma$. Then for some k, the kth coordinate function of the vector field must be non zero at P, $f_k(P) \neq 0$. We take the hyper-plane $\Sigma = \{x : x_k = P_k\}$. This hyper-plane is called *cross section* or *transversal* at P. For $x \in \Sigma$ near P, the flow $\varphi^+(x)$ returns to Σ in time $\tau(x)$, which is about T.

Let $V \subset \Sigma$ be an open set in Σ on which $\tau(x)$ is a differentiable function. The first return map or Poincare map is defined to be $P(x) = \varphi^{\tau(x)}(x)$ for $x \in V$.

Remark

With the above description, example and definition of a Poincare map, a question can be raised as to on what aspects of qualitative behaviour of a system of differential equations, a Poincare map can throw some light. Why should we go about the determining the derivatives of $P(r_0)$, $P'(r_0)$ etc.? Let us see how we can make use of them. We confine ourselves to planar systems.

10.14(A) Poincare map of planar systems

For planar systems, let us translate the origin to the point $x_0 \in \Gamma \cap \Sigma$; the normal line Σ will be a line through the origin as shown in Fig. 10.7.

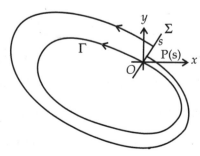

The point $O \in \Gamma \cap \Sigma$ divides the line Σ into two segments Σ^+ and Σ^- where Σ^+ lies entirely in the exterior of Γ. Let s be the distance along Σ with $s > 0$ for points in Σ^+ and $s < 0$ for points in Σ^-. We have then the

Fig. 10.7

Poincare map $P(s)$ defined for $|s|<\delta$ and we have $P(0)=0$. Let us define also the *displacement function* $d(s)$ given by

$$d(s)=P(s)-s$$

Then $d(0)=0$ *and* $d'(s)=P'(s)-1$.

Applying mean value theorem for $|s|<\delta$, we have $d(s)=d'(\delta)s$ for some δ where $0<\delta<s$. If $d'(0)\neq 0$ and for $|s|$ for sufficiently small, the sign of $d'(s)$ will be the same as the sign of $d'(0)$ and so, if $d'(0)<0$, then $d(s)<0$ for $s>0$ and $d(s)>0$ for $s<0$. Therefore, the cycle Γ is said to be a stable limit cycle or an ω–limit cycle, as shown in Fig. 10.7. Similarly, if $d'(0)>0$, Γ becomes an unstable limit cycle or an $\alpha-$ limit cycle. Further, if Γ is a stable or unstable limit cycle according as $P'(0)<1$ or >1 with $P'(0)=0$. So we can say that the stability of Γ is determined by the derivative of the Poincare map.

The formula for $P'(0)$ is given by the formula

$$P'(0)=\exp\int_0^T \nabla\cdot f(\gamma(t))dt$$

with $P(s)$ being defined above and $\gamma(t)$ being a periodic solution of $\dot{x}=f(x)$ of period T. It is to be noted that the derivative of the Poincare map is along a straight line Σ normal to $\Gamma=\{x\in R^2 | x=\gamma(t)-\gamma(t_0),\ 0\leq t\leq T\}$. We take the expression of $P'(0)$ without proof.

Further, we can state the following a corollary (without proof) and a definition :

Corollary

The periodic solution $\gamma(t)$ is a stable or unstable limit cycle

$$\text{if } \exp\int_0^T \nabla\cdot f(\gamma(t))dt<0 \text{ or } >0.$$

What happens if the integral is zero? One cannot say in definite terms; it may be stable, unstable or semi-stable limit cycle or it may belong to a continuous band of cycles.

Let us illustrate this by the above example.

$$\dot{x} = -y + x\left(1 - x^2 - y^2\right)$$

$$\dot{y} = x + y\left(1 - x^2 - y^2\right)$$

$$\vec{\nabla} \cdot f(x, y) = 2 - 4x^2 - 4y^2$$

$$\gamma(t) : (x = \cos t, y = \sin t)$$

$$T = 2\pi$$

$$\therefore \int_0^{2\pi} \vec{\nabla} \cdot f(\gamma(t))dt = \int_0^{2\pi}\left(2 - 4\cos^2 t - 4\sin^2 t\right)dt$$

$$= -4\pi$$

$$\therefore P'(0) = e^{-4\pi} < 1$$

Therefore the cycle is a stable limit cycle.

Definition

If $P(s)$ be the Poincare map for a cycle Γ of a planar analytic system $\dot{x} = f(x)$ and if $d(s) = P(s) - s$ be the displacement function, then P is called a multiple limit cycle of multiplicity k when

$$d(0) = d^1(0) = \cdots\cdots = d^{k-1}(0) = 0 \text{ and } d^k(0) \neq 0$$

Γ is called a multiple limit cycle of multiplicity k.

If $k=1$, then Γ is called a *simple limit* cycle.

It follows that $\Gamma = \left\{x \in R^2 \mid x = \gamma(t) - \gamma(t_0),\ 0 \le t \le T\right\}$ happens to be a simple limit cycle of $\dot{x} = f(x)$, iff $\int_0^T \vec{\nabla} \cdot f(\gamma(t))dt \neq 0$.

One can deduce a variety of conclusions from such results on the stability of limit cycles depending on distance d's.

Remark

A query that naturally arises at this stage is that : what can be said about the number of limit cycles that can possibly accumulate on a cycle Γ in the context of band of cycles mentioned earlier? Did Poincare establish anything about this? The answer is yes, way back in 1881.

In order to establish that we require the notion of the Poincare map in the neighbourhood of a critical point, say, a focus. We shall show this after stating simply a Poincare theorem.

10.14(B) Poincare's theorem

Statement: A planar analytic system cannot have an infinite number of limit cycles that accumulate on a cycle of the system.

Let the system, as usual, be taken as

$$\dot{x} = f(x) \tag{1}$$

having the focus, at the origin. We assume as before

$Df(0) \neq 0$. Then, a planar version of (1) is linearly equivalent to the system

$$\left.\begin{array}{l} \dot{x} = ax - by + p(x, y) \\ \dot{y} = bx + ay + q(x, y) \end{array}\right\} \tag{2}$$

with $b \neq 0$; p and q represent squares and higher degree terms. It is convenient to work on (2) in terms of polar coordinates, so that the system (2) has the form

$$\left.\begin{array}{l} \dot{r} = ar + 0(r^2) \\ \dot{\theta} = b + 0(r) \end{array}\right\} \tag{3}$$

Let $r(t, r_0, \theta_0)$ and $\theta(t, r_0, \theta_0)$ be the solution of this system, with the initial conditions $r(0, r_0, \theta_0) - r_0$ and $\theta(0, r_0, \theta_0) - \theta_0$

Then for $r_0 > 0$ sufficiently small and $b > 0$, $\theta(t, r_0, \theta_0)$ is a strictly increasing function with $t(0, r_0, \theta_0)$ as its strictly inverse function. Let us define the function

$$P(r_0) = r\left(t\left(\theta_0 + 2\pi, r_0, \theta_0\right), r_0, \theta_0\right)$$

for a fixed θ_0. Then for all sufficiently small $r_0 > 0$, $P(r_0)$ is an analytic function of r_0 and this can be taken as the *Poincare map for the focus* at the origin of the system (2). Likewise for $x(T) = 0$, $\theta(t, r_0, \theta_0)$ being a strictly decreasing function of t, we can take

$$P(r_0) = r\left(t\left(\theta_0 - 2\pi, r_0, \theta_0\right), r_0, \theta_0\right)$$

as the Poincare map for the focus at the origin in this case, as shown in Figs. 10.8.

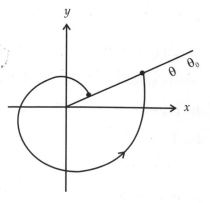

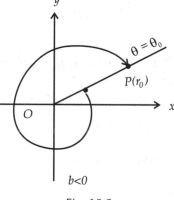

Fig. 10.8

Remark

We could have moved further with more interesting theorems and definitions relating to Poincare map for a focus at the origin of a planar analytic the system. For instance, a result which enables one to see that the Poincare map $P(s)$, with the above stipulation, has the values $P(0) = 0$, $P'(0) = \exp\left(\dfrac{2\pi a}{|b|}\right)$; also, $d(s)d(-s) < 0$, for $|s| < \delta\,(>0)$, where, as before, $d(s) = P(s) - s$.

Further, $d(0) = d^1(0) = \ldots \ldots = d^{K-1}(0) = 0$ and $d^K(0) \neq 0$ only when k is odd, say, equal to 2^{2m+1}, so that the integer $m = \dfrac{k-1}{2}$ can be designated as the *multiplicity* of the focus; $m = 0$, a simple focus.

10.14(C) Poincaré section

This version of a Poincare map is a bit involved. Let us introduce, a new terminology,

Poincare section.

Let $\dot{x} = f_\mu(x)$, μ being a parameter and $x \in R^n$

Let us think of Γ as a periodic trajectory in R^n and let the flow map generated by the vector field $f_\mu(x)$ of $\dot{x} = f_\mu(x)$ be $\varphi_\mu(x)$. Then, we define a Poincare section for the flow ϕ_1 in the nbd of Γ as an $(m-1)$ dimensional hyper-surface Σ, transverse to the flow (transverse, as usual, meaning normal or perpendicular to the surface Σ), $\hat{n}(x)$ being nowhere normal to $f_\mu(x)$ for $x \in \Sigma$ i.e. $f_\mu(x) \cdot \hat{n}(x) \neq 0$, for $x \in \Sigma \subset R^n$. Σ ought to be such that there is a single intersection of Γ with Σ, as shown in Fig. 10.9.

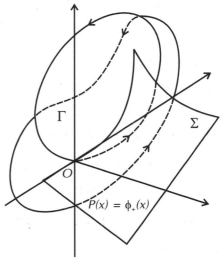

Fig. 10.9

The Poincare map or the first return map is defined for points in a nbd. $U \subseteq \Sigma$ of x_0 where x_0 is the point of intersection of the limit cycle Γ with the surface Σ. If x be such a point in the nbd, then the Poincare map $\Gamma : U \to \Sigma$ is defined by $P(x) = \varphi_\tau(x)$ where τ is the period for the trajectory with the initial point x_0 to return to Σ for the first time. Γ, it is to be noted, is no way related to the point x but may not be equal to the period of the periodic orbit Γ.

Remark

Poincare's map, being so important in the study on periodic orbits, can be looked at, rather introduced in a variety of ways, without one being in conflict with the other.

One way is to begin with idea of a *transversal*. A smooth curve '*l*' can be called a *transversal* of the orbits of

$$\dot{x} = f(x) \tag{1}$$

if l contains ordinary points only and is nowhere tangent to an orbit, as shown in the accompanying Fig. 10.10(a) . We take l_0 as the interior of l which is taken as a closed set. Let us consider a subset $V \subset l_0$ containing of the point p mapping the planar phase flow into l_0. So one can assume that there exists a t_p such that the solution beginning in $p_1 \in l_0$ vide Fig. 10.10(b)

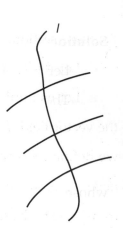

$$x(t_p, p_1) = p_2 \in l_0$$

The mapping of this subset V into l_0 can be taken as *Poincare mapping* or first return map.

Fig. 10.10(a)

Let us now move on to a periodic orbit of (1), $x \in R^n$ through $x_0 \in R^n$. Let Σ be a hyper-plane perpendicular to Γ at x_0. This is not so far new. Then, also, as before, for any point $x \in \Sigma$ sufficiently close to x_0, the solution $x \in \Sigma$ of (1) through x_0 at $t = 0$, say, $\varphi_t(x)$ will cross Σ again at $P(x)$ near x_0. Then mapping $x \to P(x)$ is taken as *Poincare mapping*. How to make use of transversality? Let Σ be a smooth surface through a point $x_0 \in \Gamma$ which is not a tangent to Γ at x_0. We say then that the surface Γ intersects the curve Γ transversally at x_0 *vide* Fig. 10.11.

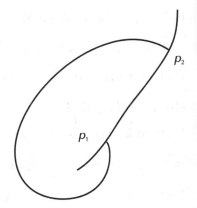

Fig. 10.10(b)

10.15 An exemplar

Investigate the behaviour of the system

$$\dot{x} = -y + \mu x - \mu x \sqrt{x^2 + y^2}$$
$$\dot{y} = x + \mu y - \mu y \sqrt{x^2 + y^2}$$

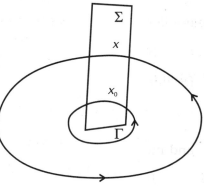

Fig. 10.11

Solution

Let $x = r\cos\theta$, $y = r\sin\theta$

Then the given system becomes

$$\dot{r} = \mu r(1-r)$$

$$\dot{\theta} = 1$$

whose solutions are given by

$$r = \frac{r_0}{r_0 - (r_0 - 1)e^{-\mu t}}$$

$$\theta = \theta_0 + t$$

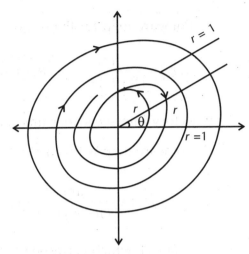

Fig. 10.12

where $r(\theta) = r_0$, $\theta(0) = \theta_0$ see Fig. 10.12.

The circle $r = 1$ (limit cycle) is attracting or repelling according as $\mu >$ or < 0.

Let Σ be taken here as $y = 0$, $x > 0$ and $\theta = 0$ as the ray. Then the Poincare map is given by

$$P(r) = \frac{r}{r - (r-1)e^{-2\pi\mu}}$$

The map P has a fixed point at $r = 1$, reflecting the intersection of the stable circle trajectory at $r = 1$.

Also, $DP(1) \neq \dfrac{d}{dr}\Gamma(\ldots)\big|_{r=1} = e^{-2\pi\mu} > 0$ or < 0 according as $\mu < 0$ or > 0 which implies (a sort of) linearization.

So, $\mu < 0$ implies stability or $\mu > 0$ implies instability. We may, however, proceed for linearization, putting $r(t) = 1 + \delta(t)$ so that

$$\dot{\delta} = -\mu$$

$$\dot{\theta} = 1$$

and move ahead.

If we take the system as

$$\dot{x} - \mu x \mid y \quad x\sqrt{x^2 + y^2}$$

$$\dot{y} = -x + y - y\sqrt{x^2 + y^2}$$

for the Poincare map for the section $y = 0$, $x > 0$. Proceeding as before, we have

$$r(t, r_0) = \frac{\mu r_0 e^{\mu t}}{(\mu - r_0) + r_0 e^{\mu t}}, \quad \theta(t, 0) = -t$$

The trajectory intersects after time $t = 2\pi$

So, the Poincare map is given by

$$P(r_0) = \frac{\mu r_0 e^{2\pi\mu}}{\left[(\mu - r_0) + r_0 e^{2\pi\mu}\right]}$$

Clearly $P(1) = 1$ which corresponds to the (limit) cycle.

Remark

It may appear that we have considered Liapunov functions somewhat in isolation. Let us recall them in order to see if it has anything to do with periodic orbits or not. To explore this, we recall that the system

$$\left.\begin{array}{l} \dot{x} = f(x, y) \\ \dot{y} = g(x, y) \end{array}\right\}, \quad t \geq 0 \qquad (1)$$

where $(f, g) \in C^{(1)}$ have a Liapunov function V so that

(a)   all solutions are bounded in $(0, \infty)$ and $\lim\limits_{t \to \infty} v(t)$ exists

(b)   if $\dot{V}$ is negative definite, then $\lim\limits_{t \to \infty} v(t) = 0$

(c)   if $\dot{V}$ is negative definite, and V is positive definite, then the origin is globally asymptotically stable.

Here, $v(t) = V\{\xi(t), \eta(t)\}$ is the value of V on the trajectory defined by $x = \xi(t)$, $y = \eta(t)$. We know how difficult it often becomes to get the required Liapunov function.

The American mathematician Joseph P. L. Salle could show how to go about in the direction. As a pre-requisite to this, we need few new notions such as limit points of a trajectory, limit sets etc.

10.16 Some notions

Definition : A limit point of a trajectory $x = \xi(t)$, $y = \eta(t)$ is a point (x_1, y_1) such that

$$\lim_{n \to \infty} \xi(t_n) = x_1$$

$$\lim_{n \to \infty} \eta(t_n) = y_1$$

for some sequence $\{t_n\}$, $t_n \to \infty$. The set of all limit points of a given trajectory Λ is called the limit set and is denoted by Λ^+.

For example, if $\lim_{n \to \infty} \xi(t) = x_0$ and $\lim_{n \to \infty} \eta(t) = y_0$ then Λ^+ consists of the single point (x_0, y_0).

Conversely, if Λ^+ consists of a single point, then the solution tends to this point as a limit.

As an another example, if the trajectory has the period T then

$$\lim_{n \to \infty} \xi(t + nT) = \lim_{n \to \infty} \xi(t) = \xi(t)$$

$$\lim_{n \to \infty} \eta(t + nT) = \lim_{n \to \infty} \eta(t) = \eta(t)$$

This holds at each t and shows that in the case of a periodic solution, Λ^+ coincides with Λ^-.

10.17 La Salle's theorem

Statement : Let $(f, g) \in C^{(1)}$ and let V be a Liapunov function for

$$\dot{x} = f(x, y)$$
$$\dot{y} = g(x, y)$$

(1)

Then the limit set Λ^+, for any given trajectory, is contained in the set of all orbits whose trajectories satisfy $\dot{V}(x, y) = 0$.

We give only a partial proof.

In view of $(f, g) \in C^{(1)}$ and the system (1) has a Liapunov function V; then

(a)   all solutions are bounded on $(0, \infty)$ and $\lim\limits_{t \to \infty} v(t)$ exists.

(b)   if $\dot{V}$ is negative definite then $\lim\limits_{t \to \infty} v(t) = 0$

(c)   if $\dot{V}$ is negative definite, the origin is globally asymptotically stable.

The function $v(t) = V(\xi(t), \eta(t))$ has a limit as $t \to \infty$. If we denote the limit by β, this gives $\lim\limits_{n \to \infty} v(t_n) = \beta$ for every sequence $\{t_n\}$ as $t \to \infty$. Let us choose a sequence that generates the given point $(x_1, y_1) \in \Lambda^+$. Since V is continuous, the above remarks yield

$$
\begin{aligned}
V(x_1, y_1) &= \lim\limits_{n \to \infty} V(\xi(t_n), \eta(t_n)) \\
&= \lim\limits_{n \to \infty} v(t_n) = \beta
\end{aligned}
$$

which being true for every $(x_1, y_1) \in \Lambda^+$, V is constant on Λ^+ which establishes that $\dot{V}(x, y) = 0$.

Remarks

1.   It can be shown that any trajectory starting in Λ^+ remains in Λ^+ throughout the entire interval of definition. In otherwords, Λ^+ is an *invariant set* for the differential equation. The fact that V is constant in Λ^+ now gives $\dot{V} = 0$ on the trajectory containing (x_1, y_1). Thus, every point of Λ^+ is contained in an orbit satisfying $\dot{V} = 0$ and this is essentially what La Salle's theorem says.

2.   It can be, later on, seen that La Salle's theorem contains the main result of Liapunov, for $C^{(1)}$. To see to it, let $\dot{V}$ be negative definite. Then the only trajectory satisfying

$\dot{V} = 0$ is $x = y = 0$. Hence, the limit set consists of the single point $(0, 0)$. This shows that the origin is globally asymptotically stable and provides requirements for $V(x, y)$ to be a Liapunov function, without V being positive definite.

10.18 Theorem on a periodic orbit

If M is an odd (and a minimal) set of equation $\dot{x} = f(x)$ in R^2 then M is a critical point or a periodic orbit.

Proof : The set M is non-empty, closed and invariant and so contains at least one orbit, say, r.

$\therefore (Rf)_x + (Rg)_y \neq 0$. Hence there is no closed curve.

10.19 Example

Show that the system $\dot{x} = y - x^3 + x$, $\dot{y} = -x - y^3 + y$ has at least one closed path in the phase plane.

Let $V(x, y) = x^2 + y^2$

$$\therefore \quad \frac{dV}{dt} = 2x(y - x^3 + x) + 2y(-x - y^3 + y)$$

$$= 2(x^2 + y^2 - x^4 - y^4)$$

If $(x^2 + y^2) < 1$ then $x^2 + y^2 > (x^2 + y^2)^2 = x^4 + 2x^2 y^2 + y^4 \geq x^4 + y^4$

Hence $\frac{dV}{dt}$ is strictly positive on the circle $x^2 + y^2 = r$ for any r, such that $0 < r < 1$.

On the otherhand, for $x^2 + y^2 = 2$

$$2(x^4 + y^4) \geq (x^2 + y^2)^2 > 2(x^2 + y^2)$$

As a result $\frac{dV}{dt}$ is strictly negative on the circle $x^2 + y^2 = r$ for $r > 2$.

$\therefore$ The system has at least one closed path lying between the two concentric circles.

10.20 Limit sets for an autonomous plane system

We consider an autonomous plane system defined by

$$\dot{x} = f(x) \tag{1}$$

where f is a map which satisfies everything to do with Lipschitz criteria (existence, differentiability, uniqueness). We can write $F(t, x_0)$ as the unique solution of (1), satisfying $F(0, x_0) = 0$

Definitions

I.   **Limit Sets :** A point P_ω in R^2 (or R^n) is in the ω – limit set $\omega(x_0)$ of the solution $F(t, x_0)$ if there be a sequence of points moving far along the orbit, as $t \to +\infty$, which converges to P. In other words, $P_\omega(t) \in \omega(v_0)$ if $\exists$ an unbounded increasing sequence $\{t_n\}$ of real numbers with $\lim_{n \to \infty} F(t_n, v_0) = P_\omega$

A point P_α is in the α – limit set $\alpha(x_0)$ if $\exists$ an unbounded decreasing sequence $\{t_n\}$ of real numbers $\{t_n \to -\infty\}$ with $\lim_{n \to \infty} F(t_n, v_0) = P_\alpha$

Observations

1.   If x_0 is an equilibrium, then $\omega(x_0) = \alpha(x_0) = x_0$

2.   For any x_0, the α – limit set of equation $\dot{x} = f(x)$ is the limit set of $\dot{x} = -f(x)$

3. ω – limit set is nothing short of the asymptotic behaviour for any bounded orbit of an autonomous differential equation, as shown by the following example

Example : Let us have $x = x(a - x)$, with $a > 0$. There are two equilibria in R, at $x = 0$ and $x = a$. All trajectories with $x > 0$ converge to the stable equilibrium $x = a$. Therefore $\omega(x_0) = 0$ for $x_0 > 0$. If $x_0 < 0$, the trajectory diverges to $-\infty$ and since O is an equilibrium, $\omega(x_0)$ is the empty set.

II.   Positive and Negative Limit Points

Let us consider a solution $x(t)$ of the system $\dot{x} = f(x)$ with $x(0) = x_0$.

This corresponds in phase space to an orbit which we indicate by $C^+(x_0)$ and for negative orbit, $C^-(x_0)$. In case of a periodic solution

$$C^+(x_0) = C^-(x_0)$$

A point P is called *positive limit point* of the orbit $C^+(x_0)$ corresponding to the solution $x(t)$ if an increasing sequence of numbers $t_1, t_2, \cdots\cdots$ tending to $+\infty$, exists such that the points of $C^+(x_0)$ corresponding to $x(t_1), x(t_2), \cdots\cdots$ have the limit point P. This can be illustrated by an example that the asymptotically stable equilibrium is the positive limit set of every solution staying sufficiently near the equilibrium point.

In the same way, one can define *negative limit point* using a decreasing sequence of numbers.

The set of all *positive limit points* of an orbit is called the $\omega -$ limit set of C^+ and is denoted by ω^+.

The set of all negative limit points is called i.e. $\alpha -$ limit set of C^- and is denoted by α^-.

III.   Invariant Set

A set M in R^n is said to be an invariant set if $x(0)$ is contained in M, then $x(t)$ is also contained in $M \forall t \in R$.

In general, a set A in the domain W of a system is invariant, if for every set $x \in A$, $\phi_t(x)$, the solution of $\dot{x} = f(x)$, is defined in A for all $t \in R$

IV.   **Minimal Set**

A set $N \in R$ is called a minimal set if M is closed, invariant, non-empty and if N has no smaller subset with these three properties.

Thus we state that A is a non empty, compact (bounded and closed) invariant set of $\dot{x} = f(x)$ in R^n, if there exists a minimal set $M \in A$.

Example

Let us consider the autonomous system given by

$$\dot{x} = x - y - x(x^2 + y^2)$$
$$\dot{y} = y + x - y(x^2 + y^2)$$

This corresponds to, in polar co-ordinates ($x = r\cos\theta$, $y = r\sin\theta$),

$$\dot{r} = r(1 - r^2)$$
$$\dot{\theta} = 1$$

All circular domains with centre $(0,0)$ and radius larger than 1 are positive invariant. Also $(0,0)$ and the circle $r = 1$ are invariant sets but the origin is a α-limit set for each orbit which starts with $r(0) < 1$. This circle $r = 1$ which corresponds to the periodic solution $(x_1, x_2) = (\cos t, \sin t)$ is the ω-limit set for all orbits except the critical point at the origin. Both α- and ω-limit sets are minimal.

V.   **Properties of an invariant set**

Let the sets $\alpha(\gamma)$ and $\omega(\gamma)$ be closed and invariant sets. Furthermore, if the positive orbit γ^+ is bounded then the ω-limit set is, compact, connected and not empty.

If $x(t, x_0)$ corresponds to the orbit $\gamma^+(x_0)$ for $t \geq 0$, then the distance $d(x(t, x_0), \omega(\gamma)) \to 0$ as $t \to \infty$.

To establish this, we proceed as follows:

That $\alpha(\gamma)$ and $\omega(\gamma)$ are closed follows from the definition. Let us first prove that $\omega(\gamma)$ is positive invariant. Let us suppose that the limit point p is contained in $\omega(\gamma)$; therefore, there exists a sequence $\{t_n\} \to \infty$ as $n \to \infty$ such that $x(t_n, x_0) \to p$ which corresponds to the orbit $\gamma^+(x_0)$ as $n \to \infty$.

For these values of t, using the translation property, we can write

$$x(t + t_n, x_0) = x(t, x(t_n, x_0))$$

By the translation property, we take the limit as $n \to \infty$ with fixed t; then we have

$$x(t + t_n, x_0) \to x(t, p)$$

Therefore, we conclude that the orbit which contains 'p' lies in $\omega(\gamma)$ and therefore, $\omega(\gamma)$ is positive invariant.

If γ^+ is bounded then $\omega(\gamma)$ is also bounded and not empty, as each bounded set in R^n with an infinite number of points has at least one point of accumulation.

$\omega(\gamma)$ being closed, it follows that $\omega(\gamma)$ is compact. In fact, we have proved, for each t that

$$x(t + t_n, x_0) \to x(t, p) \text{ where } \gamma(p) \text{ is contained in } \omega(\gamma)$$

In case of a periodic solution $\gamma^+(x_0) = \gamma^-(x_0)$

$\therefore d\{x(t, x), \omega(\gamma)\} \to 0$ as $t \to \infty$

$\therefore \omega(\gamma)$ is connected. Similarly, $\alpha(\gamma)$ is also connected.

Remarks

1. The stable limit cycle is the positive limit set of every solution starting sufficiently near the limit cycle. The solution approaches limit cycle as $t \to \infty$.

2.   Some of the above definitions are often set forth in terms of other notions.

For instance :

A set A is said to be *invariant* with respect to a homoeomorphism φ if $A = \varphi(t, A)$ for any t.

Here $\varphi(t, A)$ represents the set $U = \{x \varepsilon A \mid \varphi(t, x)\}$.

Homoeomorphism is one to one, continuous mapping with continuous inverse. If we consider, as before, the system

$$\dot{x} = f(x) \text{ where } f : W \to R^n \text{ is a } C' \text{ map as an open set } W \subset R^n .$$

Let L be the set of all points in W :

$L = \{a \in W \mid \text{ there exists } t_n \to \infty \text{ with } x(t_n) \to a\}$ with $x(t)$ as the trajectory. The set L can also be called the set of $\omega - $limit of the trajectory (or of any point on the trajectory). Likewise, we may define the set of $\alpha - $limit points or the $\alpha - $limit set of a trajectory $\gamma(t)$ to be the set of all points b such that $\lim\limits_{n \to \infty} y(t_n) = b$ for some sequence $\{t_n\} \to -\infty$.

Let $x = \varphi(t)$ be the equation representing the trajectory L. The point x_0 is called an $\omega - $limiting point of the trajectory L if $\exists$ a sequence $\{t_n\}$ where $t_n \to +\infty$ as $n \to \infty$ such that

$$\lim_{n \to \infty} \varphi(t_n) = x_0$$

A similar definition for an $\alpha - $limiting point is when $t_n \to -\infty$ as $n \to \infty$. We often denote the set of all $\omega - $limiting points of the trajectory L by Ω_L and that of the $\alpha - $limiting point by A_L . We have already noted a equilibrium such has unique $\alpha - $ and $\omega - $limit points namely itself.

In particular, if the trajectory L is periodic, then $L = \Omega_L = A_L$.

10.21 Reconsidering ω–limit (as well as α–limit) sets

Having considered $\omega-$ limit and $\alpha-$ limit sets, one may well ask the questions: Why should we do so? To be more specific, what kinds of sets in R^2 can belong to $\omega-$ limit points of a bounded solution of an autonomous differential equation? Prior to responding to these and allied questions, we can illustrate $\omega-$ limit sets by the well-known pendulum problems. The equilibrium is its own $\omega-$ limit; the others (limit sets) are provided by the equilibrium solutions approaching $\{(2n+1)\pi, 0\}$ $(n=\pm1,\pm2,\cdots\cdots)$, as $t\to\pm\infty$; the other type of $\omega-$ limit set is a cycle which happens to be its own limit set. Let us deal with some of its properties.

We should recall here the definition. Moving further, a set A that contains all its limit points can be taken as a *closed set*. Let

$$\dot{x} = f(x), \quad x \in R^n$$

be an autonomous differential equation and let $\omega(x_0)$ be the limit set of its orbit say, $F(t, x_0)$, a sequence $\{F(n, x_0): n=2,3\cdots\}$ either is bounded for all $t \geq 0$, and so it must have a limit-point, as per elementary analysis or repeats the same point infinitely many times. This ensures the existence of the $\omega(x_0)$. It satisfies the property of being a closed set. Isn't it invariant? Yes, it is so; for if $\omega(x_0)$ is invariant under the flow i.e. $y \in \omega(x_0)$, then the entire orbit is in $\omega(x_0)$.

We have already described what a connected set is in the context of a Jordan curve. Can we say, if $\{F(t, x_0)\}$ is a bounded set, then $\omega(x_0)$ is a connected set?

Let $\omega(x_0) = A \cup B$ where, A and B, are two sets distant 'd' apart. One can think of a number of disjoint segments of solution curves moving from within $\dfrac{d}{4}$ on A to, with $\dfrac{d}{4}$ on B. Since $A \cup B$ is separated by d, there must be a point on each segment, that is, $\dfrac{d}{2}$ from A. Such points are at least $\dfrac{d}{?}$ from B and these points form a bounded infinite set that has a limit point lying at least $\dfrac{d}{2}$ from $\omega(x_0)$. Hence 'd' must be zero.

Its property of transitivity follows readily. If $\alpha \in \omega(x)$, and $x \in \omega(x_0)$, then $\alpha \in \omega(x_0)$. Next, the point is how to determine the behaviour of Liapunov functions on limit process. Let us seek its answer, if any. Let the Liapunov function be $V: R^n \rightarrow R$ and we know that, with time along an orbit,

$$\frac{d}{dt}\{F(t,x)\}=0$$

For any positive real number c, let

$$W_c = \{x \in R^n : V(x) \le c\}$$

Let $x_0 \in W_c$, for some $c > 0$. Then $\exists\, d$, $0 \le d \le c$, such that $V(x) = d$ for every $x \in \omega(x_0)$. Since V is constant on $\omega(x_0)$ and $\omega(x_0)$ is an invariant set, we see that $V(x) = 0$ for each x in $\omega(x_0)$.

10.22 Some consequences leading to invariance principle

The Liapunov function still continues to be our starting point. Let us recall that a requirement of asymptotic stability, for example, in the case of energy Liapunov function, $\dot{V}(x) = -by^2$ has to be only negative semi-definite. Further, we observe that, even if $\dot{V}(x)$ is negative everywhere except on the line $y = 0$ where $V(x) = 0$, the trajectory of the system has to be confined to the line $y = 0$. This is impossible unless $x = 0$, for the governing equation of the pendulum, it is to be remembered, is of the form :

$$y(t) \equiv 0 \Rightarrow \dot{y}(t) = 0 \Rightarrow \sin x = 0$$

Hence, on the segment $-\pi < x < \pi$ of the line $y = 0$, the system can have the condition $V(x) = 0$ only at the origin $x = 0$. Therefore, $V(x(t)) = 0$ must decrease towards zero and so $x(t) \rightarrow 0$ as $t \rightarrow \infty$ (which obviously does not contradict the physics of the system). Arguably, it may be possible to show that, if a negative semi-definite Liapunov function with its derivative, decreasing along the trajectories of the system, can be obtained in a domain around the origin and further, if it can be shown that no trajectory can pass through points where $\dot{V}(x)=0$ (except at the origin), then the origin is asymptotically stable. Let us seek to establish from what is called the Invariance Principle through La Salle's invariance theorem. For the purpose, we require now to recall the definitions of *positive limit points* of $x(t)$, positive limit set, *an invariant set* with respect to $\dot{x}=f(x)$. We have not so far defined a *positively invariant set*. We say a set M to be an invariant set if with respect to $\dot{x}=f(x)$

$$x(0)\in M \Rightarrow x(t)\in M, \ \forall t\in 0$$

A set M is said to be a *positively invariant set* if

$$x(0)\in M \Rightarrow x(t)\in M, \ \forall t\geq 0$$

and we also say that $x(t)$ approaches a set M as $t\to\infty$, if for each $\varepsilon>0$, there is a $T>0$ such that

$$\text{dist}\ (x(t), M)<\varepsilon, \ \forall t>T$$

where dist (P, M), as before, is the distance of a point P to a set M, i.e. the smallest distance from P to any point in M or in symbols

$$\text{dist}\ (P, M)=\inf_{x\in M}. \ \|P-x\|$$

The set $\Omega_c =\{x\in R^n \ |V(x)\leq c\}$ with $\dot{V}(x)\leq 0$ for all $x\in \Omega_c$ is a positively invariant set since the solution starting in Ω_c remains in Ω_c for all $t\geq 0$. The equilibrium point and the limit cycle are invariant sets.

With all these, we can state (without proof) that :

If a solution $x(t)$ of $\dot{x}=f(x)$ is bounded always in the domain D for $t\geq 0$, then the positive limit set L^+ is a non-empty, compact, invariant set. Further, $x(t)$ approaches L^+ as $t\to\infty$. We shall make use of this (lemma) to prove La Salle's theorem.

10.23 La Salle's theorem
   (on Invariance Principle)

Statement : Let $\Omega \subset D$ be a compact set that is positively invariant with respect to $\dot{x} = f(x)$. Let $V : D \to R$ be a continuously differentiable function such that $\dot{V}(x) \leq 0$ in Ω. Let E be the set of all points in Ω where $\dot{V}(x) = 0$. Let M be the largest invariant set in E. Then every solution starting in Ω approaches M as $t \to \infty$.

Proof

Let $x(t)$ be solution of

$$\dot{x} = f(x) \tag{1}$$

starting in Ω. Since $\dot{V}(x) \leq 0$ in Ω, $V(x(t))$ is a decreasing function of t. Since $V(x)$ is continuous on the compact set Ω, it is bounded from below. So the limit of $V(x)$ exists as $t \to \infty$ and let it be 'a'. Also, the positive limit set L^{+} is in Ω, as Ω is a closed set. For any $p \in L^{+}$, there is a sequence t_n, with $t_n \to \infty$ and $x(t_n) \to p$ as $n \to \infty$. Since $V(x)$ is continuous

$$V(p) = \lim_{n \to \infty} V(x(t_n)) = a$$

$$\therefore \qquad V(x) = a \text{ on } L^{+}$$

Now, by the above lemma, L^{+} is an invariant set and so

$$\dot{V}(x) = 0 \text{ on } L^{+}. \text{ Thus}$$

$$L^{+} \subset M \subset E \subset \Omega$$

Since $x(t)$ is bounded, $x(t)$ approaches L^{+} as $t \to \infty$, by the above lemma. Hence $x(t)$ tends towards M as $t \to \infty$.

Remarks

1. This theorem does not need the function $V(x)$ to be positive definite, as required in Liapunov's theorem

2. The construction of the Liapunov function $V(x)$, which we need to do in problems, does not have to be linked any way, with developing Ω. That the very construction of $V(x)$ reckons the existence of a set Ω is well illustrated by the following specific example :

    If $\Omega_c = \{x \in R^n \mid V(x) \le C\}$ is bounded and $\dot{V}(x) \le 0$ is Ω_c, then we can take $\Omega = \Omega_c$.

    When $\dot{V}(x)$ is positive definite, Ω_c is bounded for sufficiently small $c > 0$; this may not hold when $V(x)$ is not positive definite.

    For example, let $V(x) = (x-y)^2$. The set Ω_c is not bounded, no matter how small c is. If $V(x) \to \infty$, as $\|x\| \to \infty$ the set Ω_c is bounded for all values of c. This holds whether $V(x)$ is positive definite or not.

3. A function $V(x)$ satisfying $V(x) \to \infty$, as $\|x\| \to \infty$, is said to radially unbounded.

4. All the above remarks, consequences, or theorems preceded by a lemma, show that the leading ideas, concepts and notions are all linked in one way or the other in that they are deducible from others; some are precursors of others, some are amenable to modifications etc. The above delineation is in no way exhaustive. For example, in the light of invariant sets, limit points etc. one may cast afresh the criteria for stability or globally asymptotic stability in regard to Liapunov functions. These are often taken as corollaries.

Corollary 1 : Let $x=0$ be an equilibrium point for

$$\dot{x} = f(x)$$

Let $V:D \to R$ be a continuously differentiable positive definite function on a domain D containing the origin $x=0$ such that $\dot{V}(x) \le 0$ in D. Let $S = \{x \in D \mid V(x) = 0\}$ and suppose that no solution can stay identically in S, other than the (trivial) solution $x(t) = 0$. Then the origin is asymptotically stable.

Corollary 2 : Let $x=0$ be an equilibrium point for $x = f(x)$. Let $V:R^n \to R$ be a continuously differentiable, radially unbounded, positive definite function such that $\dot{V}(x) \le 0$ for all $x \in R^n$. Let $S = \{x \in R^n \mid \dot{V}(x) = 0\}$ and let us suppose that no solution can stay identically in S, other than the (trivial) solution $x(t) = 0$. Then the origin is globally asymptotically stable.

Now, with $\dot{V}(x)$ being taken as negative definite, $S = \{0\}$. The above corollaries are the same as those stated earlier.

In lieu of these or as a sequel to the previous statements, in terms of a positively invariant set, one can have a statement on asymptotic stability.

Statement : Let $\bar{x} \in W$ be an equilibrium of the system $\dot{x} = f(x)$ and let $V:U \to R$ be a Liapunov function for $\bar{x}$, U an nbd of $\bar{x}$. Let $P \subset U$ be a nbd of $\bar{x}$ which is closed in W. Let P be positively invariant and let there be no entire orbit in $P - \bar{x}$ on which V is constant. Then, $\bar{x}$ is asymptotically stable. A part of the hint to the proof has already been given earlier, with the choice of L as the set of other points :

$$L = a \in W \mid \text{ such that } t_n \to \infty \text{ with } x(t_n) \to a$$

It may be remarked that those statements, along with earlier ones, show La Salle's theorem enabling us to wider domain of its applications, from an isolated equilibrium point to an equilibrium set.

10.24 A flavour of Poincare-Bendixson theorem

Although we have put off the formal proof of Poincare-Bendixson Theorem, because of its very rigorous tenor, let us have another approach how to look at it in some depth, in the light of ideas on invariant and minimal sets we have so far acquired.

Statement : Let us consider the equation $\dot{x} = f(x)$ in R^2 and assume that γ^+ is a bounded positive orbit and that $\omega(\gamma^+)$ is a periodic orbit.

In particular if $\omega(\gamma^+) \neq \gamma^+$, the periodic orbit is a limit cycle.

As for proof, we have already indicated it earlier in this chapter; the particular case is left as an exercise.

10.25 Illustrative examples

Example 1

Let us have the system

$$\dot{x} = x - y - x(x^2 + y^2)$$
$$\dot{y} = y + x - y(x^2 + y^2)$$

Let
$$x = r\cos\theta$$
$$y = r\sin\theta$$

Then we have $\dot{r} = r(1 - r^2)$
$$\dot{\theta} = 1$$

The only critical point is $(0,0)$ which is a spiral.

Let us construct an annular domain with centre at $(0,0)$ and radii $r_1 < 1, r_2 < 1$.

The orbits which start inside the smallest circle will enter the annulus, contain no critical points according to Poincare Bendixson theorem and contain a periodic orbit.

$\therefore \; \exists$ one periodic solution

$$r(t)=1$$
$$\theta = \theta_0 + t$$

which is a limit cycle.

Example 2

Let us consider the system

$$\dot{x} = x\left(x^2 + y^2 - 2x - 3\right) - y$$
$$\dot{y} = y\left(x^2 + y^2 - 2x - 3\right) + x$$

Here the only one critical point $(0,0)$ is a spiral. Transforming to polar co-ordinates by

$$x = r\cos\theta$$
$$y = r\sin\theta$$

we have $\dot{r} = r\left(r^2 - 2r\cos\theta - 3\right)$

$$\dot{\theta} = 1$$

If $r < 1$ then $\dot{r} < 0$

If $r > 3$, then $\dot{r} > 0$

Hence, according to previous theorem, the annulus is $1 < r < 3$ and must contain one or more limit cycles.

10.26 Stability of fixed points for nonlinear differential equations

We consider a nonlinear differential equation

$$\dot{x} = f(x) \text{ with } x \in R^n \tag{1}$$

The point P is, it is to be recalled, a fixed point if $f(P) = 0$ i.e. $\varphi^t(P) = P$ for all t. After linearizing the flow around P, we get $\dot{x} = A(x - P)$, where $A = Df_P$ is the matrix of partial derivatives.

Let P be a fixed point of $\dot{x} = f(x)$. As we may recall, the fixed point P is to be called a *hyperbolic fixed point* if $R_e(\lambda) \neq 0$ for all the eigen values λ of Df_P. We shall call this hyperbolic fixed point, a *sink* (or attracting) if the real parts of all eigen values of Df_P are negative and a *source* (or repelling) if the real parts of eigen values of Df_P are positive. The hyperbolic fixed point is a saddle point, if it is neither a sink nor a source so that there are two eigen values λ_+ and λ_- with $R_e(\lambda_+) > 0$ and $R_e(\lambda_-) < 0$ (of course, the real parts of all the other eigen values are non zero). A non-hyperbolic fixed point is said to be a centre whose types are known earlier.

We state below (without proof) the theorem on the behaviour (stability) on non-linear hyperbolic fixed points.

10.27 Hartman-Grobman theorem

Let p be a hyperbolic fixed point for $\dot{x} = f(x)$. Then the flow φ^t of f is conjugate in a nbd of p to the flow $p + e^{At}(y - p)$ where $A = Dl_p$. Specifically speaking, there is a nbd U of p and a homoeomorphism $h : U \rightarrow V$ such that

$$\varphi^t(h(x)) = h\left(p + e^{At}(y - p)\right) \text{ as long as } p + e^{At}(y - p) \in U$$

The following corollary is a stronger enabler for determining the stability of hyperbolic fixed points.

Corollary :

Let p be a hyperbolic fixed point p for $\dot{x} = f(x)$.

If p is a source or a saddle, then the fixed point p is not Liapunov stable (or unstable).

If p is a sink, then it is asymptotically stable (attracting).

A more general form of Hartman-Grobman theorem :

Statement : Let $f : R^m - R^n$ be a $C^{(1)}$ homoeomorphism with a hyperbolic fixed point p. Then there exist nbds. U of p and V of 0 and a homoemorphism $h : V \rightarrow U$ such that $f(h_{(n)}) = h(A_x)$ for all $x \in V$, where $A = Df_p$.

Corollary

Let $f : R^m \rightarrow R^n$ be a C^1 diffeomorphism with a hyperbolic fixed point p. If p is a source or a saddle, then the fixed point p is not Liapunov stable. If p is a sink, then it is asymptotically stable.

Exercise

1. Does the system

$$\frac{dx}{dt} = 2x + y + x^3$$

$$\frac{dy}{dt} = 3x - y + y^3$$

have periodic solutions? Justify your answer.

2. Can you show that, by using Poincare-Bendixson theorem,

$$\dot{x} = x - y - \left(x^2 + \frac{3}{2} y^2 \right) x$$

$$\dot{y} = x + y - \left(x^2 + \frac{1}{2} y^2 \right) y$$

has a periodic solution? Justify.

3. Transform the system

$$\frac{dx}{dt} = 4(x - y) - x(x^2 + y^2)$$

$$\frac{dy}{dt} = 4(x + y) - y(x^2 + y^2)$$

using polar coordinates (r, θ).

Can the well-known Poincare-Bendixson theorem be applied to show whether the system has a limit cycle or not? Where is it situated? Is it in a similar region? Justify your answer.

4. Apply the Poincare-Bendixson theorem to the nonlinear autonomous system

$$\frac{dx}{dt} = 4(x+y) - x(x^2 + y^2)$$

$$\frac{dy}{dt} = -4(x-y) - y(x^2 + y^2)$$

to show that there is a closed path between the circles $r = 1$ and $r = 3$.

5. Does the system

$$\frac{d^2x}{dt^2} + (5x^4 - 6x^2)\frac{dx}{dt} + x^3 = 0$$

have a periodic solution?

6. For what values of μ does the system

$$\frac{dx}{dt} = y - x^3 + \mu x$$

$$\frac{dy}{dt} = -x$$

have periodic solutions?

bifurcations : a prelude $\boxed{11}$

11.1 Introduction

In our earlier attempts on qualitative study of nonlinear systems, we have been, in a way
stuck up, back and forth, to ideas on stability of such systems. Several characteristics of
systems concerned emerge in regard to their types of responses, relating to changes in
initial conditions or values of parameters of systems. Do such systems lose their stabilities?
Such a poser is likely to arise. Going back to classical works of Poincare, one finds him
involved with the problem of sudden loss of stability of a system consisting of rotating
planetary masses. What sort of violation of stability is this? Do the instabilities appear as
eigen values of a linearized small amplitude power which we have already encountered?
If the system happened to have stable equilibrium paths in initial stages, how could it
become unstable? Can we seek the answer through the variation of parameters of the
system? Bifurcation theory explains and classifies the ways in which a stable equilibrium
trajectory can become unstable and hence, the rationale for the initial part of this chapter.
Having explored what structural stability is all about, we ought to explore as well,

whether equations of the system can be stable against arbitrarily small perturbations. In other words, the (global) topological form of the solutions should not be lost by a small change in the form of the equations. This brings us close to the catastrophe theory of René Thom. In the following chapter, we shall successively draw upon these two approaches of how to deal with equilibrium points of a system which suddenly becomes unstable. These theories, as will be shown later, are essentially nonlinear.

11.2 Bifurcations

The word 'bifurcation' means splitting and in the context of non-linear differential equations, it means a situation where, at some critical parameter λ, the number of solutions of the equation changes.

Let us begin with few examples :

We consider the system

$$\left.\begin{array}{l} \dot{x} = y \\ \dot{y} = -\lambda x \end{array}\right\}$$

containing a parameter λ with values in $(-\infty, \infty)$. The phase diagram is a centre for $\lambda = 0$ and a saddle point for $\lambda < 0$. These classifications represent radically different types of system behaviour. The change in nature occurs as λ passes through $\lambda = 0$ and a bifurcation is said to occur at $\lambda = 0$. This point $\lambda = 0$ is called *bifurcation point*.

To understand the concept of change in the number of solutions of a differential equation, let us now recall the basic eigen value problem

$$-u''(x) = \lambda u(x), 0 < x < \pi$$

$$u(0) = u(\pi) = 0$$

The solution of the eigen functions $u_n(x) = c_n \sin nx$ at the eigen values $\lambda_n = 1, 4, 9, ..., n^2, ...$ where c_n is an arbitrary constant. If we now plot the eigen value parameter λ along the horizontal axis and the solution $\|u\|$'s along the y-axis, the solution diagram is as follows :

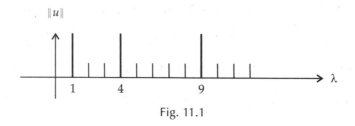

Fig. 11.1

For all other values of λ, the only solution is a trivial solution $u = 0$ which is the solution branch from which others emanate. This is a bifurcation interesting only for the nonlinear problem.

The bifurcation diagram can also be plotted by taking the vertical axis to be C_n rather than $\|u\|$, as shown below :

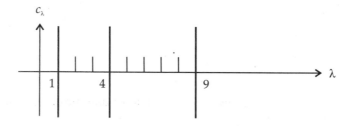

Fig. 11.2

The eigen values λ_n are the bifurcation points for both the above figures and at each of the λ_n, the number of solutions changes from one solution (often called the trivial solution) to an infinite number of solutions.

Apparently these are linear problems. How to go about with non-linearities? Let us choose the problem.

$$-u''(x) = \lambda \|u\|^2 u(x), \quad 0 < x < \pi$$

$$u(0) = u(\pi) = 0$$

$u = 0$ is of course, the trivial solution for all λ. Now for any non-trivial solution u, $\lambda \|u\|^2$ is constant having the same sign as λ. Therefore, as before, subject to the boundary conditions, we have the solution as

$$u_n(x) = c_n \sin nx \text{ which gives}$$

$$\lambda \|u\|^2 = n$$

so that

$$c_n = \pm \left(\frac{2}{\pi}\right)^{\frac{1}{2}} \frac{n}{\lambda^{\frac{1}{2}}}$$

The corresponding bifurcation diagram is given below:

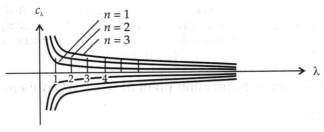

Fig. 11.3

The only bifurcation point is obtained by letting $\lambda \to \infty$.

Example

Find the bifurcation points of the system

$$\dot{x} = -\lambda x + y$$
$$\dot{y} = -\lambda x - 3y$$

Solution

Let $X = \begin{pmatrix} x \\ y \end{pmatrix}$, $A(\lambda) = \begin{pmatrix} -\lambda & 1 \\ -\lambda & -3 \end{pmatrix}$

so that the matrix form of the system is equivalent to $\dot{X} = A(\lambda)X$.

The characteristic equation is given by

$$\begin{vmatrix} -\lambda - m & 1 \\ -\lambda & -3 - m \end{vmatrix} = 0$$

$$\Rightarrow \quad m^2 + (3 + \lambda)m + 4\lambda = 0$$

$$m_1, m_2 = \frac{1}{2}\left[(-\lambda - 3) \pm \sqrt{(\lambda - 1)(\lambda - 4)}\right]$$

Let us look for bifurcations where the roots change, also whether real or complex and also about the sign of the real part when they are complex.

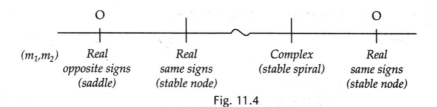

Fig. 11.4

Clearly, the system has a single bifurcation point at $\lambda = 1$ when there is a change from a stable node to a saddle.

11.3 Some types of bifurcations

We wish to study the qualitative behaviour of solution set of the system $\dot{x} = f(x, \lambda)$ depending on the parameter $\lambda \in R$. A value λ_0 of the parameter in the equation $\dot{x} = f(x, \lambda)$ for which the field $f(x, \lambda_0)$ is not *structurally stable* is called a *bifurcation value*. Let us now study some bifurcations of some chosen vector fields.

Type I

Let us consider the one-dimensional system

$$\frac{dx}{dt} = \lambda - x^2$$

For $\lambda > 0$, there are two critical points, $x = \pm\sqrt{\lambda}$

$$Df(x,\lambda)=-2x$$

$$Df(\pm\sqrt{\lambda},\lambda)=\mp 2\sqrt{\lambda} \quad [D\equiv\text{derivative with respect to } x]$$

The critical point, $x=\sqrt{\lambda}$ is stable while the critical point $x=-\sqrt{\lambda}$ is unstable.

For $\lambda=0$, there is only one critical point at $x=0$.

$$Df(0,0)=0$$

The vector field $f(x)=-x^2$ is structurally unstable and $\lambda=0$ is a bifurcation value.

For $\lambda<0$, there are no critical points.

The phase portraits for the equation $\dot{x}=f(x,\lambda)$ are shown the figures below.

$\lambda<0$

Fig. 11.5(a)

$\lambda=0$

Fig. 11.5(b)

The phase portraits are given below. The curve $\lambda=-x^2$ determines the position of the critical points of the system. The solid curve indicates a family of stable critical points and dashed portion curve indicates a family of unstable critical points. This type of bifurcation is called *saddle-node bifurcation*. The figure is the bifurcation diagram for the saddle node bifurcation.

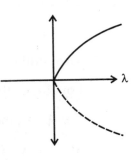

Fig. 11.6

Type II

Let us consider the system

$$\dot{x}=\lambda x-x^2$$

The critical points are $x=0$ and $x=\lambda$.

For $\lambda=0$, there is only one critical point at $x=0$.

$$Df(0,0)=0$$

The vector field $f(x) = -x^2$ is structurally unstable.

$\lambda = 0$ is the bifurcation value.

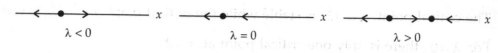

Fig. 11.7

We see here there is a change of stability at the critical points of this system at the bifurcation value $\lambda = 0$. This type of bifurcation is called a *transcritical bifurcation*, as shown by the bifurcation diagram (Fig. 11.8).

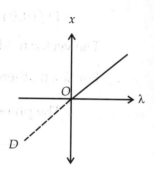

Type III

Fig. 11.8

Let us consider the system

$$\dot{x} = \lambda x - x^3$$

The equilibrium set M is given by $\lambda x - x^3 = 0$ i.e. critical points are $x = 0$, $x = \pm\sqrt{\lambda}$,

For $\lambda < 0$, there is a stable equilibrium at $x = 0$.

For $\lambda > 0$, there are two attractors at $x = \pm\sqrt{\lambda}$ separated by an unstable equilibrium at $x = 0$ which is shown by dotted points.

For $\lambda \leq 0$, $x = 0$ is the only critical point.

For $\lambda = 0$, there is a critical point at $x = 0$.

$$\left\{ \because\ Df(0,0) = 0 \right\}$$

The vector field $f(x) = -x^3$ is structurally unstable.

$\lambda = 0$ is the bifurcation value.

The phase diagram is given by (Fig. 11.9).

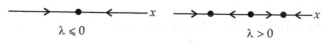

Fig. 11.9

This shows that if the parameter is increased from negative to positive, the stable equilibrium splits into two as λ passes through 0. We say that the bifurcation set is the single point $\lambda = 0$ and the λ-axis.

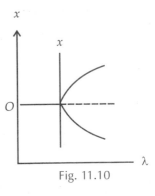

Fig. 11.10

This is called a *pitch-fork bifurcation* (Fig. 11.10). It is unstable in the sense that there are arbitrarily small perturbations with a topologically different equilibrium set.

Remarks

1. The saddle-node, the pitch-fork and the trans-vertical bifurcations, as in the above, illustrate the most important types of bifurcations that occur in 1 dimensional dynamical system. But there are certainly many other types of bifurcations that are possible in one dimensional systems.

   In the Types (I) and (II)

   if $Df(0,0) = \cdots = D^{m-1} f(0,0) = 0$

   but $D^m f(0,0) \neq 0$.

   Then the 1 dimensional system is said to have a critical point of multiplicity m at $x = 0$.

   We also say that at most m critical points can be made to bifurcate from the origin and there is a bifurcation which causes exactly m critical points to bifurcate from the origin. e.g. at the bifurcation value $\lambda = 0$, the origin is the critical point of multiplicity 2 in the Types I and II. The origin is the critical point of multiplicity 3 in the Type III; in fact, it can also be looked upon as a critical point of multiplicity 4 in the Type I.

2.   We often write $F_\lambda(x)$ in lieu of $F(x,\lambda)$ or $F(\lambda,x)$

Regarding critical point(s) of systems of differential equations $F(\lambda,x)=0$ where $\lambda \in R^m$, $x \in R^n$, our main concern is whether the solutions of such equations can bifurcate at certain values of the parameters $\lambda=(\lambda_1,.....\lambda_m)$. By translation, we can take up, without any loss of generality, studying the bifurcation of the trivial solution $x=0$ and so $F(\lambda,0)=0$. In particular, for $\dot{x}=\lambda x-x^2$, $F(\lambda,0)=0$, the value of the parameter $\lambda=\lambda_c$ is called a bifurcation value if $\exists$ a nontrivial solution in each nbd. of $(x_{c,\partial})$ in R^m/R^n.

11.4 An example on bifurcation mechanics—Buckling of a stick

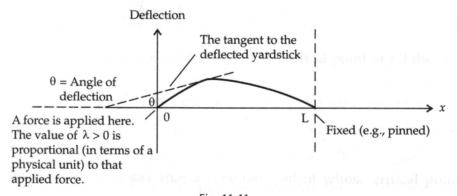

Fig. 11.11

Here a stick is pushed to a fixed wall (denoted by the shaded line) parallel to the direction of deflection, θ being the angle of deflection i.e. the direction made by the tangent to the deflected stick. The governing equations are known to be

$$-\theta''(x)=\lambda \sin \theta(x), \qquad 0<x<L$$

with $\theta'(O)=\theta'(L)=0$

Let $\theta(0)=\theta_0$ be the maximum value of the angle of deflection (at the ends), for each given

form for $\lambda \geq 0$. Let us first solve the governing equation, on the lines, we did in the beginning.

$$-f''(x) = \lambda u(x), \qquad 0 < x < \pi,$$
$$f(0) = f(\pi) = 0$$

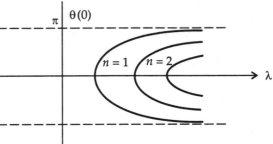

Fig. 11.12

in terms of eigen functions $f_n(x) = c_n \sin nx$ at the eigen values $\lambda_n = 1, 4, \cdots n^2, \cdots, \quad c_n$ being arbitrary constants. We obtain the bifurcation diagrams as shown on the side Fig. 11.12.

The first branch is the node, as in the original figure, when drawn, and the second branch is the node now being shown on the side Fig. 11.13.

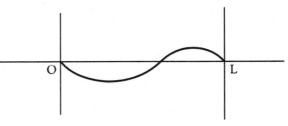

Fig. 11.13

11.5 Hopf-bifurcation—Motivation from an electrical circuit

We consider the circuit with the resistor, characterized by a parameter λ say, the temperature of the resistor. Let the resistor be

$$f_\lambda : R \to R, \ -1 \leq \lambda \leq 1.$$

Then the behaviour of the circuit is governed by the equation in R^2 :

$$\left.\begin{array}{l} \dot{x} = y - f_\lambda(x) \\ \dot{y} = -x \end{array}\right\} \tag{1}$$

$$\left(\dot{x} = \frac{dx}{dt}, \quad \dot{y} = \frac{dy}{dt} \right)$$

Let us consider, in particular, $f_\lambda(x) = x^3 - \lambda x$.

We, thus, have the differential equation with the parameter λ. Given $C^{(1)}$ map $\sqrt{\lambda}: W \rightarrow E$ where W is an open set of the vector space E and λ is allowed to vary over some parameter space, i.e. $\lambda \in J = [-1, 1]$

Moreover f_λ is differentiable in λ i.e. the map

$$J \times W \rightarrow E, \ (\lambda, x) \rightarrow F_\lambda(x)$$

is C^1. We have then the differential equation

$$\dot{x} = f_\lambda(x) \tag{2}$$

with $f_\lambda(x) = x^3 - \lambda x$; we take the (equivalent) form, namely (1) and let us see what happens as λ is varied from -1 to 1. For each λ, $-1 \leq \lambda \leq 0$, imply that the resistor is passive and solutions can be shown to tend to zero (asymptotically) as $t \rightarrow \infty$. Physically, this circuit is no longer alive in that after a period of transition, all the electrical entities (say, currents and voltages) remain at O or at least in the nbd of O.

But the circuit becomes alive as λ passes through O and begins to oscillate, when $0 \leq \lambda \leq 1$; there is a periodic solution say C_λ and the origin becomes an attractor. Indeed, every non-trivial solution tends to C_λ as $t \rightarrow \infty$. It can also be shown that $C_\lambda \rightarrow 0$ as $\lambda \rightarrow 0$, $\lambda > 0$. $\lambda = 0$ is the bifurcation value of the parameter; the portrait is essentially shown in the Fig. 11.14, as λ phase passes through the value O.

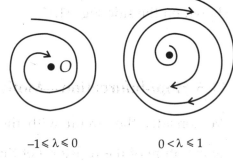

$-1 \leqslant \lambda \leqslant 0$ $0 < \lambda \leqslant 1$

Fig. 11.14

Remark

What we find, in general terms, from the above, is that we may identify one parameter families of equations $\dot{x} = f_\lambda(x)$, a closed orbit for $\lambda > \lambda_0$ if the eigen value (characterizing the equilibrium) changes at λ_0 from a sink to a source. This is precisely the essence of what the mathematician E. Hopf could establish. We shall have now occasions to consider Hopf-bifurcation of this sort.

Let us consider again a particular kind of bifurcation which generate limit cycles (or other periodic solutions).

11.6 Few exemplars on bifurcations

A. Let us consider the system

$$\dot{x} = \lambda x + y - x(x^2 + y^2)$$

$$\dot{y} = -x + \lambda y - y(x^2 + y^2)$$

where λ is a bifurcation parameter.

The system has a critical point at the origin.

In polar co-ordinates, the equation becomes

$$\dot{r} = r(\lambda - r^2)$$

$$\dot{\theta} = -1$$

If $\lambda \le 0$ then the entire diagram consists of a stable spiral given in 11.15(a).

For $\lambda > 0$, there is an unstable spiral at the origin surrounded by stable limit cycle which grows out of the origin as in shown Fig. 11.15(b).

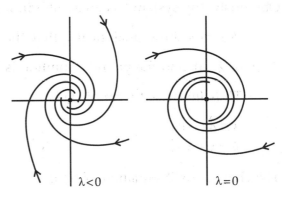

Fig. 11.15(a)

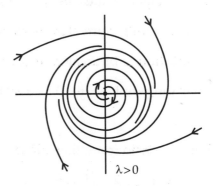

Fig. 11.15(b) : Development of a limit cycle
In a Hopf bifurcation

Remark

Hopf-bifurcation is thus the bifurcation which occurs when the periodic solution is being bifurcated from a steady solution as the bifurcation parameter reaches the critical value which we show next.

B.   Let us consider the two-dimensional system

$$\dot{x} = \lambda x - y - x^3 \tag{1}$$

$$\dot{y} = x + \lambda y - y^3$$

Obviously, the system has an equilibrium point at $x = y = 0$

We can show analytically that the solution is stable or unstable according as $\lambda < 0$ or $\lambda > 0$ and the periodic solution is bifurcated at $\lambda = 0$

Thus linearised form of (1) is

$$\left. \begin{array}{l} \dot{x} = \lambda x - y \\ \dot{y} = x + \lambda y \end{array} \right\} \tag{2}$$

The characteristic equation of (2) is

$$\begin{vmatrix} \lambda - 1 & -1 \\ -1 & \lambda - 1 \end{vmatrix} = 0$$

∴   The eigen values are $p = \lambda \pm i$

∴   The equilibrium state is stable for $\lambda < 0$ and unstable for $\lambda > 0$ and the periodic solution is bifurcated at $\lambda = 0$.

Further the point $x = y = 0$ is a stable focus for $\lambda < 0$ and unstable focus for $\lambda > 0$.

C. Let us consider another planar system

$$\dot{x} = -y + x(\lambda - x^2 - y^2) \tag{1}$$

$$\dot{y} = x + y(\lambda - x^2 - y^2)$$

Now the critical point is at the origin

$$Df(0,\lambda) = \begin{bmatrix} \lambda & -1 \\ 1 & \lambda \end{bmatrix}$$

The origin is a stable or an unstable focus of this non-linear system according as $\lambda < 0$ or $\lambda > 0$.

For $\lambda = 0$, $Df(0,0)$ has a pair of purely imaginary values. Therefore, by Dulac's theorem, this is either a centre or focus for this nonlinear system $\lambda = 0$.

In polar co-ordinates, the system is

$$\dot{r} = r(\lambda - r^2)$$

$$\dot{\theta} = 1$$

Here, we see that at $\lambda = 0$, the origin is a stable focus and for $\lambda > 0$ there is a stable limit cycle.

The phase portraits are given by Fig. 11.16 (a) & Fig. 11.16(b)

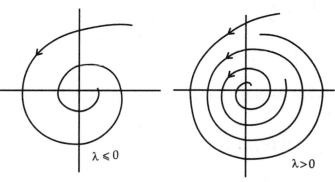

$\lambda \leqslant 0$

Fig. 11.16 (a)   Fig. 11.16(b)

Let us have the bifurcation diagrams Fig. 11.17(a) & Fig. 11.17(b) :

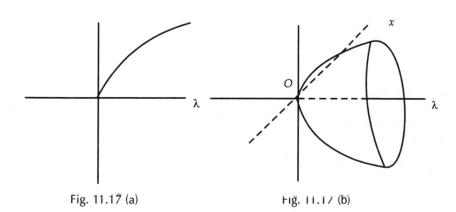

Fig. 11.17 (a)   Fig. 11.17 (b)

The curve Γ_λ represents 1 parameter family of limit cycles of the system. The upper curve in the bifurcation diagram represents one parameter family of limit cycles which defines the surface $R^2 \times R$. The bifurcation of the limit cycle from the origin that occurs at the bifurcation value $\lambda = 0$, as the origin changes its stability, is thus Hopf bifurcation.

The equation $\dot{r} = r(\lambda - r^2)$ can be solved as

$$r(t, r_0, \lambda) = \left[\frac{1}{\lambda} + \left(\frac{1}{r_0^2} - \frac{1}{\lambda} \right) \times e^{-2\lambda t} \right]^{-\frac{1}{2}}$$

For $\lambda > 0$ with $r(0) = r_0$, on any ray from the origin, the Poincare map $P(r_0, \lambda) = r(2\pi, r_0, \lambda)$ is given by

$$P(r_0, \lambda) = \left[\frac{1}{\lambda} + \left(\frac{1}{r_0^2} - \frac{1}{\lambda} \right) \times e^{-4\pi\lambda} \right]^{-\frac{1}{2}}$$

If we differentiate it with respect to r_0 we find

$$DP(r_0, \lambda) = e^{-4\lambda\pi} r_0^{-3} \left[\frac{1}{\lambda} + \left(\frac{1}{r_0^2} - \frac{1}{\lambda} \right) e^{-4\lambda\pi} \right]^{-\frac{3}{2}}$$

For, $r_\lambda = \sqrt{\lambda}$ for $\lambda > 0$, $P(r_\lambda, \lambda) = \sqrt{\lambda}$ and $DP(r_\lambda, \lambda) = e^{-4\pi\lambda}$

$\therefore$ for $\lambda > 0$, $DP(r_\lambda, \lambda) < 1$

$\therefore$ the periodic orbits Γ_λ are all stable.

This is an example to show how a Poincare map $P(r, \lambda)$ depends on the parameter λ.

D. Andronov Hopf-bifurcation

The relevant system is given by

$$\left. \begin{array}{l} \dot{x} = y + x\left(c + a\left(x^2 + y^2\right)\right) \\ \dot{y} = -x + y\left(c + a\left(x^2 + y^2\right)\right) \end{array} \right\} \tag{1}$$

We write the whole system, in polar coordinates, as

$$\dot{r} = r(c + ar^2)$$

$$\dot{\theta} = 1$$

We solve for r and θ, as before, in terms of t.

The origin is a stable-focus for $c < 0$ and unstable for $c > 0$ and for

$$c = 0, \quad r = \frac{r_0}{[2r_0^2 t + 1]^{1/2}}$$

This represents a slower approach to r_0 than when

$c < 0 \quad [r \approx r_0 \exp(ct)]$

If $a < 0$, then there is a stable periodic orbit when

$c > 0$ at $r = \left(-\dfrac{c}{a}\right)^{1/2}$

If $a < 0$, the system has what is called a *super critical*

bifurcation, which is a Hopf bifurcation as well, at $c = 0$.

If $a > 0$, an unstable periodic orbit occurs for $c < 0$ and

we say that the system has a *sub-critical* Hopf bifurcation at

$c = 0$.

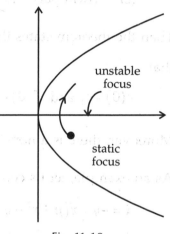

unstable
focus

static
focus

Fig. 11.18

We note that the system (1) having characteristic exponents of the linearised equation of the form $c = \pm i$, changes from the stable focus to unstable focus as c goes from negative to positive. Further the real part at $c = 0$ is 1. These are the essential features of Hopf bifurcation theorem which we state as follows:

Hopf-bifurcation theorem

Statement : Let us assume that $\dot{x} = F(x,c)\,(x \in R^n, c \in R)$. $F(x,c)$ is analytic in x having a fixed point $x_0(c_0)$ so that $F(x_0(c_0)) = 0$. Then linearised equations about the fixed point are

$$\dot{x}_i = \sum_{j=1}^{n} \left(\frac{\partial F_i}{\partial x_j}\right)_0 x_j \quad (l = 1, 2, \cdots, n)$$

These are assumed to have solutions $x_j = A_j \exp(\lambda_i t)$ whose characteristic components $\{\lambda_i\}$ satisfy the following conditions :

(a)   for $c = c_0$, the roots are purely imaginary and conjugate, say

$\lambda_1(c_0) = -\lambda_2 * (c_0)$ (complex conjugate)

(b)   no other purely imaginary roots satisfy

$\lambda_j(c_0) = m\lambda_1(c_0)$

(c)   (Real part) $\mathrm{Re}\left(\dfrac{\partial \lambda_j}{\partial c}\right)_{c_0} \neq 0$ for $j = 1, 2, \cdots,$

Then the theorem states that there are analytic functions $c(\varepsilon)$ and $T(\varepsilon)$ near $\varepsilon = 0$ such that

$$c(0) = c_0 \text{ and } T(0) = \frac{2r}{\lambda_1(c_0)}$$

Moreover, there is a non-constant solution $x(t, c(\varepsilon))$ which has the period $T(\varepsilon)$.

As an example, let us consider the system

$$\left. \begin{array}{l} \dot{x} = -y + x\left(\mu - x^2 - y^2\right) \\ \dot{y} = x + y\left(\mu - x^2 - y^2\right) \end{array} \right\} \tag{1}$$

Let us see whether the system is stable or not

Here , the critical point is $(0,0)$. As per usual conditions,

$$DF(0,\mu) = \begin{bmatrix} \mu & -1 \\ 1 & \mu \end{bmatrix}$$

The origin is a stable or an unstable focus of the non-linear system according as $\mu < 0$ or $\mu > 0$. In fact for $\mu = 0$, $DF(0,0)$ has a pair of imaginary eigen values and, therefore, by Dulac's theorem, the origin is either a centre or a focus, for the non-linear system for $\mu = 0$.

We can get the phase portraits by transforming to polar coordinates.

$$\dot{r} = r\left(\mu - r^2\right)$$

$$\dot{\theta} = 1$$

and at $\mu = 0$, the origin is a stable focus and at $\mu > 0$, there is a stable limit cycle as shown below.

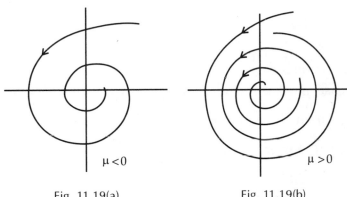

Fig. 11.19(a)   Fig. 11.19(b)

Theorem on limit cycle

Given the equation $\dot{x} = \mu x + y - xf(r)$

$$\dot{y} = -x + \mu y - yf(r)$$

where $r = \sqrt{x^2 + y^2}$, $f(r)$ is continuous for $r \geq 0$ and $f(0) = 0$, $f(r) > 0$ for $r > 0$

Then (i)   for $\mu < 0$, the origin is a stable spiral covering the entire plane

(ii)   for $\mu = 0$, the origin is a stable spiral and

(iii)   for $\mu > 0$, there is a stable limit cycle whose radius increases from zero as μ increases from zero.

Proof : Let us choose a Liapunov function

$$V(x, y) = \frac{1}{2}\left(x^2 + y^2\right)$$

Then $\dot{V}(x, y) = \dfrac{\partial V}{\partial x}\dot{x} + \dfrac{\partial V}{\partial y}\dot{y}$

$$= r^2(\mu - f(r)) < 0 \text{ for } \mu \le 0 \text{ and } r > 0.$$

Therefore, by Liapunov stability theorem, the origin is asymptotically stable and its domain of attraction is the entire plane.

To have from it, a spiral, we write the given equation in polar form given by

$$\dot{r} = r(\mu - f(r))$$

$$\dot{\theta} = -1$$

Note that the case $\mu = 0$ is included. Let us now imagine that the time is reversed and t is replaced by $-t$ in the equation and see that for the same Liapunov function $\dot{V}(x, y) = r^2(f(r) - \mu) < 0$ for $\mu > 0$ in some interval $0 < r < r_1$ because of continuity of $f(r)$ and the inequality $f(r) > 0$ for r>0.

This proves that the origin is unstable and it confirms that it is a spiral $0 < r < r_1$. Finally, in some interval $0 < \mu < \mu_1$, $\mu - f(r) = 0$ must have exactly one solution for μ_1 sufficiently small and again, for the polar equation, we find that these limit cycles must be stable.

11.7 Illustrative example

Show that the equation

$$\ddot{x} + (x^2 + \dot{x}^2 - \mu)\dot{x} + x = 0$$

exhibits a Hopf bifurcation as μ passes though zero.

Solution

Putting $\dot{x} = y$, the given system is equivalent to

$$\dot{x} = y$$
$$\dot{y} = -(x^2 + y^2 - \mu)y - x$$

which can be expressed in the form

$$\left. \begin{array}{l} \dot{x} = P(x, y) \\ \dot{y} = Q(x, y) \end{array} \right\} \tag{1}$$

where $P(x, y) = y$ and $Q(x, y) = -(x^2 + y^2 - \mu)y - x$

$$\therefore \quad \frac{\partial P}{\partial x} + \frac{\partial Q}{\partial y} = -x^2 - 3y^2 + \mu < 0 \text{ for } \mu < 0 \text{ and for all } (x, y)$$

Hence, by the Poincare-Bendixson theorem there can be no closed paths in the phase plane. For the critical case $\mu = 0$, we take the Liapunov function as $V(x, y) = \frac{1}{2}(x^2 + y^2)$

Then $V(x, y) = x \cdot \dfrac{dx}{dt} + y \cdot \dfrac{dy}{dt}$

$$= -(x^2 + y^2)y^2$$

Since $\dot{V}(x, y)$ vanishes at the isolated value $x = 0, y = 0$ but is otherwise strictly negative, the origin is an asymptotically stable equilibrium point. For $\mu > 0$ the system has a stable limit cycle with path $x^2 + y^2 = \mu$ which evidently emerges from the origin at $\mu = 0$ with a radius which increases with μ.

As μ passes through O, there is thus the bifurcation called the Hopf bifurcation.

Remark

Having introduced bits of bifurcations, there should be an expectation that there should be some kind of theorization on bifurcation. We shall do it in a chapter later. We take up in the next chapter another genre of applications, that comes within the ambit of what is called catastrophe theory

Exercise

1. How do you have the bifurcation diagram for the nonlinear system.

   $$-u(x) = \lambda u(x) + \|u^2\| u(x)$$

   $$u(0) = u(\pi) = 0 ?$$

   [Hint : $\because C_n = \pm \left(\dfrac{2}{\pi}\right)^{\frac{1}{2}} \left(u^2 - x^2\right)^{\frac{1}{2}}$]

2. Does the system

   $$\dot{x} = y$$

   $$\dot{y} = -\lambda x, \ (\lambda, \text{ a parameter})$$

   exhibit any bifurcation? What can you say about the behaviour of

   $$\dot{x} = y$$

   $$\dot{y} = -ky - w^2 x, \ (w \text{ and } k, \text{ the parameters}) \text{ in regard to bifurcation? Justify your}$$

   answer.

3. Find, for all values of μ, the bifurcation points of the system.

   $$\frac{dx}{dt} = \mu x + y$$

   $$\frac{dy}{dt} = x - 2y$$

4. Does the system

   $$\ddot{x} + (x^3 + x^2 - \mu)\dot{x} + x = 0$$

   exhibit a Hopf bifurcation as μ passes through origin? Justify.

5. Find the bifurcation value, if any, of the system

   $$\dot{x} = 1 - 2(1 + \mu)x + x^2$$

   Does it have an unique solution if $x \neq (1 + \mu)$? When can it have the equilibrium solution?

6. Does the system

$$\dot{x} = \mu x + y - x$$

$$\dot{y} = -x - \mu y - y\left(x^2 + y^2\right)$$

show Hopf-bifurcation? Justify your answer.

7. Investigate the behaviour of the system

$$\dot{x} = y + x[c + a(x^2 + y^2)]$$

$$\dot{y} = -x + y[c + a(x^2 + y^2)]$$

for negative and positive values of c.

When does its Hopf bifurcation occur, if any?

8. Investigate the behaviour of the system

$$\dot{x} = \mu x - x^3 + xy$$

$$\dot{y} = -y + y^2 - x^2$$

in regard(s) to bifurcations, if any.

catastrophes : a prelude

12.1 Introduction

In the preceding chapter, a different way of looking at qualitative aspects of studies has been presented, indicating what can happen if the variables and parameters change through some values. In this chapter, we take up another motivation that leads to what are called 'catastrophes' dealing again with qualitative aspects of mathematical systems. We begin with the genesis of the ideas as 'catastrophes', and then consider the mathematics of it followed by exemplars that become applicable at this stage.

12.2 Genesis

Stability continues to be our fundamental concern. The whole universe including biological organisms has some kind of stability as its basis. However, it was the great French mathematician René Thom who in his classic book, published in 1975, pioneered the technique of applying a theory of stability to mathematical models of various kinds. This technique naturally did advance the cause of qualitative insight and could also demonstrate that the qualitative understanding of a problem was as adequate as its quantitative understanding. A combination of qualitative information as well as quantitative details tends to make the solution of many problems from diverse areas not only easier but more complete, as well. Sometimes, quantitative methods applied to obtain answers to practical problems such as the structural survival of a certain bridge in high winds, or may be, the continuation of roughly elliptical planetary orbits in the solar system are, in effect, qualitative answers.

We know that the concept of stable equilibrium is of immense importance in physical systems. We are all quite familiar with the idea of stable equilibrium in a dynamical system. But this concept can be further extended to the study of more general kinds of dynamical systems, such as, economic, social, biological, ecological, geological and so on. As is well known, there are various kinds of the state of equilibrium, termed as 'highly stable', 'just stable', 'unstable' etc. But in some cases, we come across some very interesting phenomena, which may be posed in the following way.

Suppose, we have a kind of system in equilibrium, but the system itself is changing slowly as its various important parameters are changing. What happens to the equilibrium? From common sense, we may expect, that the equilibrium will also change slowly. But in a number of instances, we observe quite the reverse kind of phenomena. We give some more concrete examples as follows. It is well known, in fluid dynamics, that the flow of water suddenly turns from smooth to turbulent, if the velocity (or strictly speaking Reynold's number) exceeds a critical value. We also know how a crystalline metal starts melting after the temperature exceeds a certain characteristic value. In these two situations, we really have, what can be called a 'discontinuous response' to a smooth change in one or more parameters, the parameter in the first case being the Reynold's number, and in the second case, the temperature. There are other such examples too; for example, the case of rain drops turning to snow crystals. There are evidences from fossil records, that phenotypes remain unchanged for relatively long periods, suddenly giving rise to fresh phenotypes which, in turn, remain relatively unchanged for long periods. It is easy to surmise that these abrupt changes might have occurred on account of the fact that the environment underwent some drastic changes at that time. There being no evidence of changes of environment, which may, therefore, be taken to have undergone smooth changes, one can attribute evolution to long periods of gradual changes alternating with rapid periods of drastic structural changes in phenotypes. There is a problem in embryology with regard to developments of organisms to which the celebrated biologist C.H. Waddington has drawn our attention. It is about the process of gastrulation in which the embryo is in the form of a spherical shell. On its surface, the crescent grows from a point till an entire circle is formed. Along with this crescent, certain processes take place between the tissues and the interior of the spherical shell, so as to form the primitive core of the animal. The process is related to inter-cellular concentrations of one or more characteristic substances called morphogens. Essentially, all these relate to forms or changes of forms or in other words, morphogenesis. In mathematical terms, we may say that in the above cases, we are led to discontinuous responses to a continuous change in one or more parameters. Hence, systems with continuous inputs, giving discontinuous outputs, are of great interest to us. Any mathematical analysis to unfold the reasons for such abrupt changes with possible predictions is naturally going to be of equally great interest in emerging aspects of mathematical sciences.

The general nature of such discontinuous changes was not very well known until René Thom classified these discontinuous jumps into a small number of classifiable types. These types are called 'elementary catastrophes'. The catastrophe theory is concerned with descriptions of the ways in which the equilibrium states of a dynamical system can change, as the system varies with respect to certain parameters. In the next article, we consider a mechanical model to show how this motivates to the concept of certain types of 'elementary catastrophes.'

12.3 Motivation to elementary catastrophes : A mechanical model

Here we first take up the case of a simple arch.

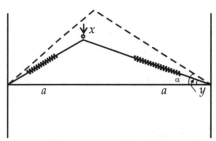

A simple arch is, in general position, as depicted by Fig. 12.1. Two very light springs situated at a distance 2 a apart constitutes the arch. The springs are smoothly hinged to each other and to two supports at a distance 2 a from each other. The springs, in the

Fig. 12.1: Simple arch

general position, with load x make an angle y with the horizontal. The angle of the springs with the horizontal at the initial unloaded position is α. Obviously, the P.E. (V) of the system is given by

$$V = x\, a \tan y + k\left(a \sec \alpha - a \sec y\right)^2$$

Assuming that the arch is shallow and making appropriate approximations, we get,

$$V = axy + \frac{1}{4} ka^2 \left(\alpha^2 - y^2\right)^2$$

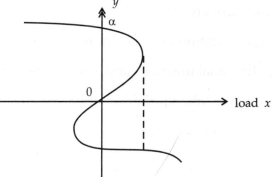

Fig. 12.2: Equilibrium curve for simple arch

The equilibrium curve $V_y = 0$, is evidently given by the relation $x = aky\left(\alpha^2 - y^2\right)$ and depicted by the figure in Fig. 12.2.

This is obviously a cubic curve. Since $V_{yy} > 0$ for $|y| > \dfrac{\alpha}{\sqrt{3}}$, we have minima of V, and so a stable equilibrium, for the ranges of values as shown by continuous lines. The dotted lines depict the unstable equilibrium.

If we increase the load, y decreases, slowly at first, and more rapidly later, as we move along the equilibrium curve, until we reach the load $\dfrac{\alpha}{\sqrt{3}}$, at which the equilibrium is unstable and the arch snaps through along a vertical line to a position of stable equilibrium. A further increase of the load produces further depression of the inverted arch and decreasing it, we arrive at another unloaded position of the stable equilibrium, the reflection in the line joining the supports of the first. By using a negative load, i.e., pushing it upwards, we can eventually make the arch snap back.

Obviously, in this model, the sudden snap which occurs from the unstable maximum or minimum load is an example of a catastrophe.

12.4 Geometrical approach to catastrophe theory

As already mentioned in the beginning, change of forms in biological processes is the moot concern in catastrophe theory. As analogues to biological morphogenesis, mechanical situations like deformation, buckling, bending etc. of structural systems can be qualitatively analysed. As a first step towards this direction, we take recourse to representation of these forms by some mathematical entities which are well known as polynomial functions and observe their structures with varying parameters and variables.

We take up the simplest case (one parameter)

$$V_a(x) = x^3 + ax.$$

which is often written as

$$V(a, x) = \frac{1}{3}x^3 + ax.$$

If $a > 0$, $V_a(x)$ is a monotonically increasing function of x; therefore there are no points for which $V_a'(x) = 0$; i.e. there are no stationary points. On the other hand, if $a < 0$, there are two stationary points $x = \pm\left(-\dfrac{a}{3}\right)^{1/3}$, one of them being a maximum and the other, a minimum. At the intermediate stage $a = 0$, there is exactly one stationary point $x = 0$;

it is a degenerate function, in that it is a repeated root of $V_a(x)=0$ and hence, a root of $V_a'(x)=0$.

$V_a(x)$ has the following graphs :

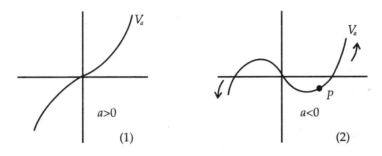

Fig. 12.3

One can think of $a=0$ as the instantaneous coalescence of a maximum and minimum as 'a' moves through the value 0 as shown above.

Further, we may think of this as follows :

For $a<0$, a particle P rests at a minimum point as long as that minimum exists; this is as long as $a<0$. If we now increase the value of a progressively, i.e., if the curve is slowly pulled, eventually we reach a configuration for which $a=0$ and the minimum ceases to exist. In such a case, the particle

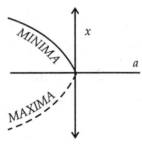

Fig. 12.4

falls to the left. A continuous input has then given rise to a sudden jump or discontinuous output. This kind of sudden change is termed catastrophe. Another aspect to be remembered is as follows :

$V_a(x)$ is stable for $a>0$ or $a<0$ under sufficiently small perturbations of the paramotor but $V_0(x)$ is unstable, for arbitrarily small perturbations of a parameter can destroy the form. In the language of Thom, the point $a=0$ is a catastrophe point for the family of functions $V_a(x)$ and it forms the common boundary of two stable regions $a > 0$ and $a < 0$. This is a fold catastrophe.

We next consider a biquadratic polynomial function of two parameters. As for example,

$$V_{(a,b)}(x) = x^4 + ax^2 + bx$$

$$\therefore V'_{(a,b)}(x) = 0 \Rightarrow 4x^3 + 2ax + b = 0 \tag{1}$$

and also

$$V''_{(a,b)}(x) = 0 \Rightarrow 12x^2 + 2a = 0 \tag{2}$$

Eliminating x between equations (1) and (2), we get,

$$27b^2 + 8a^3 = 0$$

which is the equation of a *cusp* in the (a, b)-plane describing the set of points (a, b) for which $V_{(a,b)}(x)$ has coalescing stationary points. In other words, cusp is the set of catastrophe points and we call it the catastrophe set K for the family of functions $V_{(a,b)}(x)$. For various values of the parameters the graphs of $V_{(a,b)}(x)$ are given in Figs. 12.5 (i)-(viii). $V_{(a,b)}(x)$ looks like (i) or (ii) if $27b^2 + 8a^3 > 0$ and like Fig. (iii) or Fig. (iv) if $27b^2 + 8a^3 < 0$. The situation can be summed up in Fig. 12.5.

We next consider a three-parameter polynomial of the type

$$V_{(a,b,c)}(x, y) = x^4 + ax^2 + y^2 + bx + c.$$

The stationary points are given by

$$\frac{\partial V}{\partial x} = 0, \quad \frac{\partial V}{\partial y} = 0$$

$$\Rightarrow \quad 4x^3 + 2ax + b = 0$$

$$ay = 0$$

Now $\begin{vmatrix} V_{xx} & V_{xy} \\ V_{yx} & V_{yy} \end{vmatrix} = 0 \quad \Rightarrow 2(12x^2 + 2a) = 0.$

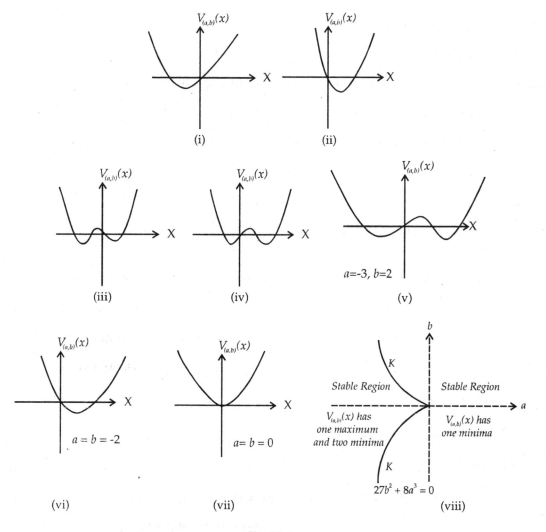

Fig. 12.5

Eliminating x and y, we have,

$27b^2 + 8a^3 = 0$ as the catastrophe set K.

So we now have on the (a, b, c)-space a surface whose projection on the (a, b)-plane is a cusp, as in Fig. 12.6.

12.4 Classification of elementary catastrophes

The above examples are essentially simple cases of families of functions $V(x, y, z, \cdots\cdots)$

varying with parameters $(a, b, c, \cdots\cdots)$. We obtain for each of the catastrophe set K in $(a, b, c, \cdots\cdots)$ spaces. Also, the state which the function represents can change discontinuously with respect to parameters $(a, b, c, \cdots\cdots)$ even though V itself varies smoothly. If we analyse catastrophe sets of all families of functions $V_{(a, b, c, t)}(x_1, x_2, \cdots\cdots, x_n)$ which is a pretty difficult task and more so, when n increases, we take recourse to Thom's powerful Theorem of Seven, which we state as follows :

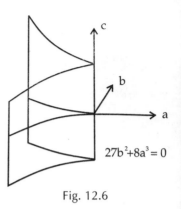

$27b^2 + 8a^3 = 0$

Fig. 12.6

Thom's theorem (The theorem of Seven on Classification of Elementary Catastrophes) : For systems governed by smooth functions with at most four parameters (but any number of variables) there are essentially only seven possible types of local geometric structures for stable catastrophe sets. René Thom has made a list of seven explicit functions (catastrophe models).

These may be stated as follows :

1.   **The Fold**

    If $V_a(x)$ be any function having the properties

    (i) $V_a(x)$ has one (control) parameter and one state variable x,

    (ii) $V_a(x)$ has a catastrophe set K which is stable,

    then we have a fold catastrophe. The fold catastrophe has been discussed in details in the last section.

2.   **The cusp**

    If we have a function defined as before, then $V_{(a, b)}(x) = x^4 + ax^2 + bx$ has two control parameters, a, b, and one state variable x. This kind of a polynomial function represents a cusp catastrophe, provided, the critical points occur when $V_{(a, b)}(x) = 0$.

The cusp has been discussed in details in the previous section. As in the previous section, elimination of x gives $27b^2 + 8a^3 = 0$ for the equation of the catastrophe set K, easily found to be a cusp in the (a, b)-plane as indicated in the Figs. 12.7 below.

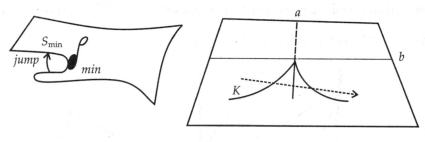

Fig. 12.7

Remark

For the latter models the calculations are very involved; hence we will simply state the functions and sketch the catastrophe sets K in the control space and indicate the nature of the critical points on the polynomial functions for control parameters in each region (that is complementary to K). In all the cases that will follow, the control space has three dimensions.

3.   The Swallow-tail

Here $V_{(a,b,c)}(x) = x^5 + ax^3 + bx^2 + cx$, is a function having one state variable x and three control parameters a, b, c. The following figure shows the schematic diagram of a swallow-tail catastrophe.

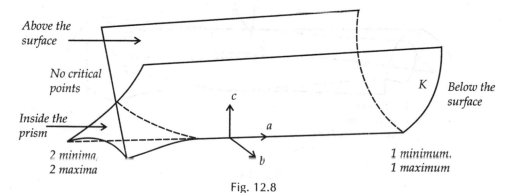

Fig. 12.8

4. The Elliptic Umbilic (or Hair)

Here $V_{(a,b,c)}(x,y) = x^2 + 3xy^2 + a(x^2 + y^2) + bx + cy$ has two state variables x and y, and three control parameters a, b, c. If it has a catastrophe set K which is stable, then the above polynomial function represents the elliptic umbilic catastrophe. It is schematically represented in Fig. 12.9.

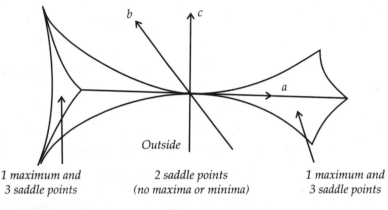

Outside

1 maximum and	2 saddle points	1 maximum and
3 saddle points	*(no maxima or minima)*	*3 saddle points*

Fig. 12.9

5. The Hyperbolic umbilic (or breaking wave)

If we have a polynomial function $V_{(a,b,c)}(x,y) = x^3 + y^3 + axy + bx + cy$ defined as before, then it represents the hyperbolic umbilic or the breaking wave. The function has three control variables a, b, c and two state variables x, y. The schematic diagram of such a catastrophe is shown in the Fig. 12.10

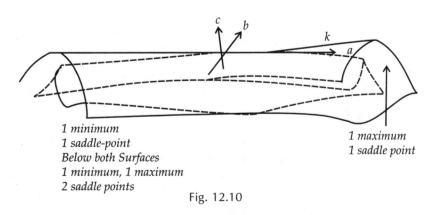

1 minimum
1 saddle-point
Below both Surfaces
1 minimum, 1 maximum
2 saddle points

1 maximum
1 saddle point

Fig. 12.10

6.   **The butterfly**

A polynomial function $V_{(a,b,c,t)}(x) = x^6 + ax^4 + bx^3 + cx^2 + tx$, defined as before, and having four control variables a, b, c, t, and one state variable x represents a butterfly catastrophe.

7.   **The parabolic umbilic (or the mushroom)**

A polynomial function $V_{(a,b,c,t)}(x,y) = y^4 + x^2y + ax^2 + by^2 + cx + ty$ defined as before and having four control variables a, b, c, t, and one state variable x represents a mushroom catastrophe.

The above seven elementary catastrophes, as classified By René Thom, may be arranged in a tabular form as follows :

Types of Catastrophes	Polynomial
1. Fold	$Va_1(x) = x^3 + a_1x$
2. Cusp	$V_{(a_1,a_2)}(x) = x^4 + a_1x^2 + a_2x$
3. Swallow-tail	$V_{(a_1,a_2,a_3)}(x) = x^5 + a_1x^3 + a_2x^2 + a_3x$
4. The Elliptic Umbilic or Hair	$V_{(a_1,a_2,a_3)}(x_1,x_2) = x_1^3 + 3x_1x_2^2 + a_1(x_1^2 + x_2^2) + a_2x_1 + a_3x_2$
5. The Hyperbolic Umbilic (or the breaking wave)	$V_{(a_1,a_2,a_3)}(x_1,x_2) = x_1^3 + x_2^3 + a_1x_1x_2 + a_2x_1 + a_3x_2$
6. The Butterfly	$V_{(a_1,a_2,a_3,a_4)}(x) = x^6 + a_1x^4 + a_2x^3 + a_3x^2 + a_4x$
7. The Parabolic Umbilic (or the mushroom)	$V_{(a_1,a_2,a_3,a_1)}(x_1,x_2) = x_1^2x_2 + x_2^4 + a_1x_1^2 + a_2x_2^2 + a_3x_1 + a_4x_2$

12.6 Some applicable systems

I. Mechanical system

If catastrophe theory can describe events as complex as the evolution of the embryo and other types of biological morphogenesis, can it be made use of in complementing existing quantitative knowledge on problems of mechanical *morphogenesis*? This is a

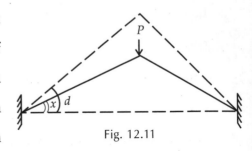

Fig. 12.11

motivation for the application of catastrophe theory to mechanical systems.

First we take up the case of a simple mechanical model which illustrates one kind of catastrophe. We begin with the simplest case of a simple arch or a shallowarch.

The planar model is shown in the above Fig. 12.11. This consists of two equal compressible elastic rods, supposed to remain straight but smoothly hinged to two fixed pivots and one centrally loaded free joint. P is the load and members of the arch make an angle x with the horizontal. When $P = 0$, $x = \pm \alpha$ *i.e.*, when unloaded, the arch takes up a position with its members making an angle α with the horizontal. The depth of the arch is $a = 2(1 - \cos \alpha) = \alpha^2 > 0$ for small α. We can calculate the potential energy V of the system with the line joining the supports as the zero of gravitational potential. If we restrict overselves to small deflections, the normalized potential energy is given by

$$V = \frac{1}{4}x^4 - \frac{1}{2}ax^2 + Px .$$

The equilibrium curve (or surface M in x, a, P-space) is obtained by setting

$$\frac{\partial V}{\partial x} = 0,$$

$$x^3 - ax + P = 0,$$

This is a cubic-equation. Again

$$V_{xx} = 3x^2 - a .$$

Since $V_{xx} > 0$ for $x > \sqrt{(a/3)}$, we have minima of V and so there is a stable equilibrium in a certain range and for $V_{xx} < 0$, the equilibrium is unstable.

The load we have referred to, may be thought of as a weight, but which may in practice, be a reaction from some other structure. We start with no load and with the angle of arch as α. If we increase the load, x decreases, at first slowly and then more rapidly as we move along the equilibrium curve, until we reach the load $\alpha^2 / \sqrt{3}$, at which the equilibrium is unstable and the arch then snaps through along a vertical line to a position of stable equilibrium. A further increase of the load produces further depression of the inverted arch and decreasing it, we arrive at another unloaded position of the stable equilibrium, the reflection, in the line joining the supports, of the first. By using a negative load *i.e.*, pushing it upwards, we can eventually make the arch snap back.

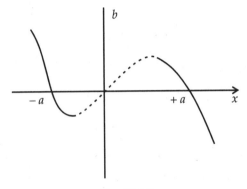

Fig. 12.12

This model can be viewed as an example of the 'cusp catastrophe' in Thom's table, the control variables being the load P and depth $a \ll 1$. The load-deflection curve for a given arch is the cross-section of M with given a as shown in Fig. 12.12.

The catastrophe is the sudden snap-through "which occurs from the unstable maximum or minimum load". The equilibrium surface M, which is also the folded surface, is shown in Fig. 12.13.

In Fig. 12.13 the fold line has the cusp-projection onto the a, P-plane. The shaded region

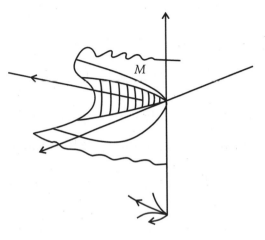

Fig. 12.13

within the fold represents unstable equilibrium states.

One can analyse in the same fashion mechanical structures such as guyed strut, propped cantilinear strut, columns and plates, curved P arches and shells. It would now be worthwhile to see how the above sort of analysis can be extended to the case of a simple continuous non-linear system, or a simple discrete non-linear system, conservative system etc. Studies on these systems have been undertaken at length and we would report here only the salient features of one of such studies.

The potential energy of a continuous non-linear system is taken as

$$V(T_0, F, x) = R\lambda\mu\left[\frac{1}{4}x^4 + \frac{1}{2\lambda\mu}(T_0 + \epsilon)x^2 - \frac{F}{R\lambda\mu}x\right] \tag{1}$$

where T_0 is the rest tension, F transverse force per unit length, x the displacement of the mid-point, λ elastic parameter and μ a definite integral over the deformed shape of the system. (1) is, in the language of catastrophe theory, the potential function for the system with the map $V: R^3 \to R$ and the critical point or points of equilibrium are given (T_0, F, x), where x is a solution of the cubic

$$x^3 + \frac{1}{\lambda\mu}(T_0 + \epsilon)x - \frac{F}{R\lambda\mu} = 0 \tag{2}$$

The potential function in (1) has two controls or external parameters, namely, the rest tension T_0 and the transverse force F and that the potential function and its surface

$$(T_0, F, x): x^3 + \frac{1}{\lambda\mu}(T_0 + \epsilon)x - \frac{F}{R\lambda\mu} = 0$$

of critical points with respect to x are related to the cusp catastrophe already described. Further, we can state that the simple linear transformations.

$$T_0 \to \mu = \frac{1}{\lambda}, \quad \mu(T_0 + \epsilon) \text{ and } F \to V = -\frac{F}{R\lambda\mu}$$

are diffeomorphisms which take the potential $V(T_0, F, x)$ to

$$V(u, v, x) = R\lambda\mu\left(\frac{1}{4}x^4 + \frac{1}{2}ux^2 + vx\right)$$

which is essentially the potential function (1) associated with the cusp catastrophe. Thus, the rest tension T_0 and the transverse force F can be identified with what are called splitting variables u and v. The catastrophe set is given by

$$4R^2(T_0+\in)^3 + 27\lambda\mu F^2 = 0$$

which is the well-known semi-cubical parabola.

II. Electro-magnetic system

In the classical theory of electricity and magnetism, there occurs a situation where catastrophe theory provides some understanding into some qualitative details of the phenomena.

We consider an axisymmetric, electrically conducting body about its principal axis with an angular velocity Ω in the presence of an externally applied uniform magnetic field of strength B_0. The rotation is opposed by a frictional torque taken to be proportional to Ω and is produced by a constant driving torque which can be characterised by the angular velocity Ω_0 for which the drive is balanced by friction alone. The question is: how does the equilibrium rotation rate depend on two control parameters Ω and B_0?

We consider a rectangular coil whose width is taken to be $2b$ and the height, $h \square b$ (Fig. 12.14). It rotates about its axis normal to the applied magnetic field B_0. This body produces a vertical oscillating applied electric field

$$E_1 = \mathrm{Re}\left(E_0\, e^{i\Omega t}\right) \text{ where } E_0 = -\Omega b B_0,$$

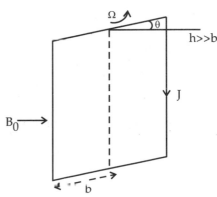

Fig. 12.14

Ω being the angular velocity $\dot{\theta}$ where θ is the angle as shown in the figure.

The phase is so chosen that

$$\theta = \frac{\pi}{2} \text{ when } E_1 = 0$$

If R is the resistance of the coil, L the inductance (per unit length), then the electric current J satisfies the equation

$$L\frac{dJ}{dt} + RJ = E_1$$

The quasi-steady current is given by

$$J = \text{Re}\left(J_0 e^{i\Omega t}\right) \text{ where } J_0 = \frac{E_0}{R + \Omega L}$$

The electromagnetic couple $\vec{\mu}$ exerted on the coil about the vertical axis is $AB_0 J \cos \Omega t$. The couple averaged over one cycle is thus

$$\vec{\mu} = \frac{1}{2}AB_0 \text{Re}\left(J_0\right) = \frac{v}{\lambda \tau}B_0^2\left[\frac{\Omega R}{R^2 + \Omega^2 L^2}\right]$$

where A = amplitude of the coil,

$$v = \pi b^2 h \ = \text{volume enclosed by the rotating coil.}$$

Now $\vec{\mu} \rightarrow 0$ as $\Omega \rightarrow 0$ and also as $\Omega \rightarrow \infty$. The maximum value of $\vec{\mu}$ occurs at $\Omega = \frac{R}{L}$. The equation for component of angular momentum parallel to the axis of rotation is given by

$$I = \frac{d\Omega}{dt} = \lambda\Omega_0 - \lambda\Omega + \vec{\mu}$$

where I = moment of inertia

$\lambda\Omega$ = frictional torque opposing rotation,

λ = coefficient of friction

Ω_0 = equilibrium rotation rate in the absence of the magnetic field

If dimensionless rotation rates are defined as

$$\omega = \frac{\Omega L}{R}, \quad \omega_0 = \frac{\Omega_0 L}{R},$$

and the dimensionless coupling parameter as

$$Q = \frac{\upsilon B_0^2}{2\pi\lambda R}$$

then for a steady rotation rate, the dimensionless angular momentum equation is given by

$$f(\omega) = \omega_0 - \omega - \frac{2Q\omega}{1+\omega^2} = 0$$

This is an equation in ω, ω_0, Q being the control variables. Plotting equilibrium values of ω against Q and ω_0, as shown in Fig. 12.15 we find that the dimensionless driving torque has a critical value $\omega_{0c} = \sqrt[3]{3}$. If $\omega < \omega_{0c}$ then ω is a monotonic decreasing function of Q, with $\omega \propto Q^{-1}$ for large Q. If $\omega > \omega_{0c}$ then $\omega(Q)$ is folded giving rise to three equilibrium values of

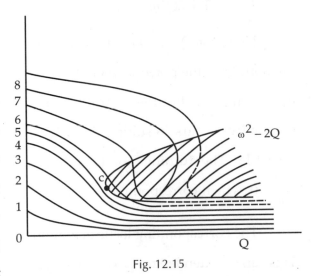

Fig. 12.15

Q. The re-entrant knee occurs for all $\omega_{0c} > \sqrt[3]{3}$. The shaded parts of the graph represent unstable equilibria. It can be seen that the upper and lower equilibria are stable. To demonstrate that it is an example of Thom's cusp catastrophe, we introduce a 'potential function' such that

$$f(\omega) = -\frac{\partial \psi}{\partial \omega}$$

$f(\omega) = 0$ indicates steady states of the system which correspond to turning points of ψ which have the form

$$\psi = \frac{1}{2}\omega^2 - \omega\omega_0 + Q\log(1+\omega^2)$$

Fig. 12.16 shows the potential function $\psi(\omega)$ for a rectangular coil for $\omega_0 = 10$, i.e. for values of Q between 8 and 14.

The necessary and sufficient condition for stability against small perturbations in the rotation is

$$\psi_{\omega\omega} < 0$$

or in other words,

$$(1+\omega^2)^2 < 2Q(\omega^2 - 1)$$

Here, for $Q = 8$, there is a single equilibrium at the bottom of the potential well. For $Q = 11$, there are three equilibria, but the central one is unstable. The instability occurs resulting in $\psi_{\omega\omega} > 0$, which is unstable. The turning points in Fig. 12.16 where $\dfrac{dQ}{d\omega} = 0$ which correspond $\psi_\omega = \psi_{\omega\omega} = 0$.

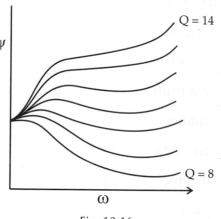

Fig. 12.16

The corresponding locus of equilibria, where $f(\omega) = \dfrac{\partial \psi}{\partial \omega} = 0$, is shown in Fig. 12.17. This can be extended to the case of a cylindrical shell and other axisymmetric bodies. The detailed analysis when carried out shows that an axisymmetric body rotating in a transverse applied magnetic field can suffer a sudden large jump in the rotation rate, if the controlling parameters, the strength of the magnetic field and the strength of the driving torque are varied slightly. This becomes obvious if it is explained in terms of Thom's cusp catastrophe. The above examples show how one can identify the gradient system i.e. system characterised by smooth potential functions which fall under the set of

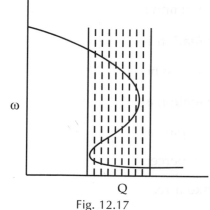

Fig. 12.17

elementary catastrophes of Thom. Therefore, if the situations, biological or mechanical, are such that they do not admit of a potential like the above, one has to look for other types of catastrophes viz. the advanced catastrophes. It is also to be pointed out in this connection that the catastrophe theory provides a qualitative understanding of some of the biological and mechanical phenomena without being extra-predictive in character.

III. A Biological system

There is a lot of biological systems to which catastrophe theory may be applied. We choose the one which is perhaps earliest of the kind and most successful and illuminating, shown by a brilliant exponent of catastrophe theory, namely, E.C. Zeeman. We recall now the situation about heartbeat and nerve impulse which we had occasion to refer to in the first section. Zeeman could show how these phenomena are related to Thom's theory. The procedure of Zeeman is to set forth first three dynamical qualities displayed by heart muscle fibres and nerve axioms and then go on building up a sequence of mathematical models step by step in order of complexities. To him, the words 'dynamical system', 'differential equation' , 'flow' and 'vector field' are synomous. The three dynamical qualities displayed by heart muscle fibre and nerve axioms are : (1) stable equilibrium (2) threshold, for triggering action (3) return to equilibrium, which is a jump is case of heart and smooth, in case of nerve. Let us seek to represent the qualities by a differential equation in the Euclidean plan R^2. The quality (1) requires a fixed point which can be taken to be the origin $O \in R^2$. Let $V' = AV$ be the linear approximation to the differential equation at O, where A is a real 2×2 matrix. Two eigen-values of A have each a negative real part as the equilibrium is stable. As for the second quality, namely, *action* which, if it is perceptible, has to have a reasonably large change in one of the coordinates and to take a reasonably short time. Hence an action is to be represented by large number of vector fields or in other words, by part of an orbit along which we call the fast orbit. Thus quality (2) implies a *fast orbit* near O. If the vectors O are to have large values, we need to conclude that eigen values must have large moduli, which we call fast eigen values while others are called *slow eigen values*. We start with a trivial linear case where we take (x, b) as coordinates in R^2. If ϵ be a small positive constant then the equations are

$$\epsilon x' = -x$$
$$b' = -b$$

Therefore in the matrix

$$A = \begin{pmatrix} -\epsilon^{-1} & 0 \\ 0 & -1 \end{pmatrix}$$

the fast eigen values is $1/\epsilon$. We call $\epsilon x' = -x$ as the fast equation as x dies exponentially as fast as $e^{-t/\epsilon}$. The slow eigen value is -1 so that $b' = -b$ is the slow equation, because b dies more slowly as e^{-t}. In general, the fast equation will be of the from $\epsilon x' = -f(x, b)$ where $f(x, b)$ is a function of x and b that vanishes at the origin. We define the *slow manifold* by putting $\epsilon = 0$; in other words, the slow manifold is a curve through the origin given by $f(x, b) = 0$. In the first example, the *fast solution* is defined to be the family of lines parallel to x-axis. We may remark that the fast equation determines the slow manifold and the slow equation determines behaviour as the slow manifold. It can be proved that the tangents at the origin to the fast solution and the slow manifold are, to first order in ϵ, the eigen spaces of the fast and slow equations, respectively. Let us consider more examples. Let us consider the equations

$$\epsilon x' = -(x + b),$$
$$b' = -b.$$

The slow manifold is clearly given by $x + b = 0$. It may be verified that the invariant submanifold determined by the eigen value -1 is the fact the line $(1 - \epsilon)x + b = 0$ to which the slow manifold is an approximation. Let us consider another set of equations

$$\epsilon x' = -(x+b),$$
$$b' = x.$$

The slow manifold is the same as before; the fast equation is unchanged. The behaviour on the low manifold is the same, because on the slow manifold $-b = x$ and so the slow equation which determines the behaviour is in effect the same. What possible biological systems can the three equations so far considered represent? Mathematically if one has a dynamical system which is allowed to vary along a specific 1-dimensional slow manifold M, one can have a slowing down of one eigen value. This corresponds in biological terms, to *homeostasis* which every developing cell has to pass through in course of its effort to seek what is called its identity. This situation is represented by adjoining to the above examples, other fast equations of the form $\epsilon \gamma' = -\gamma$.

Let us turn to an example which is non-linear in character, given by

$$\epsilon x' = -(x^3 + x + b),$$
$$b' = x.$$

Its local behaviour is the same as in the earlier examples. By changing the sign of a term in the above set, one gets

$$x' = -(x^3 - x + b),$$
$$b' = x - x_0.$$

where x_0 is greater than $1/\sqrt{3}$. We set forth the 'jump return' solution as in Zeeman. If we are to make use of these equations for the problem of heartbeat, we need to identify the variables a and b with measurable qualities and use the differential equations for prediction. Here x is taken as the length of the muscle fibre (a positive constant) so that the action represents contraction and the jump return—the relaxation. b is then to be taken some form of electrochemical control. The pace-maker wave will change the control from b_0 and b_1, say, thus triggering off the heartbeat cycle. We might delve deeper into the underlying chemistry but our main objective is to study the dynamics of the heartbeat and even if we represent the dynamical system in R^n, the heartbeat cycle would still be represented by a one-dimensional path in R^n, consisting of 2 pieces of slow orbit and 2 pieces of fast orbit. This gives, in brief, a flavour of the kind of analysis undertaken by Zeeman and for details the interested reader is advised to go through the appendix IV.

We take up the following example from physiology and demonstrate how Zeeman applied catastrophe theory to the case of heart beating and tried to explain how many of the complexities of the beat could be seen from a simple behaviour of muscle fibre. The three dynamic qualities displayed by heart muscle are

(i)   stable equilibrium

(ii) threshold, for triggering an action

(iii) return to equilibrium.

The above three qualities are taken as axioms. The quality (iii) is of the type 'jump return' in the case of heart beat. If the heart stops beating, it stays relaxed in diastole, which is the stable equilibrium as listed in quality (i). The global electrochemical wave emanating from a pacemaker and reaching each individual muscle fibre triggers off the action of quality (ii). Each fibre remains contracted in the systole state for about $\frac{1}{5}$ second, and then rapidly relaxes agains thus obeying the jump return to equilibrium of quality (iii). These three qualities describe the local behaviour for an individual muscle fibre and Zeeman represented this phenomenon by a differential equation in the Euclidean plane R^2. The theorem he deduced may be stated as follows :

Zeeman's theorem

There exists a dynamical system on R^2 possessing above qualities (i), (ii), and (iii).

The simplest example is as follows :

$$\varepsilon \dot{x} = -\left(x^3 - x + b\right)$$

$$\dot{b} = x - x_0$$

where x_0 is a constant greater than $\dfrac{1}{\sqrt{3}}$, x, b being coordinates in R^2, ε being a small positive quantity (constant). In order to identify the variables x, b with measurable qualities, we find that x is the length of the muscle fibre, so that the action represents the contraction and the jump return—the relaxation is to be of some form of electro-chemical control. The pacemaker wave will change the control from b_0 to b_1, as depicted in Figs. 12.18.

Rybak's experiment showed that the heart can stop beating even though the pacemaker is still on. Thus, if the tension drops, the threshold must disappear and conversely, which leads to the cusp catastrophe

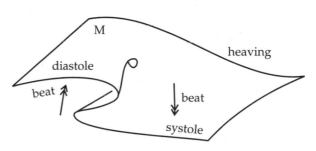

Fig. 12.18(i)

$$\dot{x} = -\left(x^3 + ax + b\right)$$

where

        x = length of fibre,

        b = chemical control,

        $-a$ = tension.

From the point of view of catastrophe theory, a and b are two parameters of control in the control space. In the Fig. 12.18(i) above, the slow manifold M illustrates how these

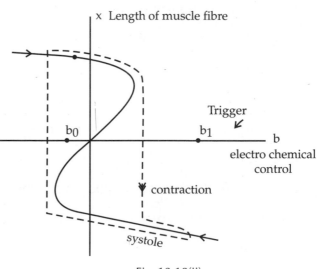

Fig. 12.18(ii)

two controls determine the length of the muscle fibre. The feedback on M is determined by the slow equation $b = x$. Let the chemical control b take up the values b_0 and b_1 in diastole and systole respectively.

Then $b_0 = b_1$ is the equilibrium position and the trigger moves b from b_0 to b_1 after which the slow equation returns b to b_0. Thus, during diastole, b is fixed at b_0 and during systole, b is changing, with a maximum at b_1 as shown in Fig. 12.19.

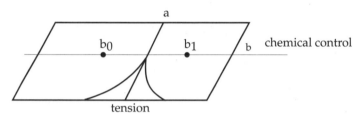

Fig. 12.19

Exercise

1. What is a fold catastrophe?

2. What kind of a polynomial leads to a cusp catastrophe? Establish the same.

3. Give an applicable example of a cusp catastrophe.

4. Does a polynomial with two variables and with some parameter(s) lead to a cusp catastrophe? Justify your answer.

5. How do you set forth the idea of an elementary catastrophe? How do you classify them in some types, if feasible?

6. How do you formulate the problem of heart beat? How does it lead to a catastrophe, if any?

7. State Thom's theorem on elementary catastrophes. What are its implications?

8. What is an electromagnetic catastrophe?

9. How do you construct an example of a catastrophe from a mechanical structure?

10. How many variables and parameters are needed for a swallow-tail catastrophe? What is the control space, if any, here?

theorizing, further, bifurcations and catastrophes

13

The last two chapters provide means how to grapple with some real systems with variables and parameters that keep on changing. Although these could be mathematized, there exist approaches that require few more notions, types, definitions, theorems etc. There are many for theorizing, in some more depth, ideas on bifurcation, and catastrophes. We begin with a resumé of what we have learnt in the earlier chapters. We take bifurcation first, then catastrophes and after that, interweaving one with the other to the extent they facilitate both in understanding of and pushing further concepts. But at every stage, we reckon non-linearity whose effect is to bend the solution branches, which we have already met in the example $-u''(x) = \lambda \|u\|^2 u(x), 0 < x < \pi$. We can call this as a mildly non-linear problem, in the sense, that $\|u\|^2 u$ does not reflect a genuine non-linearity (or pseudo non-linearity) so well represented by, say, $f(xu)u$ where $f(u)$ is nothing but a vector, which turns the vector $\bar{u}$ to a new direction in the space.

13.1   Resumé on Bifurcations

Let us recall that our objective has been not merely to solve the system of equations in variables $x = (x_1, x_2, \cdots, x_n) \in R^n$ of the form

$$F(\lambda; x) = 0 \qquad (1)$$

but also to investigate the behaviour of solution of (1) as the real scalar parameter λ varies; $F = (F_1, F_2, \cdots, F_m)$ is a non-linear mapping with the values in R^m. In particular if $m = n$, the solutions of (1) form a discrete set of points in R^n. The mapping F is taken to be smooth i.e. infinitely differentiable.

For $\lambda = \lambda_0$ (say), let there be a solution $x = p$ of (1). The process of seeking solutions x close to p, with the choice of values close to λ_0, comes within the purview of what is called local bifurcation theory, which we have already touched upon earlier.

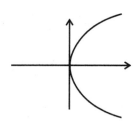

Fig. 13.1

We have considered few types of bifurcations and let us add on, few more with corresponding figures :

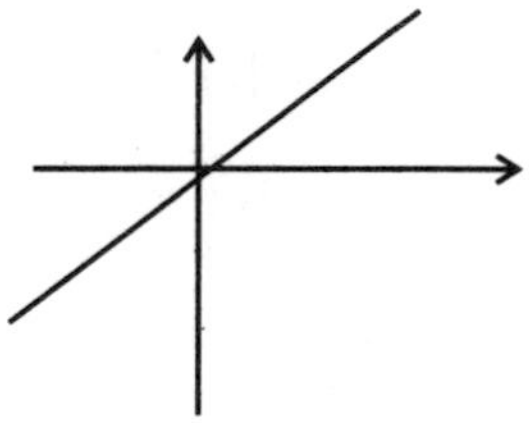

1.   With $m = n = 1$, a single variable x and a single parameter λ, we have the fold (limit point) (See Fig. 13.1)

Fig. 13.2

2. $F(\lambda; x) = x^2 - \lambda$, we have trans-critical anti-symmetric bifurcation (See Fig. 13.2)

3. $F(\lambda; x) = x^3 - \lambda$, we have what is called hysteresis point. (See Fig. 13.3)

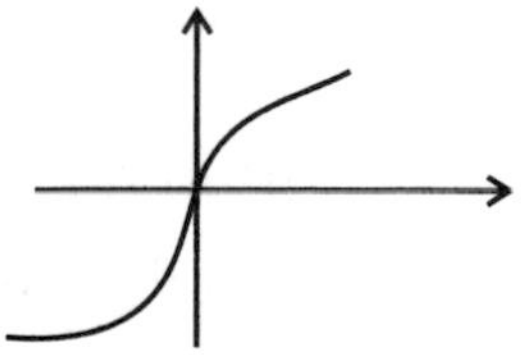

Fig. 13.3

4    $F(\lambda; x) = x^3 - \lambda x$, we have the pitch-fork symmetric bifurcation. (See Fig. 13.4)

5. $F(\lambda; x) = x^4 - \lambda$ (See Fig. 13.5)

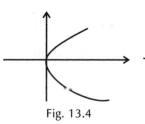
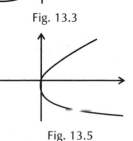

Fig. 13.4   Fig. 13.5

The above remarks do not rule out the possibility of increasing the number of variables.

With $m = n = 2$, $F(\lambda;x,y) = (x^3 + xy^2 - \lambda x, x^2 y + y^3 - \lambda y)$

which has the figure (See Fig. 13.6)

Another is $F(\lambda;x,y) = (y^3 - \lambda x, x^3 + \lambda y)$ in Fig. 13.7.

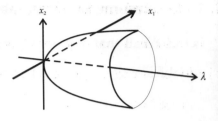

Fig. 13.6

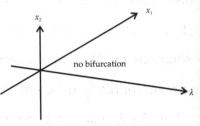

Fig. 13.7

Let us note that, in case of two variables here, we need to see if the relevant Implicit Function Theorem is applicable or not.

Here, it is $F(\lambda;x) = 0$ has a unique solution, $x = x(\lambda)$ for small λ and so, there is no bifurcation.

Remarks

1. In terms of reality of mathematical sciences in regard to its form of mathematization, we have to see if $F(\lambda;x) = 0$ responds to small perturbations or not. In a way, we ought to be aware if the behaviour of solutions of $F(\lambda;x) = 0$ in $(\lambda;x)$ space does itself change qualitatively when the mapping F is subjected to arbitrarily small perturbations. Doesn't this bring us back to structural stability ?

    The approach should, therefore, be to consider the whole families of problems $F(\alpha;\lambda;x) = 0$ with $\alpha = (\alpha_1, \alpha_2, \cdots, \alpha_n)$ is a collection of more parameters (small) and F is a function of all variables $(\alpha;\lambda;x)$.

2. It should also be stated, without proof, that for most bifurcation problems represented by $F(\alpha;\lambda;x) = 0$, there exist particular families $F(\alpha;\lambda;x) = 0$ which dominate all other families that arise as perturbations. These dominant families are called *universal perturbations* or *universal deformations* of the original problem $F(\lambda;x) = 0$.

3. It is a matter of history of mathematical pursuits that these ideas have come up in sixties of the last century because of the seminal works by the Russian mathematician V. I. Arnold and the French mathematician M. René Thom. The following figures represent those of related perturbations (with $m = n = 1$):

(i) $F(\alpha;\lambda;x)=x^2+\alpha x-\lambda \ (\alpha>0)$

(See Fig. 13.8)

(ii) $F(\alpha;\lambda;x)=x^2-\lambda x+\alpha \ (\alpha>0)$

(See Fig. 13.9)

(iii) $F(\alpha;\lambda;x)=x^3-\alpha x-\lambda \ (\alpha>0)$

(See Fig. 13.10)

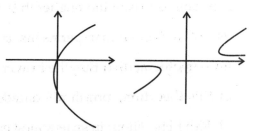

Fig. 13.8   Fig. 13.9

(iv) $F(\alpha_1;\alpha_2;\lambda;x)=x^3+\alpha_1 x^2-\lambda x+\alpha_2$

$[(\alpha_1,\alpha_2>0)$ by choice]

(See Fig. 13.11)

(v) $F(\alpha_1;\alpha_2;\lambda;x)=x^4-\alpha_1 x^2+\alpha_2 x+\lambda$

$[(\alpha_1,\alpha_2>0)$ by choice]

(See Fig. 13.12)

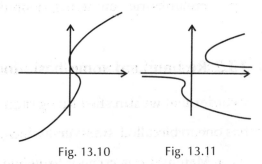

Fig. 13.10   Fig. 13.11

4. Some of the earlier figures (unperturbed ones) show that there are reflectional and other symmetries. One can say that every bifurcation may occur as a consequence of the breaking of symmetry; indeed symmetry can even be observed as the source of bifurcation itself in the arena of mathematical

Fig. 13.12

sciences. Non-linearities can hardly dispense with symmetry of one kind or the other. Physicists talk about symmetry breaking phenomena. Indeed, many advances of mathematical sciences show in abundance a synergy, between mathematical symmetry and symmetries e.g., in physical, biological, technological, ecological sciences etc. So symmetry does occupy a central status in bifurcation theory.

5.   With the foregoing results and remarks, we are led to a theory that may form the basis of a general theory of local bifurcation, i.e. perturbations would certainly facilitate us in moving further in this direction. First, we should look for admissible list of universal perturbations and then, which sort of criteria ought to be investigated so that they fit in with any one or others, of this list. The endeavour in this direction, in a limited case, was initiated by the French mathematician M. René Thom in sixties; as stated earlier, through his cardinal work on Catastrophe Theory. For this and for bifurcation theory as well, we need some mathematical preliminaries on new terms, definitions, propositions etc.

13.2 Resumé and some basic motions

In order that we can shed further light on stability of systems, we need to consider what has one to be called 'transversality' which, in turn, requires the knowledge of 'manifold'.

Manifold has come into vogue just as higher dimensional entity analogous to a smooth curve (or a surface). If it is to be a smooth manifold of R^n, it has to be a subset M having the following properties :

(a)   locally speaking, it can be taken as a small portion of spaces R^m.

(b)   it is inextricably built into R^n, without losing smoothness. This is often expressed by saying that $\exists$ a tangent hyper-plane at each point.

'D', as before, is the dimension of the manifold; for example, 1D manifold is a curve, 2D manifold is a surface etc.

In order to express these attributes of a manifold a bit more mathematically for (a) we should say that $\exists$ a local diffeomorphism $f : U \rightarrow M$ where U is an open set in R^n and $f(U)$ is a nbd of $x \in M$.

Let us now introduce the notion of 'transversality'. We have an intuitive feeling about this term. Transversality is often identified with general position and negatively speaking, two manifolds seldom meet non-transversely (e.g. in the way a real number can scarcely be a real number equal to π). Thom put forward what has come to be known as "Transversality theorem" to which we shall return a bit later. Now we know of intersection of curves through the joint of intersection of tangents. Can we thus think of in the nbd of a point of transverse intersection, two manifolds, being approximated by their tangents? For this, we are to associate the local nature of intersection with the dimensions of manifolds for a pair of spaces (of given dimensions). For reasons of simplicity, let us choose two vector spaces U and V with a basis $u^1, \cdots, u^p$ for $U \cap V$ being extended to a basis for U by adding $u^{p+1}, \cdots, u^s$ and to a basis of V by adding $v^{p+1}, \cdots, v^t$. Then

$$u^1, \cdots, u^s, v^{p+1}, \cdots, v^t$$

becomes a basis for R^n. Hence, in terms of a linear transformation, the subspaces need to be replaced by :

U^s spanned by $e^t, \cdots, e^s$

V^n spanned by $e^1, \cdots, e^p, e^{s+1}, \cdots, e^n$

with $e^t = (0, \cdots, 0, 1, 0, \cdots, 0)$ with 1 in the i th place.

This formally represents a transverse intersection of an s-manifold with a t-manifold in R^n.

In R^3, we can have thus a sketch for 2-manifolds. If there be a transverse crossing, we can intuitively think of another in the close nbd; for transversality conditions can be taken to have directions in one manifold, along with those in the other, equalling the totality of directions in R^n. R^n can well be realized by a suitable choice of coordinates in algebraic terms; so we find transverse intersections in the neighbourhood. Can't we then afford to say that transversality has the property of being stable under small perturbations and so, transversality brings us back to our concern on stability and more than that, transversality crossings being stable as well. Having talked about stability in this context, can we explore if structural stability can well be taken care of ? For this, we ought to recast transversality in terms of mapping. Let $C: R \to R^2$ be a curve, t (may be time) be its parameter and the curve as the (locus of) a moving point. Can this C be associated with an unparameterized curve C' through its transversality ? This implies that if $C(t)$ lies on C', then the velocity vector of the moving point at 't' must be linearly independent of tangent vector to C' at $C(t)$. Further if C' is, for instance, on the y-axis and $C(t)$ is represented by the point $(t', 0)$ then the image of C is just the x-axis which obviously is transverse to C'. Let us suppose we replace $(t^3, 0)$ by $(t' - \varepsilon t, 0)$ for $\varepsilon > 0$, i.e. we perturb C a bit, we have a path crossing C' more than once which is, indeed, qualitatively meaningful, for the velocity $\left(\dfrac{d}{dt} t^3 |_0, 0 \right)$ of C' is 0, as it crosses C'. Thus, we have a notion that keeps up structural stability.

Remarks

1. If we replace the velocity vector by space spanning, as shown earlier, by all velocities through $f(x)$ in R^n, that can be obtained by the other curves $f(g(t))$ through x, we can have an analogous condition for a function $f: R^m \to R$ to be transverse to a manifold.

2. With the above observation on transversality, let us set forth when two affine spaces are said to be transverse to R^n. By an affine space, we mean a linear subspace K_0,

translated, so that it does not necessarily pass through the origin; $K = K_0 + C$, $C \in R^n$. Two affine spaces, K, M, as indicated earlier; K_0, M_0 span R^n if the corresponding linear spaces K_0, M_0, span R^n as linear subspaces : $K_0 + M_0 = R^n$.

We make now the following statement (without proof) :

Let K, M be the affine spaces of dimensions k, m respectively, located in R^n. In general, K, M will not meet if $k+m<n$. On the otherhand, if $k+m>n$ then K and M will meet in an affine space of dimension $k+m-n$, while K and M, in totality, will span the space R^n, in which case K and M are said to be transverse in R^n.

This leads to the formula $\dim K \cap M = k + m - n$

The above proposition is not being established. But its plausibility stems from a process of generalisation when we seek meeting points of geometrical entities with higher dimensions.

3.   The last remark is obviously about *linear* transversality; can we move on what may transpire as 'nonlinear transversality' ? We can explore this as follows. Let us think of the nonlinear analogue of a k-dimensional affine space in R^n ; what can it be ? We can have it as a smooth *k-dimensional manifold* (or *k-manifold*). This means a subset K of R^n, which appears locally as a k-dimensional affine space K' in R^n in terms of some appropriate local conditions in R^n, as shown in Fig. 13.13.

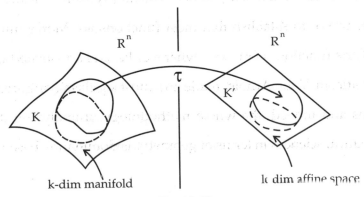

Fig. 13.13

4.   That transversality, implies something more in the light of what is called 'co-dimension' as taken up in the next section. Let us do this, in several stages, beginning with a naïve one.

13.3 More notions

Having related 'transversality' with 'stability', in non-linearity which happens to be the main concern, how can we relate this to critical points ?

We recall the definition of a critical point of $f : U \to R^n$, a smooth (infinitely differentiable) function in some open region U in R^n. A point $x \in R^n$ is a critical point of f if the $1 \times n$ matrix

$$D f(x) = \left(\frac{\partial f}{\partial x_1}(x), \cdots, \frac{\partial f}{\partial x_n}(x) \right)$$

is the zero-matrix and then x is a non-degenerate critical point of f if the $n \times n$ matrix

$$H f(x) = \left(\frac{\partial^2 f}{\partial x_i \partial x_j}(x) \right) \quad 1 \le i, j \le n$$

is non-singular.

In passing, one can say that a function f all of whose critical points are non-degenerate is called a *Morse function*. We simply state that the idea of transversality can be made use of to establish that most functions are Morse functions. Also every critical point of the function $f(x) + a x_1$, whatever be a, is an isolated critical point. The Russian mathematician V. I. Arnold made the most of classifying degenerate critical points of functions and indeed, the whole methodology of analyzing degenerate phenomena of mathematical sciences in terms of geometry is dominantly based on ideas of transversality.

13.4 Co-dimension

Generally speaking, we know that the number of equations to represent a geometrical object is equal to the difference between the dimension of the object and that of the space in which it is embedded. We call this quantity the co-dimension of the object and is often denoted by co-dim. Objects with the same co-dimension have certain properties in common, apart from requiring the same number of equations. That is, let us consider an object of co-dimension 1. It can divide the space R^n into disjoint parts. Thus a point divides a line, a line divides a plane; so does a simple closed curve, a plane divides R^3. If we change the dimension (dim) of the problem by ignoring inessential coordinates, then codim is preserved.

In the (Fig. 13.14), we have shown a part of R^3 with a curve on it. Let us now ignore the z-coordinate and restrict ourselves to $x\text{-}y$ plane; then the curve becomes a single point with a different dim, namely, zero but not 1, but has the same co-dimension 2. In general, a one parameter continuous family of objects of dim p is an object of dim $p+1$: a family of points is a curve, a family of lines a is a surface and so on. The reason for this is as follows. We have to set up a coordinate system; each member of the family and

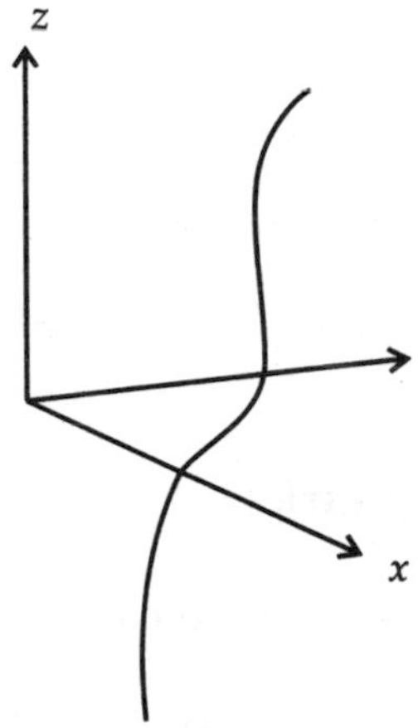

Fig. 13.14

then, any point in the new geometric object will be specified with $p+1$ coordinates. An r parameter continuous family of objects of dim p is an object of dim $p+r$. Equally an r parameter family of objects of co-dim p is an object of co-dim $p-r$.

Let us now consider a point P lying on an object of co-dimension r in some Euclidean space R^n. Let us suppose we want to construct a family of similar objects such that (s.t.) there is a nbd of P, every point of which lies on the member of that family. This can only be done in geometric objects generated by the family of dim m and we have an

r parameter family. We can interpret R^m as the parameter space for polynomials in one variable x and of degree not greater than m having a critical point at the origin. Let us consider a subset of parameter values which corresponds to f s.t $f_{xx} = 0$. It is a geometric object of co-dim 1 for it is specified by only one equation. Similarly a subset of parameter values for which $f_{xx} = f_{xxx} = 0$ is a geometric object of co-dim 2, since it is specified by 2 equations.

We can thus afford to have a definition of co-dimension of a function $f(x)$.

Definition: The co-dimension of a function $f(x)$ is the number of possible terms which independently are not generated by $f_{ji}(x)$.

As an example, we can say the function $x_1{}^3 + x_2{}^3$ has co-dimension 3, for x_1, x_2 and $x_1 x_2$ are not generated. Another example : $x_1{}^3 - 3x_1 x_2{}^2$ has co-dimension 3; $x_1, x_2, x_1{}^2, x_2{}^2$ are not generated but $x_1{}^2 - x_2{}^3$ is. Similarly, $x_1{}^2 x_2$ has co-dimension ∞; $x_2{}^k$ is not being generated for any value of x.

Remarks

1. If we recall about dimensions of affine spaces, in the context of transversality, we can say $(n-k)$ to be the co-dimension of K in R^n. We have then

    co-dim of $K \cap M$ in K = co-dim of M in R^n

    $(k\text{-}\dim K \cap M = n - m)$, given that K and M together span R^n. Thus, while interactions reduce dimensions, they preserve co-dimension.

2. In this chapter as well as in others, we have had terminologies that are in no way unrelated to each other; rather they are so structured that they, when taken together, bring out some revealing aspects of non-linearities from a qualitative standpoint; be it transversality, co-dimension, manifolds, structural stability, often each on its

own, often along with others. We now bring up another term called 'unfolding' in the next article but we will soon find how we are led to it through co-dimensions and hence, the title of the article; next to the next, we shall see how a couplet or triplet or more of such terms we have so encountered or are going to do so, shed better insights into qualitative ways of looking at systems through 'catastrophe theory', often along with 'bifurcation theory'.

3.   **Codimension and universal unfolding**

A general cubic is of the form

$$V = x^3 + ax \tag{1}$$

and the degenerate form

$$V = x^3 \tag{2}$$

is obtained when we put special value

$$a = 0 \tag{3}$$

Similarly, the most general form of a quartic is

$$V = x^4 + ax^2 + bx \tag{4}$$

which acquires the form $y = x^4$ being, of course, doubly degenerate.

$$V = x^4 + \sum_{i=1}^{N} a_i \varphi_1(x) \tag{5}$$

where the a_i's are N parameters, may be taken small, and φ_i's are N, C^∞ functions. (i.e. all derivatives of each of C^∞ function, exist at the point whatever be the order) and hence representable by their Taylor's expansions. Obviously (4) is a particular representation of the general perturbation given by (5), with two parameters a and b. One may think as well of perturbation in the form

$$V = x_1^3 + x_2^3 \tag{6}$$

which can be further generalized to have the form

$$V = x_1^3 + x_2^3 + ax_1 + bx_2 + ux_1x_2 \tag{7}$$

Thus, in general, we can have the perturbed function

$$V = f(x) + \sum_{i=1}^{N} a_i \varphi_i(x) \tag{8}$$

The minimal value of N in (8) is the co-dimension of the function $f(x)$. If (8) can be simplified to obtain a precise form, we call that form to be the universal unfolding of $f(x)$. For example in (1), the function x^3 has the co-dimension 1 and (1) is the universal unfolding. In (4), x^4 has the co-dimension 2 and the universal unfolding is given by (4); the function $x_1^3 + x_2^3$ has the co-dimension 3 and equation (7) gives that universal unfolding.

Observations

We find that each term of the universal unfolding has coefficient(s) so that c being the co-dimension, there are c parameters displayed by the universal folding. These parameters are often called control variables and the variable x_j are called state variables. Control variables are so named because any changes in their values may affect the form of the curve or the surface given by the universal unfolding.

Haven't we met this in the earlier chapter on elementary catastrophes? For example, $V(x) = x^3 + ax$; graphs differ for $a < 0$, $a > 0$ and $a = 0$.

The same is true for two parameters a and b. The boundary in a-b (control space) between the two types of potential functions is defined by

$$27b^2 + 8a^3 = 0$$

whose graph in the earlier chapter can also be recalled. Such a curve (or strictly speaking, a surface or hyper-surface) is known as the bifurcation set equation e.g. $a = 0$ is the bifurcation set for $V = x^3 + ax$.

In general, in order to determine the bifurcation set, we need to solve

$$\frac{\partial V}{\partial x_i} = 0 \quad (1 \le i \le n) \tag{9}$$

$$\det \left(\frac{\partial^2 V}{\partial x_i \partial x_j} \right) = 0 \tag{10}$$

Equation (9) gives the condition that the origin be a singular point and equation (10), being of degenerate type. We obtain the equation, as shown earlier, in control variables by eliminating state variables. We have already classified earlier 'universal unfolding' as seven elementary catastrophes with relevant names. But how to go about with the match between these two terms? Structural stability may be of use in this direction. Let us decide to begin with such a motivation. Before we do so in the next article, let us have the table on the functions of co-dimension, 1 to 4, as follows :

Co-dimension	Function	Universal Unfolding	Name
1	x^3	$x^3 + a_1 x$	Fold
2	x^4	$x^4 + a_1 x^2 + a_2 x$	Cusp
3	x^5	$x^5 + a_2 x^3 + a_1 x^2 + a_3 x$	Dovetail
			Swallow tail
4	x^6	$x^6 + a_1 x^4 + a_2 x^3 + a_3 x^3 + a_4 x$	Butterfly
3	$x_1^3 - 3x_1 x_2^2$	$x_1^3 - 3x_1 x_2^2 + a_1(x_1^2 + x_2^2) + a_2 x_1 + a_3 x_2$	Elliptical Umbilic
3	$x_1^3 + x_2^3$	$x_1^3 + x_2^3 + a_1 x_1 x_2 + a_2 x_1 + a_3 x_3$	Hyperbolic Umbilic
4	$x_1^2 x_2 + x_2^4$	$x_1^2 x_2 + x_2^4 + a_2 x_2^3 + a_3 x_1 + a_2 x_2$	Parabolic Umbilic

13.5 Revisiting structural stability with a view to catastrophe theory

We know about the concept of structural stability. Let us recall it. This concerns a system of equations

$$\dot{x} = F(x,c), \quad x \in R^n, \quad c \in R^k.$$

Let us think of a slight change in F i.e. $F \to F + \delta F$, such that it does not bring about remarkable change(s) in the solution of the system. A system $\dot{x} = F(x)$ is said to be structurally stable if any small change in F, say δF, the phase portraits of $\dot{x} = F(x)$ and $\dot{x} = F(x) + \delta F(x)$ are topologically equivalent.

For example, we have the system $\dot{x} = 0$. Suppose we change it to $\dot{x} = \varepsilon x \exp(-x^2)$. So we get a phase portrait of this, which is not equivalent; obviously because of the change, we are not getting a phase portrait, which is equivalent to the earlier one, however small, ε may be.

Let us consider a special kind of system called the *gradient system* defined by

$$F = -\nabla V(x,c), \quad x \in R^n \tag{1}$$

For gradient systems with the fixed points $x*$ we have

$$F(x*,c) = 0. \tag{2}$$

The fixed points are said to be attractors if $L(x) = V(x) - V(x*) > 0$ in a small nbd of $x*$. Also $F \Box \nabla L = (-\nabla V)(\nabla V) = -(\nabla V)^2 < 0$,

so that L is a strict Liapunov's function. René Thom calls these attractors as structurally stable, for a perturbation $F \to F + \delta F$ generates a corresponding perturbation in the fixed point $x* \to x* + \delta x*$; the condition for this is $F(x) + \delta F(x)$ evaluated at $x* + \delta x*$ should be 0 for small $\delta x*$.

Using Taylor's expansion for small $\delta x*$,

$$F_j(x*) + \delta x* \left(\frac{\partial F}{\partial x} \right)_{x*} + \delta F_j(x*) = 0. \qquad j = 1, 2, \cdots n$$

The first term is 0 because of (2). These equations give a solution for the $\delta F_j(x^*)$, provided the determinants of the coefficients do not vanish

i.e. $\det \left[\dfrac{\partial F}{\partial x_i}\right] = \det \left[\dfrac{\partial^2 V}{\partial x_i \partial x_j}\right] \neq 0$ at $x = x^*$

If such conditions are satisfied then the fixed point x^* becomes structurally stable. To look for an example, let us go back to Morse function.

A Morse function $M(x): R^n \to R$ is any function such that if $\left(\dfrac{\partial M}{\partial x_i}\right) = 0$ at some point for all $i = 1, 2, \dots, n$ for which the Hessian does not also vanish at this point i.e. to say if $\nabla M = 0$ then $\det \left(\dfrac{\partial^2 M}{\partial x_i \partial x_j}\right) \neq 0$.

Such a function is structurally stable in the sense that if $\delta M(x)$ is a small perturbation at $M(x)$, there is a diffeomorphism $h(x)$ s. t.

$M(h(x)) + \delta M(h(x)) = M(x) + \alpha$, where α is some constant.

Morse functions are equivalent to the function $\pm x_1^2 \pm x_2^2 \pm x_3^2 \pm \dots \pm x_n^2$.

The important point here is that near the extreme point(s), $\nabla F = 0$

Hence, most fixed points of gradient systems become structurally stable.

Let us recall about control parameters c variations of which can bring about variations of $F(x,c)$. This change is represented by

$\delta F = F(x, c + \delta c) - F(x, c)$

If $F(x,c) = 0$ has the solution for $x \in R$, $c \in D$ and if the Jacobian of F does not vanish, then by the well known Implicit Function theorem, there is a subregion of D for which there is an unique solution, $x = g(c)$ in R

We have already seen that the fixed point of gradient system $\dot{x} = F(x,c) = -\nabla V(x,c)$ is structurally stable.

René Thom calls these sets : $\nabla V(x,c) = 0$ and $\det \left[\dfrac{\partial^2 V}{\partial x_i \partial x_j}\right] = 0$, the elementary catastrophe sets.

If the two fixed points say $x_1(c)$ and $x_2(c)$ become equal as $c \to K$ (c–control space formed by the values of c) the fixed points are clearly degenerate. The catastrophe set thus represents the values of c, where fixed points become degenerate. We have also seen that such a degeneracy occurs at a bifurcation point in the c-space. Thus, we can conclude that the catastrophe set K is a set of bifurcation points. The catastrophe set K is said to be structurally stable, if the set K^* associated with $V^*(x,c) = V(x,c) + \delta V$ can be mapped into K by a homeomorphism $h(c): K^* \to K$ for arbitrarily small δV.

Let us now consider some possible forms of $V(x,c)$ and in particular, about the nature of catastrophe set given by the solution of $\nabla V(x,c) = 0$ and $\det \left[\dfrac{\partial^2 V}{\partial x_i \partial x_j} \right] = 0$

Can we go back to universal unfolding?

Let us explore this.

Let us consider the nature of the catastrophe set $C \in K$ given by the solutions of :

$$\nabla V(x,c) = 0 \text{ and } \det \left[\frac{\partial^2 V}{\partial x_i dx_j} \right] = 0$$

For $n=1$ there is only one variable x and the equations to give rise to the catastrophe set are

$$\left(\frac{\partial V}{\partial x} \right)_{x^*} = 0 \text{ and } \left(\frac{\partial^2 V}{\partial x^2} \right)_{x^*} = 0$$

In other words, the catastrophe K consists only the values of c which give fixed points $x^* = 0$ for the equation $x^* = -\nabla V$.

In particular, we consider $x^* = 0$ and in particular, we consider $c \in K$ which we can also take for convenience as $c = 0$.

Then $V(x)$ must be of the form

$$V(x) = a_3 x^3 + a_4 x^4 + a_5 x^5 + \cdots$$

Let us now distinguish two cases :

Case 1 $a_3 \neq 0$

Assuming x to be sufficiently small, we can neglect higher order terms and for reasons of simplicity, taking $a_3 = 1$ we can write $V(x)$ as $V(x) \approx x^3$ near the find point if $c = 0$.

$\therefore V(x)$ is of the order x^3 near the point if $c = 0$.

Thom called this function as organising centre.

Mathematically, our problem should be to determine the catastrophes c associated with the functionary, $U(x)$ s.t. it reduces to this particular organising centre when $c = 0$. Mathematically this means, if $V(x,c)$ satisfy $\dfrac{\partial V}{\partial x} = 0$, $\dfrac{\partial^2 V}{\partial x^2} = 0$ for $x^* = 0$ then $V(x,c) = x^3$

This development of a catastrophe set in the control space away from the origin $c = 0$ is called by Thom, the unfolding of the set K.

Next, let us consider the only variation of V for small x i.e. of

$$V(x,c) = c_1 x + c_2 x^2 + c_3 x^3$$

Let us ignore the constant term c_2 and then by shifting the origin, we can express this in the canonical form given by

$$V(x,c) = c_1 x + c_3 x^3$$

For simplicity, we can write $c_1 = c$, $c_3 = 1$

then $V(x,c) = cx + x^3$

This expression is the universal unfolding of the organising centre $V(x,c) = x^3$ and here, we have only one parameter c, which Thom calls the co-dimension one.

A small deduction

Let us consider the polynomial for

$$V(x) = cx + x^3$$

$$\frac{\partial V}{\partial x} = 3x^2 + c, \quad \frac{\partial^2 V}{\partial x^2} = 6x$$

The catastrophe set is given by the point $c = 0$. The dimension of the k-set can be defined as one less than the co-dimension.

$$\therefore \ \dim\ (k) = k - 1$$

Here $\dim\ (k) = 1 - 1 = 0$.

The flow in the phase control space is obtained from the equation

$$\ddot{x} = -\frac{\partial V}{\partial x} = -3x^2 - c$$

This structure in the phase control pace is called fold catastrophe with its representations given below :

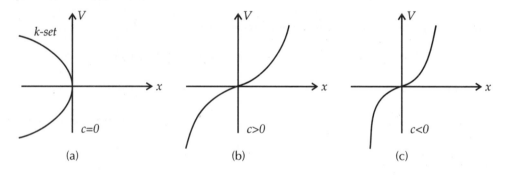

Fig. 13.15

Case 2 $a_3 = 0$, but $a_4 \neq 0$

Then, near $x = 0$, the significant term is $a_4 x^4$

We can write this as $V(x) = x^4$ near $x = 0$.

$\therefore$ For $c \neq 0$, and by shifting the origin, we can write this as

$$V(x) = x^4 + c_2 x^2 + c_1 x$$

which is the universal unfolding of the organising centre $V(x) = x^4$?

There are now two essential control parameters and the co-dimension is 2.

The catastrophe set K is given by

$$\frac{\partial V}{\partial x} = 0 \text{ and } \frac{\partial^2 V}{\partial x^2} = 0$$

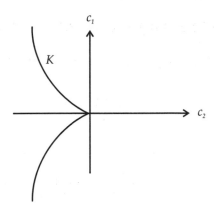

i.e. $\quad 4x^3 + 2c_2 x + c_1 = 0$

and $\quad 12x^2 + 2c_2 = 0$

i.e. $\quad c_2 + 6x^2 = 0$

$\quad\quad c_1 + \dfrac{4}{3} c_2 x = 0$

Fig. 13.16: Cusp Catastrophe

$\therefore \quad 8c_2{}^2 + 27c_1{}^2 = 0$ which is the catastrophe set K

Remarks

1. The above analysis and discussions show that catastrophe theory is concerned how a dynamic gradient system that exhibits discontinuous changes, by a suitable transformation, be reparameterized into one of the seven canonical forms which, in turn, are often referred to as catastrophe manifolds.

2. We have studied, in general, bifurcation sets that occur in C^1 system given by $\dot{x} = f(x, \lambda)$ depending on a parameter $\lambda \in R$ or in several parameters $\lambda \in R^n$. If we confine ourselves to changes that occur in the nbd of equilibrium points of periodic orbits, the bifurcation is called a local bifurcation. Bifurcations of limit cycles from one periodic parameter family of orbits such as those of surrounding a centre are called global bifurcations.

3. Bifurcations are closely related to catastrophes. We consider this relation by an example.

13.6 An example on bifurcation & catastrophe

Let us consider a system given by

$$V(\lambda,x)=\frac{1}{3}x^3+\lambda x \tag{1}$$

x being the state variable and λ the parameter.

The equilibrium points occur where

$$\frac{\partial V}{\partial x}=0 \;\; \text{i.e.} \;\; x^2+\lambda=0 \tag{2}$$

for, $\lambda<0$, there are two equilibrium points

$\lambda=0$, there is one equilibrium point

$\lambda>0$, there is one equilibrium point

The phase portraits are given below :

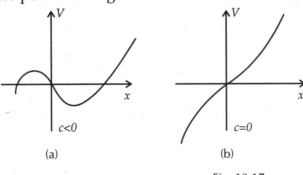

    (a)   c<0   (b)   c=0   (c)   c>0

Fig. 13.17

If $\lambda<0$, then V has a minimum at $x=\sqrt{\lambda}$, indicating a centre at that point and a minimum at $x=-\sqrt{\lambda}$ indicating a saddle at that point. Similarly, for the case $\lambda=0$ and $\lambda>0$ we have already found them as catastrophe manifolds.

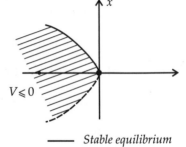

——— *Stable equilibrium*

- - - *Unstable equilibrium*

Fig. 13.18

The last figure shows the position of equilibrium point, in terms of the values of λ; an important feature is that $\lambda = 0$ is the bifurcation set where the nature of the solution undergoes changes.

Exercise

If the potential function is given by

$$V(\lambda, \mu, x) = \frac{1}{4}x^4 - \frac{1}{2}\lambda x^2 + \mu x$$

with λ and μ are parameters, what is the catastrophe manifold? Draw a sketch of a catastrophe manifold for this sort of catastrophe. How can you indicate the critical values of parameter(s) at which sudden changes in the nature of the equation can expectedly occur (catastrophe map)? Draw its sketch and also the relevant bifurcations.

dynamical systems

14

The preceding pages show, in some measure, ways how to deal with non-linear systems. Qualitative approach has necessarily been a conditioning element and so, other emerging facets such as stability or otherwise of systems concerned. The perspective, historically speaking, has been largely due to Jules Henri Poincare (1854-1912) who could hardly be explicit in his cardinal pieces of work on qualitative theory of differential equations but left the same to his successors like Arnold, Thom and many others. The work, to date, has been enormously prolific and we cannot cover the bulk of it through an introduction. The area of concern has been 'dynamical systems' without being perfectly and specifically, repetitive about it. This chapter is intended to deal with the introductory endeavour, save the later appendices, through few more topics and themes , without which the work may appear to be unduly incomplete. While doing so, we draw upon what we have so far mentioned but studiedly seek for another view, and more so, an unified view with evolutionary characteristics, if palpably discernible.

14.1 Evolutionary system

The main purpose is to represent the evolutionary state of the system. Let us do it through examples.

Example 1 : Simple Harmonic Motion (SHM)

Here the basic equation is given by

$$\ddot{x}+\omega^2 x = 0 \qquad (x \in R) \qquad (1)$$

This is equivalent to $\left. \dot{x}_1 = x_2, \ \dot{x}_2 = -\omega^2 x_1 \right\}$ (2)   putting, $\left. x = x_1, \ \dot{x} = x_2 \right\}$

which is of the form $\dot{x} = F(x)$ where $x = (x_1, x_2) \in R^2$ and $F(x_1, x_2) = (x_2, -\omega^2 x_1)$

The solution $x(t)$, subject to $x(0) = (a, b)$ is

$$x(t) = \left(a \cos \omega t + \frac{b}{\omega} \sin \omega t, -a\omega \sin \omega t + b \cos \omega t \right)$$

where $(a, b) = (0, 0)$ obviously describes an ellipse in R^2 as t varies. Projecting this motion on to x_1-axis gives the oscillatory behaviour of x, as is expected from the original equation.

Characteristics of S.H.M.

1.   Let p be a point in R^n, then a solution with an initial state p of $\dot{x} = X(x)$ is a curve $x(t)$ in R^n with properties

$$x(0) = p, \ \dot{x}(t) = F \qquad (4)$$

for all t in some interval (α, β) where $\alpha < t < \beta$. Assuming the existence and uniqueness of solutions, we find that for a given p, there is β trajectory; precisely, one such curve $x(t)$ satisfying (4) and so, it is a trajectory through p. This is so, for it represents the changing state of the system given by

$$\dot{x} = F(x)$$

as it begins at p and moves uninterruptedly along a path in its arena of possible states. We can speak of this as evolution of the state. Where does a flow stand in this setting? For this, let us turn to family of all solutions of $\dot{x} = X(x)$ simultaneously. Let us agree to write $x(t; p)$ in place of $x(t)$ so as to emphasize the dependence on p. Let $\varphi(t)$ be a transformation here : R^n to R^n, so as to make each point correspond to its position, as per (4). We can express this by saying that the system has evolved according to (4) at time t. Then the collection $\phi = \{\varphi(t)\}$ for all t is one-parameter family of all maps $R^n \to R^n$, satisfying

$$\left.\begin{array}{l} \varphi(0) \qquad = \text{identity} \\ \varphi(s) \circ \varphi(t) = \varphi(s+t) \text{ for all } s,t \end{array}\right\} \tag{5}$$

Such a collection φ of maps can be called a flow on R^n. Also, $\{\varphi(t)\}^{-1} = \varphi(-t)$, because of (5).

2.   From the above S.H.M. we can write

$$\varphi(t;p) \equiv \Lambda(t)p \text{ where } \Lambda(t) = \begin{pmatrix} \cos\omega t & \dfrac{1}{\omega}\sin\omega t \\ -\omega\sin\omega t & \cos\omega t \end{pmatrix}$$

The conditions (5) are seen to be satisfied.

Following Poincare, we say that the configuration of the velocity of orbits (trajectories) in R^n for the phase portrait of the flow e.g. in the case of the above example, the phase portrait consists of ellipses, and also shows the oscillatory character of the motion, phase difference between the displacement x_1 and velocity $\dot{x}_1$ (i.e. x_2) and properties of the orbit.

Remark

We can have a similar glance at the behaviour of a damped oscillator represented by

$$\ddot{x} + k\ddot{x} + a^2 x = 0$$

as well as its orbits with $a > 0$ or $a < 0$.

Example 2

Let us consider the classical problem with prey populations, say x and the predator populations, say y. Left to themselves, the simplest evolution predicts the exponental growth of the prey population $(\dot{x} = kx)$ and the exponential decay of the predator population $(\dot{y} = -\varepsilon y)$, assuming they do not interact. If they do so, this decreases the prey population and increases the predator population. We, obtain, assuming the number of interaction per unit, to be proportional to both populations, the well-known Lotka-Volterra system

$$\dot{x} = kx - axy$$

$$\dot{y} = -\varepsilon y + bxy$$

We describe the state of the system—a point in the first quadrant of the plane (x, y) as shown.

The manifold of the possible states $(x > 0, y > 0)$ of a dynamical system is what we call the phase space, which we discussed earlier. The evolution of the state is described by the motion of the point of the phase space. The velocity of this motion depends only on the present

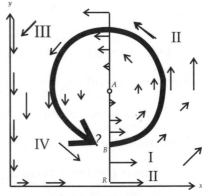

Fig. 14.1: The Lotka-Volterra vector field

state. As shown in the above Fig. 14.1, the vector field on the phase space represents the dependence of this velocity on the point of the phase space.

So we have phase velocity field as the vector field having $(kx - axy)$ and $(-\varepsilon y + bxy)$ as its components. This phase velocity field describes the (law of) evolution of the system. The study of dynamical systems concerned is, given the velocity field, to study the evolution i.e. the motion of the phases and in particular, the trajectory of this moving point. We have already seen in some ways the dynamics of this system, which population grows (I), attains its stationary state, which are in decline (II), when two population begin declining (III) allowing the other population to grow (IV). The vector field of the system has the stationary point A. What has happened to the behaviour of the populations? We have, following Arnold, an estimate of the possible behaviour scenarios of the populations.

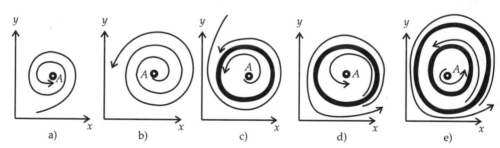

Fig. 14.2 : Different scenarios in the predator–prey systems

Fig. 14.2(a) represents the stable stationary state or we often say, the attractor; 14.2(b) is otherwise. The others represent the growth of oscillations of the populations; in particular Fig. 14.2(c) repeats stable periodic oscillations, which are denoted by close plane trajectories and we have called them, earlier, limit cycles surrounded by spirals, seeking to approach the limit cycle as limits. One can take Fig. 14.2(d) as the case, where A is attracting but the basin of attraction (we shall formally define a bit later) is bounded by a limit cycle. Fig. 14.2(e) represents limit cycles, alternatively, attracting and repelling the spiral trajectories in the nbd. We have met earlier with the term 'phase portrait' as one obtained from phase space.

As found earlier, we can see, following Poincare, the first return mapping which associates to an initial point say B on a segment, the next point of the trajectory with a segment. The sequence of the consecutive returns of the trajectories is :

$$B_0 = B, \; B_1 = f(B), \; B_2 = f(f(B)), \; B_3 = f(f(f(B))), \; ...$$

which is shown by what is often called staircase construction of the trajectory, as in Fig. 14.3.

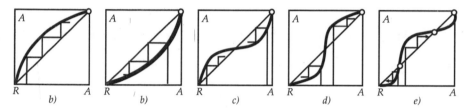

Fig. 14.3 : The Poincaré first return mapping

Thus, the Poincare mapping enables us to investigate the long time evolution behaviour of the motion.

Remarks

1. If we have a system defined by a mapping, $f : M \rightarrow M$ connecting a phase point $x \in M$ (phase space) to a new phase point $f(x) \in M$, then we have a model of evolutionary systems with continuous time t, called discrete time dynamical system. The phase trajectory in this case consists of a sequence of points $x, f(x), f(f(x)), \cdots$, the state of the system of the moments 0, 1, 2, 3, ...

    So, the Poincaré mapping is an example of such a discrete time dynamics

2. The foregoing examples show that, by transforming problems of dynamics to geometrical equations, it is possible to make a study of (non-linear) evolutionary systems having some paradigms. The basic cornerstone in such pursuits is to

reiterate the behaviour of the solutions of given systems of equations $\dot{x} = f(x)$ and widen further the query, its qualitative behaviour. How are such systems rough, robust or structurally stable? To turn to history, we should say that Poincare was the earliest of the precursors in this direction to be followed by, in the thirties and forties, of the scientists Andronov, then in the sixties by M. René Thom and Stephen Smale and also by V.I. Arnold of the school in the erstwhile Soviet Union. Conceptually speaking, what properties should we seek for, now, in the context of structurally stable systems? We should begin with some mathematical preliminaries, over and above, what we have mentioned earlier, which form the basis of dynamical systems.

14.2 Some mathematical notions

It is convenient to begin with maps and simpler it is, with maps of the circle i.e. the stable space in the circle. We are used to represent the circle T', in the complex plane as

$$\left\{ z \in C : |z| = 1 \right\} = \left\{ e^{2\pi i x}, x \in R \right\}$$

We can write the map as $f : T' = T'$ or $z \to f(z)$. We need to assume that f is continuous along with its derivatives and we can call such f to C' diffeomorphism; the orbit of a point $\omega \in T'$, denoted by $O(\omega)$ is

$$\left\{ \cdots, f^{-1}(w), \omega, f^{1}(w), f^{2}(w), \cdots \right\} = \left\{ f^{n}(w) : n \in Z \right\}$$

A homoeomorphism is a continuous map that has a continuous inverse.

We say that two homoeomorphisms $f : Y \to Y$ and $g : Z \to Z$ are topologically conjugate (orientation-preserving conjugacies) if there is a homoeomorphism $h : Y \to Z$ satisfying $f = h^{-1}gh$.

A diffeomorphism f is said to be structurally stable if any diffeomorphism g close enough in the C^1-sense to f is topologically conjugate to f. It is to be noted that f and g are close in the C^1-sense if they are close point-wise and their derivatives at each point are close.

We know what we mean by fixed points i.e. point p where $F(p)=0$, so that $\phi(p;t)=p$ for all t, and p represents the equilibrium state for the system.

We have also read about periodic orbits as those orbits Γ such if $q \in \Gamma$, then $\varphi(T;q)=q$ for some $T>0$, the least such T being the period of Γ; of course, the system beginning at state q returns to this state after time T. An off-the-track consequence is provided by the rotation of the circle $\alpha(\in R)$ of a complete turn $R_\alpha : T'$ by

$$R_\alpha\left(e^{2\pi ix}\right)=Re^{2\pi i(x+\alpha)}$$

Obviously $R_\alpha = R_{\alpha+n}$. If α is a rational number of the form $\dfrac{p}{q}$ then

$$R_\alpha^{\,q}\left(e^{2\pi ix}\right)=e^{2\pi i(x+p\alpha)}=e^{2\pi ix}$$

i.e. every point is fixed by $R_\alpha^{\,q}$ and not by $R_\alpha^{\,r}$, $0<r<q$.

Here, we say that the point is periodic of (least) period q.

If, however, α is irrational, $x\alpha$ is not an integer and

$$R_\alpha^{\,n}\left(e^{2\pi in}\right)\neq e^{2\pi ix} \text{ for any } n\neq 0.$$

So, we can conclude that under R_α, each α has its orbit $O(z)$ finite when α is rational but infinite when α is irrational.

Let us now introduce two new notions, *recurrent orbits* and *nonwandering orbits*.

If $\phi(t;r)$ returns arbitrarily close to r for sufficiently large $t>0$ (i.e. given $\varepsilon>0$ and $T>0$) then $\exists\ t>T$ with distance $\{(\phi(t;r),r)<\varepsilon\}$, then r and its orbits are called recurrent. A recurrent orbit is far from being a periodic orbit. It represents a kind of long-term oscillatory region but capable to return close to where it started.

We also define a recurrent set in terms of ω-limit set. Let us have a map $f:G\to G$; we say that a point $g\in G$ has a ω-limit set, $\omega(g)=\{v\in G:f^n(y)\to v$ for some sequence $n_i\neq\omega\}$. If $y=\omega(g)$, we say that y is recurrent.

A point w and its orbit are said to be non-wandering points if points arbitrarily close to w, eventually return close to w, even though w itself may not even return. Finally, given $\varepsilon>0$ and $T>0$, there is some v and some $t>T$ with distance $(v,w)<\varepsilon$ and distance $\{\varphi(t;v),w\}<\varepsilon$. Fig. 14.5 illustrates the non-wandering orbit.

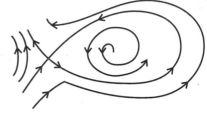

Fig. 14.5

It is to be noted that this orbit is not recurrent. Alternatively, the point w is said to be non-wandering if for each open U containing w, there is $n\geq 1$ with $f^n(U)\cap U\neq\phi$. The non-wandering set $\Omega(f)$ is the set of non-wandering points.

Non-wandering orbits, in their totality, are often denoted by U. Fixed points, periodic orbits and recurrent orbits are all examples of non-wandering orbits.

What is then a wandering point? We call a point x_0 wandering if $\exists$ is an open nbd. $U(x_0)$ of x_0 and a positive integer T such that $U(x_0)\cap\phi(t,U(x_0))=\phi$ for $t>T$.

Clearly, applying the transformation $\varphi(-t,x)$ to this, we get

$\varphi(-t,U(x_0))\cap U(x_0)=\phi$ for $t<T$

Hence, the definition of a wandering point shows this to be symmetric with respect to positive and negative values of t. Can we say anything about openness and invariance, if at all, of non-wandering sets?

A set A is said to be with respect to a homeomorphism φ if $A=\varphi(t,A)$ for any t where $\varphi(t,A)$ stands for the set $U_{x\in A}\varphi(t,x)$ and so if $x\in A$, then the trajectory $\varphi(t,x)$ lies in A.

Let us look into the properties of the set of non-wandering points.

Let U be the set of non-wandering points. That U is open follows from the fact that, together with x_0, any point in $U(x_0)$ is wandering. If x_0 is a wandering point, the point $\varphi(t_0, x_0)$ is also a wandering point for any t_0. To show this, let us choose $\varphi(t_0, U(x_0))$ to be in the nbd of the point $\varphi(t_0, x_0)$.

Then $\varphi(t_0, U(x_0)) \cap \varphi(t, \varphi(t_0, U(x_0))) = \phi$ for $t > T$ and invariance criterion is obeyed. Hence, the set U of non-wandering points is closed and invariant.

In sum, the conditions which define a *continuous dynamical system* (or *flow*) are :

(a)   a total metric space E called the phase space

(b)   a time variable t which may be either continuous i.e. $t \in R$ or discrete i.e. $t \in \Sigma$

(c)   an evolution process i.e. a mapping of any given point x in E and any t to a uniquely defined state $\varphi(t, x) \in E$ satisfying the conditions :

    (i) $\varphi(0, x) = x$

    (ii) $\varphi(t_1, \varphi(t_2, x)) = \varphi(t_1 + t_2, x)$

    (iii) $\varphi(t, x) \in C^0$ with respect to (t, x)

Remarks

1.   From the last definition, we can well say that flow is a non-parameter group of homoeomorphisms.

2.   In case, the mapping $\varphi(t, x)$ is a diffeomorphism (a one and one, differentiable mapping with differentiable inverse), the flow is a smooth dynamical system given by $\dot{x} = f(x)$, $x \in R^n$

3.   The well-known phase trajectory is obtained as a curve, by fixing x and varying t from $-\infty$ to $+\infty$. $\{x, \varphi(t, x), t \geq 0\}$ is a positive semi-trajectory and so $\{x, \varphi(t, x), t \leq 0\}$ is a negative semi-trajectory.

4.   The phase space E is usually chosen to be either R^n or $R^{n-k} \times T^k$ where T^k may be a k-dimensional manifold (or a smooth surface).

5.   Discrete dynamical systems are often called *cascades*. How to get it? Let us have a homoeomorphism $\varphi(t,x)$ and let us denote it by $\varphi(x)$. It is obvious that $\varphi(t,x) = \varphi^t(x)$ where

$$\varphi^t = \underbrace{\varphi(\varphi(\cdots, \varphi(x)))}_{t-1 \text{ times}}$$

Hence, for a cascade it suffices to have the homoeomorphism

$$\varphi : E \to E$$

For a discrete dynamical system, a sequence $\{x_k\}_{-\infty}^{+\infty}$ where $x_{k+1} = x_k$ is called a trajectory of a point x_0. Periods, cycles, periodic orbits, etc. may be defined accordingly for a discrete dynamical system.

6.   What we have not as yet discussed in the above lines, formally, is evolutionary stability or the instability of evolving systems. Let us pose it formally as follows. A system does change continuously and slowly as measured by some control parameters. Then the system, affordably, can have an initially stable equilibrium state. How can it then lose its stability? Under what conditions? We have found a partial answer to this in bifurcation theory, which classifies the ways in which a stable equilibrium path can become unstable. Further, it does investigate the stability of the whole evolutionary process against small secondary perturbations. The catastrophe theory adds reinforcement to this and provides unusual classification of stability phenomena and this theory is an upshot of mathematical topology which leads to the important concept of structural stability.

14.3 Revisiting homoeomorphism: The Hartman-Grobman theorem

Some preliminaries

Let us consider the nonlinear system

$$\dot{\vec{x}} = f(\vec{x}) \tag{1}$$

This has the same qualitative structure as the linear system

$$\dot{\vec{x}} = A\vec{x} \tag{2}$$

where, as we are aware, $A = Df(\vec{x}_0)$, x_0 being the equilibrium point.

We need now to take recourse to homoeomorphism .

Let X be a metric space and let A and B be sub-sets of X.

A homoeomorphism of A onto B is a continuous one to one map of A onto B,

$h : A \to B$ such that $h^{-1} : B \to A$ is continuous.

The sets A and B are called homoeomorphic or topologically equivalent if there is a homoeomorphism of A onto B. We write this as $A \square B$. This leads to an analogus definition of two autonomous systems of differential equations, which we haven't done so far.

Definition

Two autonomous systems of differential equations such as (1) and (2) are said to be topologically equivalent in a nbd of the origin or to have the same qualitative structure nearer the origin if there is a homoeomorphism H mapping an open set U containing the origin to an open set V containing the origin which maps trajectories of (1) in U onto trajectories of (2) in V and preserves their orientation by time in the sense that if a trajectory is directed from $\vec{x}_1$ to $\vec{x}_2$ in U, then its image is directed from $H(\vec{x}_1)$ to $H(\vec{x}_2)$ in V. As mentioned earlier, if the homoeomorphism H preserves the parameterization by time, then the systems (1) and (2) are said to be *topologically conjugate* in the nbd of the origin.

To illustrate this, let us consider an example

Let us consider the linear system

$$\dot{\vec{x}} = A\vec{x}$$
$$\dot{\vec{y}} = B\vec{y}$$

where $A = \begin{bmatrix} -1 & -3 \\ -3 & -1 \end{bmatrix}$ and $B = \begin{bmatrix} 2 & 0 \\ 0 & -4 \end{bmatrix}$

Let $H(\vec{x}) = R\vec{x}$ where $R = \dfrac{1}{\sqrt{2}}\begin{bmatrix} 1 & -1 \\ 1 & 1 \end{bmatrix}$ and $R^{-1} = \dfrac{1}{\sqrt{2}}\begin{bmatrix} 1 & 1 \\ -1 & 1 \end{bmatrix}$

Then $B = RAR^{-1}$

Let $\quad \vec{y} = H(\vec{x}) = R\vec{x}$

or, $\quad \vec{x} = R^{-1}y$

which gives $\vec{y} = RAR^{-1}y = B\vec{y}$

Thus if $\vec{x}(t) = e^{At}\vec{x}_0$ is the solution of the first system through $\vec{x}_0$ then $\vec{y}(t) = H(\vec{x}(t)) = Rx(t) = Re^{At}x_0 = e^{Bt}Rx_0$ is a solution of the second system through x_0 i.e. H maps trajectories of the first system onto the trajectories of the second system (Fig. 14.6) and it preserves the parameterization since $He^{At} = e^{Bt}H$. Now, mapping $H(x) = R\vec{x}$ is simply a homoeomorphism.

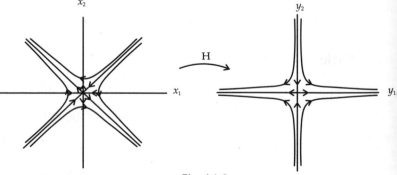

Fig. 14.6

We are now in a position to state, without proof, the well known Hartman-Grobman theorem, a generalized version on diffeomorphism in a nbd of a fixed point.

The Hartman-Grobman theorem

Statement

Let E be an open subset of R^n containing the origin, let $\vec{f} \in C'(E)$ and let ϕ_t be the flow of the system

$$\dot{\vec{x}} = f(\vec{x}) \tag{1}$$

Let us suppose $f(0) = 0$ and the matrix $A = D\vec{f}(0)$ has no eigen value with no real parts. Then there exists a homoeomorphism H of an open set U containing origin, onto an open set V containing the origin such that for each $\vec{x}_0 \in U$, there is an open interval $I_0 \subset R$ consisting of zero such that for all $\vec{x}_0 \in U$ and $t \in I_0$

$$H \circ \phi_t(\vec{x}_0) = e^{At} H(x_0)$$

i.e. H maps trajectories of (1) near the origin onto trajectories of

$$\dot{x} = A(\vec{x})$$

with $A = Df(\vec{x}_0)$ \hfill (2)

near the origin and preserving the parameterization by time.

Remarks

1. The proof of the theorem can be achieved through a variety of stages such as lemmas, partial proofs etc.

2. A remarkable spin off of this theory that, in two dimensions, Hartman could prove any C^2 diffeomorphism to be C^1 conjugate to its linearized map coordinates in the nbd of a hyperbolic fixed point . This leads to two phase portraits to be similar upto

changes which C^1 change of coordinates allow.

3.   This theorem ensures the stability of the fixed point, as in the case of a flow.

14.4 Attracting sets, attractor and basin of attraction

We have seen earlier how orbits tend to move away from a orbit (or orbits) and some move towards a orbit (or orbits). Limit cycles are good examples in such contexts. We have also used the term 'attractor', somewhat naïvely. Let us now seek to be formal about them and allied areas pertaining to dynamical systems.

Definition : A set A is called an attracting set for the dynamical system

$$\dot{x} = f(x)$$

with its flow, denoted by $\varphi(t;x)$, if there is some nbd U of A such that

$$\varphi(t;x) \subset U \text{ for } t \geq U$$

and $\varphi(t;0) \rightarrow A$ as $t \rightarrow \infty$ for all $x \in U$

Remarks

1.   Can we arrive at this notion from the standpoint of *forward limit sets*? Let us explore this.

Let f be a map and x_0 be an initial condition. The formal limit set of the orbit $\{f^n(x_0)\}$ is the set

$$\omega(x_0) = \{x : \text{for all } N \text{ and } \varepsilon \text{ there exists } n \geq N \text{ s.t. } |f^n(x_0) - x| < \varepsilon\}$$

We have called this set earlier as the ω–limit set of the orbits. If $\omega(x_0)$ is a forward limit set of some orbits and x_0 is another initial condition, then we say that the orbit $\{f^n(x_0)\}$ (or the point x_1) is attracted to $\omega(x_0)$, $\omega(x_1)$ being contained in $\omega(x_0)$.

2. Obviously, the forward limit set of an orbit $\{f^n(x_0)\}$ is the set of points x to which the orbit always makes what may be described as 'occasional nbd visits'. No matter how small $\varepsilon > 0$ is close and no matter how long N we have, there is an $n > N$ with $|f^n(x_0) - x| < \varepsilon$.

3. The kind of orbit, talked about in Remark (1), is the set of points to which the orbit may or may not be contained in its forward-limit set, which may not have even points in common with the orbit; this may converge to a sink, being approached by the orbit as closely as we may specify and as forward in time and as closely as we desire. This orbit is attracted to the sink. We can now have the definition of an attractor as follows.

Definition : Attractor

An attractor is the forward time limit of an orbit that attracts a significant portion of initial conditions. Since a sink is what attracts at least a small nbd of initial values, it can be taken as an attractor.

Another definition of an Attractor (or Sink)

Let f be a map on R^n and let p in R^n be a fixed point i.e. $f(p) = p$. If there be an $\varepsilon > 0$ so that for all v with ε-nbd $N_\varepsilon(p)$, $\lim_{k \to \infty} f^k(v) = p$, then p is an attractor or sink.

If there be an ε-nbd $N_\varepsilon(p)$ such that each v in $N_\varepsilon(p)$ except for p itself maps exterior to $N_\varepsilon(p)$ (eventually) then p is a source or repeller.

Definition : Basin of Attraction

The set of points whose orbits converge to an attracting fixed point is called the basin of attraction or just the basin of the sink. We can formally present its definition as follows :

Let f be map an R^n and let p an attracting fixed point or periodic point for f. The basin of attraction of p or just basin of p is the set of points x such that

$$\left| f^k(x) - f^k(p) \right| \to 0 \text{ as } k \to \infty.$$

Remark

We have defined earlier the attracting set; we can look upon the basin of attraction as the union of all such nbds U.

If there be a bounded nbd that a map sends into itself it can be called a *trapping region*.

In fact, the trapping region $D \subset 1$ is a simply connected set such that

$$\varphi_t(D) \subset D \text{ for all } t \geq 0 \cdot$$

Exercise

1. Show that the basis of attraction of the equilibrium $(0, 0)$ of

   $$x = -y^3 + xy$$
   $$y = -y^3 - x^2$$

   is R^2. (Is $(0, 0)$ an asymptotically stable equilibrium?)

2. Given a Liapunov function V on W let

   $$W_c = \left\{ w \in W : V_{(w)} \leq C \right\}$$

   where C is a positive real number.

   Is W a forward invariant set? As $w \to \infty$, what happens to $V_{(w)}$? Can we say W_c to be a trapping region?

3. Find the critical points of the system

$$\frac{dx}{dt} = y$$

$$\frac{d\dot{y}}{dt} = x - 2x^3$$

How do they behave? Do they have attraction properties? Justify your answer.

4. Determine the critical points of the system

$$\frac{d\dot{x}}{dt} = x^2 - y^2$$

$$\frac{dy}{dt} = 2x(x^2 - y)$$

Are there attractors of the system? Do periodic solutions exist? Justify your answer.

5. Establish the attraction points, if any, of the solutions $(0,0)$ of

$$\frac{dx}{dt} = x^3 + y$$

$$\frac{dy}{dt} = (x^3 + y^2 - 2)y$$

6. Is $(0,0)$ of the system

$$\frac{dx}{dt} = -y + x(x^2 + y^2) \sin\left(\sqrt{x^2 + y^2}\right)$$

$$\frac{dy}{dt} = x + y(x^2 + y^2) \sin\left(\sqrt{x^2 + y^2}\right)$$

an attractor?

epilogue

15

The preceding chapters have sought to present broad considerations of some leading heights of what come within the orbit of nonlinear studies. This chapter is primarily intended to wind up with another important notion, that has not merely come to stay but is amenable to applications. Applicability here, pertains to the emerging area of atmospheric sciences, which, doubtless, is an important constituent of mathematical sciences. We take care of what has gone by in the last chapter and also deal with some aspects, in appendix V, that may appear to be missing links, in one way or the other.

15.1 Lorenz system : Predictability

As we know, the great meteorological scientist Professor E. N. Lorenz of MIT, USA, investigated the phenomenon of convection in the atmosphere of the Earth because of heating from below and cooling from above. The governing equations, are

$$\left.\begin{array}{l} \dot{x} = \sigma\left(y - x\right) \\ \dot{y} = rx - y - rz \\ \dot{z} = xy - bz \end{array}\right\} \tag{1}$$

where σ, r and b are positive constants (or parameters). We have made brief studies on the behaviour of the solutions of the Lorenz system given by (1). The independent variables (x, y, z) define the phase-space. The solutions of (1) are represented by trajectories in phase-space for the dissipative system, such as the atmosphere here. Numerical forecasts on weather form the mainstay of endeavours on weather forecasting. Each forecast is treated as an initial value problem with specified boundary conditions. The physical state of the atmosphere itself is updated from observations made simultaneously over the whole globe. A question that arises is whether there is, for each scale of motion, a time limit beyond which it is not possible to make a deterministic forecast. Although Lorenz was the precursor of such studies, the excellent poser in this context was by Smagorinsky (1969) and this needs to be cited as follows :

"If we had a physically faithful model of the red atmosphere, an ability to specify fully the initial conditions for all spectral components and committed no truncation error in numerically integrating the system of nonlinear differential equations, could we expect to predict the atmospheric evolution from an initial state whole with infinite infinitely distant in the future precision? Or, would small random perturbations (noise) develop in the model and amplify to the point at which simulation departs from reality and ultimately become uncorrelated with the real atmosphere? What is the ultimate point of predictability of the atmosphere? Does this ultimate limit to predictability beyond which, no improvement, whether in models, initial conditions (observations) or computing power would increase the predictability of a given scale of atmospheric development?"

Edward Lorenz, of course, contributed to the bulk of literature on predictability studies. In particular, Lorenz had uncomfortable experiences while rerunning some experimental long range numerical forecasts and he had to round off the initial data inserted into the computer. It so happened that at the termination of the forecast, the forecasts initiated by the slightly modified data differed considerably from initial forecasts. Thus came up what is often called a paradigm of the phenomena of predictability of nonlinear systems, called the sensitivity to initial conditions. This sensitive dependence on initial conditions is said to be one of the definitions of chaos and this is typical for chaotic behaviour. Chaology, as the study is often described, has come to stay. Lorenz, in his brilliant expose 'Does the Flap of a Butterfly's Wings in Brazil Set Off a Tornado in Texas?' shows how while running a meteorological computer model, he decided to round it off to few decimal places, after being tiringly disgusted with the long number he had to be in. That this tiny change could bring about wild changes in respect of weather prediction and could be of great importance in enabling Lorenz to step across the border between order and chaos; is well borne by contemporary developments in mathematical sciences. Further, any alternative portrayal of a chaotic behaviour, not necessarily confined to atmospheric sciences, has to take recourse to 'fractal geometry', a term carried by Benoit Mandelbrot of the IBM Research Labs in USA to describe 'a self similar' shape a motif that keeps on repeating at smaller scales again and again infinitude.

According to Lorenz, if a dynamical system is to be a reasonably realistic model of earth's atmosphere, we ought to anticipate some of the properties of its attractor from our experience with weather maps. After a brilliant exposition of the salients of a dynamical system, Lorenz has sought to find out what the attractor looks like for simple atmospheric models. Lorenz reckons that an attractor set A to be a basic property of a dynamical system. Thus a point Q is in A, if the points for which Q is a limit point together form a set of non-zero volume in phase space. Each point on the orbit though Q is then in A so that the attractor is composed of orbits. Lorenz could establish from the well-known equations that the equations for weather prediction had a set of two attractors and trajectories in phase space tended to converge towards the first attractor and later, towards the second attractor. He defined these as a system of 'strange attractors' emphasizing thereby a greater sensitivity to initial conditions affecting the computer sequence of weather data. To Lorenz, the estimate of maximum period for short range weather prediction could be two weeks, fitting in the best possible date for the initial state. The allied idea of a 'climatic attractor' is very much in the offing reckoning the familiar El Nino and ENSO events. Lorenz's book "The Essence of Chaos" published by the University of Washington Press in 1993 should provide a good background in regard to chaotic behaviour. A precise knowledge of the attractor is of great practical value in NWP (Numerical Weather Prediction); to quote, Lorenz : 'Weather seems to come in random sequences; other people believe economics is a chaotic process in the way it varies; it may naturally follow certain laws but it seems random. Chaos theory unites these various fields, and also includes the testing of various sequences to discover whether they are chaotic or non-chaotic.' Here is an approach that hardly dispenses with rigours of the study of dynamical systems. The topics like manifolds, bifurcations etc. or sophisticated Cantor sets appear conspicuously in such pursuits.

15.2 A potential exemplar on FDI

Let us think aloud about the much talked FDI (Foreign Direct Investment) so as to explore whether there exists a flavour of nonlinearity around it. FDI's role in promoting economic growth across developing countries and FDI's interaction with trade are being widely discussed. To someone obviously on account of a variety of reasons, FDI is welcome or irksome and an issue to be viewed critically. There are naturally terms, mostly with economic overtones, that are associated with a conceptual framework of FDI. Of these that are of relevance to our purpose consist of : (i) g, the per capita GDP growth rate. (ii) FDI (iii) DRD, the trade (exports plus imports) of goods and services. (iv) HC, the stock of human capital (v) K, the domestic capital investment (vi) G_0, the initial GDP (initial stock) (vii) IRT, the inflation rate (viii) TX, a tax on income, profits, capital gains in the host country expressed as percentages of current revenue and (ix) GC, the government consumption. The variables FDI, TRD, K, GC are those that are measured as ratios to GDP. The effects of FDI and trade on economic growth are expressed by the nonlinear relationship:

$$g = a + b_1\,FDI + b_2 TRD + b_3 HC$$
$$+ b_4 K + b_5 G_0 + c_1 FDI * TRD$$
$$+ c_2 FDI * HC + c_3 FDI * K$$
$$+ d_1 IRT + d_2 \Gamma X + d_3 GC$$
$$+ e$$

where $a, b_1, b_2, b_3, b_4, b_5, c_1, c_2, c_3, d_1, d_2, d_3$ and e are a positive constants.

It is clear that there are three coupled terms with FDI (* between) accounting for interaction of FDI with trade, domestic investment and human capital. The coupled term, for example, (FDI* K) stands for an estimate of the combined impact of FDI and domestic investment on growth and this also indicates the nature of relationship between the two. A positive coefficient for this term suggests that FDI and domestic investment supplement and complement each other in advancing economic growth.

Quantitatively speaking, the goal should be to ascertain the effects of FDI and trade on economic growth; this unfortunately often forms the vexed complexion of the furore about FDI. To go in for a qualitative approach, we ought to have a governing system with (mean) values of per capita GDP growth rates over a certain time horizon, say, a decade. There are, of course, wider concerns with regard to investigations on FDI. Qualitative exercises ought to provide better insights into whether FDI has to have some extant scenarios for, FDI-driven growth to materialize; stability criteria have to be looked into on the basis of what we have done earlier in regard to stability from a qualitative standpoint, with data from developing countries. Here is thus a potential exemplar on nonlinearity that has a continuing concern and compelling characteristics in countries like ours, without being one of pseudo-nonlinearity or mild nonlinearity. Local, global, strong or weak stability, attraction or repulsion, sensitivity etc.—the attributes ordinarily belonging to a system, amenable to qualitative analysis, ought to figure prominently in such endeavours.

appendix I

Poincare–Bendixson theorem

Any text on nonlinear systems can hardly afford, not to refer to the celebrated result called 'Poincare–Bendixson Theorem'. It was first established by the French mathematician Henri Poincare, in 1880 and later on, simplified by the Swiss mathematician Ivan Bendixson in 1901. It is known to be an indispensably vital result that asserts the existence of a periodic solution for a general class of non-linear systems. The theorem has been stated earlier without a formal proof, in connection with periodic orbits, which, of course, focus its primary concern. The ideas in its proof are relatively difficult and so, the proof is not set forth on the first exposure to this theorem. Perhaps, it will now be fairly comfortable to have glimpses of ways and ideas leading to the proof of this theorem. The proofs are achieved apparently in different ways but they do depend on concepts and results treated in the early part of this book. Poincare-Bendixson theorem (PB) has, on the face of it, different versions, as shown below in different sections.

I. Revisiting concepts treated earlier

We look upon the PB theorem as a basic wherewithal even for understanding planar dynamical systems, which we have already met. For this, we need to bank upon some properties of the limiting behaviour of orbits at the level of abstract topological dynamics, followed by an analysis of the flow near non-equilibrium points of a dynamical system. Can we then begin with the definition of a dynamical system as an open set W in a vector space E, that is, the flow $\phi(f)$ defined by a $C^{(1)}$ vector field, $f : W \to E$? Perhaps, we can, in the light of what we have said earlier, coupled with the concepts of vector field and vector space.

Now, we recall the concept of *limit sets*, particularly, ω-limit set (α-limit set) of the form $L_\omega(y)$ or $L_\alpha(y)$, y being a ω- (or α-) limit point. We need the result, $L_\omega(x) = L_\omega(z)$, x and z being on the same trajectory; the closure and invariance of the sets are also assumed. We should remember what is meant by a *hyperplane*, which is a linear subspace with dimension one, less than dim E. If $f(x) \notin H$ for all $x \in S$ and, in particular, $f(x) \neq 0$ for $x \in S$, then $S \subset H$ is transverse to f. The origin $O \in E$, belongs to W. By a *local section* at O, of f, we mean an open set containing O in a hyperplane $H \subset E$ which is transverse to f. A sequence, finite or infinite, $[x_0, x_1, \cdots\cdots]$ of distinct points on the solution curve $C = \{\phi(t, x_0) \mid \le t \le \alpha\}$, if $\phi(t_n, x_0) = x_0$ with $0 \le t_1 \le \cdots \le \alpha$ is often taken. The appendix III on more definitions and ideas may be seen.

Let us now state two lemmas (without proof)

Lemma 1 : Let S be a local section of a $C^{(1)}$ planar dynamical system and $\{y_0, y_1, y_2 \cdots\}$ a sequence of distinct points of S that are on the same solution curve C. If the sequence is monotone along C, it is also monotone along S.

Lemma 2 : Let $y \in L_\omega(x) \cup L_\alpha(x)$. Then the trajectory of y crosses any local section at more than one point.

II. Poincare-Bendixson theorem

Here we use the term *'closed orbit'*. A trajectory Γ is a closed orbit if Γ is not in equilibrium, $\phi_p(x) = 0$ for some $x \in \Gamma$, $p \neq 0$.

Statement : A non-empty compact limit set of a C^1 planar dynamical system, which contains no critical point, is a closed orbit.

Proof : Let us assume $L_\omega(x)$ to be compact (and invariant) and $y \in L_\omega(x)$; similar is the assumption on α-limit set.

∵ $y \in L_\omega(x)$, $L_\omega(y)$ is a nonempty subset of $L_\omega(y)$. Let $z \in L_\omega(y)$; let S be a local section at z and N be a flow in the nbd of Z about some open interval $J, z \in J \subset S$. By Lemma 2, the trajectory of y intersects S exactly at one point. Also, there is a sequence t_n such that $\phi(t_n; y) \to z$ as $t_n \to \infty$ and so, there $\exists$ many $\phi(t_n; y)$ that belong to V. Therefore, $\exists$ $r, s \in R$ such that $r > s$ and $\phi(t_n; y) \in S \cap V$, $\phi(t; y) \in S \cap V$.

It follows that $\phi_r(y) = \phi_s(y)$; hence $\phi_{r-s}(y) = y$, $r - s > 0$.

∵ $L_\omega(x)$ does not have a critical point, y belongs to the closed orbit. We are yet to show that if Γ is a closed orbit in $L_\omega(x)$ then $\Gamma = L_\omega(x)$. For this, it suffices to show that $\lim_{t \to \infty} d(\phi(t; x), \Gamma) = 0$ where $d(\phi(t; x), y)$ is the distance from $\phi(t; x)$ to the nearest point of Γ. Let S be a local section at $z \in \Gamma$, so small that $S \cap \Gamma = z$. Considering a flow V_s in the nbd of z, we can say that there is a sequence $t_0 < t_1 < \cdots$ such that, $\phi(t_n; x) \in S$ and $\phi(t_n; z) \to z$, $\phi(t; x) \notin S$ for $t_{n-1} < t < t_n$, $n = 1, 2, \cdots$.

Let us put $x_n = \phi(t_n; x)$. By the above Lemma 1, $x_n \to z$ monotonically in $S, \exists$ an upper bound for the set of positive numbers $t_{n+1} - t_n$. Let $\phi(\lambda; z) = z$, $\lambda > 0$. Then for x_n sufficiently close to z, $\phi(\lambda; x_n) \in V_s$ and so, $\phi(\lambda + 1; x_n) \in S$ for some $t \in [-\varepsilon, \varepsilon]$.

∴ $t_{n-1} - t_n \leq \lambda + \varepsilon$

Let $\beta > 0$; then $\exists$ a $\delta > 0$ so that if $|x_n - u| < \delta$ and $|t| \leq \lambda + \varepsilon$ then

$|\phi(t; x_n) - \phi(t; u)| < \beta$

Let n_0 be sufficiently large that $|x_n - z| < \delta$ for all $n \geq n_\alpha$. Then

$|\phi(t; x_n) - \phi(t; z)| < \beta$

if $|t| \leq \lambda + \varepsilon$ and $n \geq n_0$. Now, let $t \geq t_{n_0}$ and $n \geq n_0$ such that $t_n \leq t \leq t_{n+1}$

Then $d\big(\phi(t,x),\Gamma\big) \;\le\; \big|\phi(t;x)-\phi(t-t_n;z)\big|$

$$= \big|\phi(t-t_n;x_n)-\phi(t-t_n;z)\big| < \beta.$$

since $|t-t_n|\le \lambda+\varepsilon$. This proves the Poincare-Bendixson threorem.

Remarks

1.   In the above proof, we have tacitly used the concept of diffeomorphism while using the term 'flow'. It is the diffeomorphism ψ given by $R\times H \supset N \xrightarrow{\;\psi\;} W$ which describes the flow in a nbd N of $O(0,0)$ onto a nbd 0 in W, transforming the vector field $f:W\to E$ into the constant vector field $(1,0)$ on $R\times H$. This is also referred to as *flow box* so as to describe completely a flow in a nbd of any non-equilibrium point, using nonlinear coordinates.

2.   We recall concepts of invariant sets and limit-sets only with their properties and minimal sets, in regard to the system

$$\dot{x}=f(x),\; x\in D<R^n,\; t\in R \tag{1}$$

We distinguish between positive and negative orbits for $t\ge 0$ and $t<0$ with

$$\Gamma^+(x_0),\; t\ge 0$$

and $\Gamma^-(x_0),\; t<0$

so that for periodic solutions, $\Gamma^+(x_0)=\Gamma^-(x_0)$; $x(t)$ is the solution of (1), $x(0)=x_0$ and the orbit is indicated by $\Gamma(x_0)$. We can now have a statement of Poincare Bendixson theorem in terms of $\omega(\Gamma^+)$ having a critical point or otherwise, recalling ideas on a 'transversal' and Poincare mapping or a first return map. Three lemmas and a theorem are of course, necessary to arrive at the PB theorem. The various stages of the proof are indicated below.

We restrict ourselves to only planar systems given by the equation

$$\dot{x}=f(x) \text{ with } x\in R^2,\; f:R^2\to R^2 \tag{1}$$

having continuous first order partial derivatives. We also assume that the solutions exist for $-\infty < t < \infty$. If we have a positive orbit Γ^+ of equation (1) which is bounded but does not correspond with the periodic solution, then the ω-limit set $\omega(\Gamma^+)$ consists of a critical point or it consists of a closed orbit.

This is really the crux of a version of a statement of Poincare-Bendixson theorem. To establish this we consider following important results expressed through lemmas.

IIIA. Lemma 1 : A lemma based on Poincare mapping

Let us take the mapping $g : W \to (-1, 1)$ caused by using h to map w on $p_1 \in l_0$ as shown here

$h : \{-1, 1\} \to l$ with $W = h^{-1}(V)$

($V \to$ Poincare mapping of V into l_0).

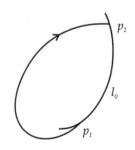

Let us now prove that, the set W is open, the function $g(w)$ is continuous and non decreasing in W. The sequence $\{g^k(w)\}_{k=0}$ is monotonic; $\{g(w) = w\}$, $g^1(w) = g(g^0(w)\}$ and so on.

Proof : We note that an open nbd of $p_1 = h(w)$ is mapped on an open nbd of p_2 in l_0. Therefore W is open. The solutions depend on the continuity of initial value of $h(w)$ and hence, follows the continuity. Let us now consider the curve C consisting of the orbit connecting p_1 and p_2 and the curve, p_1, p_2 lying in l_0. If $p_1 = p_2$, then $\Gamma(p_1)$ corresponds with periodic orbit; in that case p_1 becomes a fixed point in the mapping of V into l_0. Therefore $\{g^k\}$ consists of one point.

Let $p_1 \neq p_2$, for instance, $h^{-1}(p_1) < h^{-1}(p_2)$. Let C_i be the interior part of C and C_e be the exterior part. Now the transversal l_0 is no where tangent to the orbits and can be intersected in one direction only. Therefore $h[g(w), 1] \subset l_0$ must be contained in C_e.

Defining $g^2(w)$, we find the point $\in$ to belong to $\{g(w),1\}$. The monotonicity of the sequence can be seen through induction.

IIIB. Lemma 2

The w-limit set of an orbit $\Gamma(p)$ can intersect the interior l_0 of a transversal l in one part only. If $\exists$ such a point p_0 we have $w(\Gamma)=\Gamma$ with Γ a cycle corresponding to a periodic solution or $\exists$ a sequence $\{t_k\}$ with $t_k \to \infty$ so that $x(t_k,p) \to p_0$ monotonically in l_0.

Proof : Let $w(p)$ intersect l_0 in p_0. Obviously if $p=p_0$, the orbit is periodic. If not, $w(\Gamma)$ being the limit set of $\Gamma(p)$, $\exists$ a sequence $\{t_k^1\}$, $t_k^1 \to \infty$ as $k \to \infty$. With $x(t_k^1,p) \to p_0$ as $k \to \infty$. Then in a nbd of p_0 there must exist a sequence $\{t_k\}$, $t_k \to \infty$ as $k \to \infty$ such that $x(t_k,p) \to p_0$ in l_0. From Lemma (1), we know that this sequence is monotone in l_0. Let us now suppose that $w(\Gamma)$ intersects in l_0 at the point p_0^1. Therefore, $\exists$ a sequence $\{x(k,p)\}$ in l_0 which $\to p_o^1$. This enables us to construct a sequence $\{g^k(w)\}$ as in Lemma 1 which cannot be monotonic unless $p_0 = p_0^1$, but the existence of such a sequence which is not monotone is contradicted by Lemma 1.

Hence our assertion is justified.

IIIC. Theorem

If M is a bounded minimal set of $\dot{x} = f(x)$ in R^2 then M either contains a critical point or forms a periodic orbit.

Proof : We first note that M is not empty; it is bounded and invariant and so contains at least say one orbit Γ. Therefore limit sets $\alpha(\Gamma)$ and $w(\Gamma)$ are contained in Γ. If M contains a critical point because of M being minimal, M cannot but be identified with this critical point. If M does not contain critical points, Γ and $w(\Gamma)$ must consist of ordinary points. Again, because of being the minimal, $\Gamma \subset w(\Gamma)$. Let us now choose a point $p \in \Gamma$ and a transversal l_0 of Γ in p. Therefore, it follows from Lemma 2 that $\Gamma = w(\Gamma)$ and Γ is periodic or there should exist a sequence in l_0 which monotonically $\rightarrow p$, but the second alternative is contradicted by Lemma 1. Therefore Γ is periodic by Lemma 1.

IIID. Lemma 3

If $w(\Gamma^+)$ contains both ordinary points and a periodic point Γ_0 then we have $w(\Gamma^+) = \Gamma_0$.

Proof : Let us suppose that $w(\Gamma^+)/\Gamma_0$ is not empty. Let us choose $p_0 \in \Gamma_0$ and an open transversal l_0 which contains p_0. From Lemma 2, it follows that $w(\Gamma^+) \cap l_0 = \{p_0\}$.

Moreover, $\exists$ a sequence $\{p_n\}$ in $w(\Gamma^+)/\Gamma_0$ such that $p_n \rightarrow p_0$ as $n \rightarrow \infty$. Therefore, for n sufficiently large, $\Gamma(p_n)$ will intersect the transversal l_0. Now by Lemma 2 this can happen in one point only, which is again a contradiction.

IV. Poincare Bendixson theorem

Let us consider the equation $\dot{x} = f(x)$ in R^2 and assume that Γ^+ is a bounded positive orbit and $w(\Gamma^+)$ contains ordinary points only. Then $w(\Gamma^+)$ is a periodic orbit. If $w(\Gamma^+) \neq \Gamma^+$, then the periodic orbit is a limit cycle. A similar result is valid for a bounded negative orbit.

Proof : It follows from the above result that $w(\Gamma^+)$ is compact, connected and non empty. Then from Lemma 3, $\exists$ a bounded, minimal set $w(\Gamma^+)$; M contains only ordinary points and because of the above theorem M is a periodic orbit; we now use the Lemma 3 so as to get at the requirements of the Poincare Bendixson theorem.

Remarks

1.   In order that the theorem becomes applicable, we need to find a domain D in R^2,

which contains ordinary points only and one has to find one orbit which, for $t \geq 0$, enters the domain D without leaving it, i.e. D must contain at least one periodic orbit.

2.   The above steps bring out in explicit terms that there are penetrating aspects of studies on Poincare Bendixson theorem. To get at its proof, we break down the ideas into a series of lemmas and as we have shown just now, a portrayal of the flow in a small nbd of a non-equilibrium part is sought, and how in such nbds, solution curves behave. Transversals are used. These results are for strictly planar flows. According to the well-known Jordan Curve theorem from plane topology, a simple closed curve divides the plane into two parts : a bounded region (the interior) and an unbounded region (the exterior). This is expressed by following version of the statement of the PB theorem.

V. Poincare-Bendixson theorem

Let us consider the planar dynamical system given by

$$\frac{dx}{dt} = f(x, y)$$

$$\frac{dy}{dt} = g(x, y)$$

Here, $(f, g) \in C^{(1)}$ in a domain D and let Γ be its trajectory of the system for $t \geq 0$. Let us suppose that Γ is contained in a bounded closed subset of D that has no critical points. Then Γ^+ is an orbit of this system and is a Jordan curve.

Remark

If Γ is itself a Jordan curve, then $\Gamma = \Gamma^+$. But, in general, Γ is not a closed curve but spirals towards the closed curve Γ^+, in which case, we call this a limit cycle. There is, thus, a periodic trajectory in either case and there lies the seminal importance of Poincare-Bendixson theorem.

appendix II

Applicable nonlinear difference equations

Nonlinear phenomena, in some of its areas, have already been shown to be amenable to mathematization through differential equations. Their evolutionary characteristics have also been dealt with. The purpose of this appendix is to show, in brief, and once again, how a nonlinear phenomenon becomes not only mathematized through what are called nonlinear 'difference equations', but also revealing.

We choose again a situation from a biological system. It relates, in particular, to population biology. Let N represent some quantitative measure for a biological population. We take it that essential changes of N take place at certain discrete moments $t_1, t_2 \cdots$ which usually correspond to the birth of a new generation. Let N_0 be the initial value of N at time t_0; let the change of the variable N at a given time t_{i+1} $(i = 0, 1, 2, \cdots)$ be determined by its value at time t_i and by externalities like food, habitation, etc. Let N_i be the value of N at time t_i. We have then the difference equation of the type

$$N_{i+1} - N_i = f(N_i, \mu)$$

where $\mu \in \Lambda$, the parameter space containing the information conditioned by externalities.

It is a matter of history that Malthus, way back in 1798, proposed a *linear* dependence of f on N, assuming the change of population to be proportional to the number of individuals :

$$f(N,\mu)=C(\mu)N$$

where $C(\mu)>-1$ is the difference between the *birth rate* $B(\mu)$ and the *death rate* $D(\mu)$. Given $N_0>0$, one can say that the behaviour of the solutions N_i is determined by the sign of $C(\mu)$ as indicated below :

$$\left.\begin{array}{l} N_i \to \infty \text{ as } i \to \infty \text{ if } C(\mu)>0 \\ N_i \to 0 \text{ as } i \to \infty \text{ if } -1<C(\mu)<0 \end{array}\right\} \tag{1}$$

This sort of behaviour, as indicated in (1), of course, does not always fit in with reality. Indeed, the unbounded growth for positive values of $C(\mu)$ is far from satisfactory and one may reasonably assume that, if there are two way individuals, the effort of over crowding leads to decrease of the factor $C(\mu)$ and makes it eventually negative. So, one can take $C(\mu)$ to be dependent on N and we find a *nonlinear difference* equation of the type

$$N_{i+1}-N_i=C(N_i,\mu)N_i \text{ where } C(N,\mu)<0 \text{ if } N>N_\mu.$$

Of course, we do have choices for the function $C(N,\mu)$ and the simplest choice, as proposed by Verhulst in 1837, is : $\mu=(a,b)\in\Lambda=(-1,\infty)\times(0,\infty)\in C(N,a,b)=a-bN$.

Thus, we arrive at the logistic difference equation.

$$N_{i+1}-N_i=(a-bN_i)N_i \leftrightarrow N_{i+1}=\{(a+1)-bN_i\}N_i.$$

We note that if $a>0, N=\dfrac{a}{b}$ is an equilibrium solution i.e. $N_0=\dfrac{a}{b}$ the $N_i=\dfrac{a}{b}$ for all i. We also note that if $a+1-bN_i<0$ then $N_{i+1}<0$ and so the model ceases to be realistic. Therefore, we cannot but assume that $N_i\le\dfrac{a+1}{b}$ \hfill (2)

We can express this equation, otherwise, by putting

$$M=\frac{b}{a+1}N \text{ and } \lambda=a+1>0$$

so that

$$M_{i+1} = \lambda M_i (1 - M_i) \text{ for } i = 0, 1, 2, \cdots$$
$$M_0 \in (0, 1)$$

$$(3)$$

That $M_0 \leq 1$, follows (2). This puts a limitation on λ.

We seek $M_{i+1} \leq 1$ if $0 < M_i < 1$ i.e. $\lambda M (1 - M) \leq 1$ for all $x \in [0, 1]$.

Since the maximum of the function $M(1 - M)$ in $[0, 1]$ is $\dfrac{1}{4}$, we can assume that $0 < \lambda < 4$. Further, we can make the following observations, on the basis of solutions behaving regularly for small values of λ (assuming, of course, the existence of equilibrium solutions) :

(a)   if $0 < \lambda \leq 1$, all solutions M_i converge to the unique equilibrium solution $M = 0$. One can establish this for every solution is decreasing and its limit is necessarily an equilibrium solution.

(b)   for $\lambda > 1$, there are exactly two equilibrium solutions $M = 0$ and $M_\lambda = \dfrac{(\lambda - 1)}{\lambda}$.

We can describe $\lambda = 1$ as the *bifurcation point*. Do these solutions lead to one of these equilibrium solutions? If so, which one of the two? What about stability or otherwise? Such posers are likely to occur. We, therefore, need the definition :

Definition : An equilibrium solution x of the difference equation $x_{i+1} = f(x_i)$ is said to be stable if for any $\varepsilon > 0$, $\exists$ a $\delta > 0$ so that a solution x_i satisfies $|x_i - x| < \varepsilon$ if the initial value satisfies $|x_0 - x| < \delta$. If x is not stable, it is said to be unstable and x is said to be asymptotically stable if $\exists$ a $\delta > 0$ such that $x_i \to x$ as $i \to \infty$ for any solution x_i with $|x_0 - x| < \delta$.

It is easy to see, from earlier discussions, that $N = 0$ is an asymptotically stable solution if $0 < \lambda \leq 1$. We have another criterion about asymptotic stability/instability about the equilibrium point of the difference equation $x_{i+1} = f(x_i)$ in that (i) if $|f'(x)| < 1$, then

x is asymptotically stable and (ii) if $|f'(x)| > 1$ then x is unstable.

Let us now go back to equation (3). To ascertain the stability, we compute the derivative $\lambda(1-2M) = \lambda$ at $M = 0$; we find that $M = 0$ is asymptotically stable for $\lambda < 1$ and unstable for $\lambda > 1$. The same derivative at M_λ is equal to $-\lambda + 2$ and hence, $M = M_\lambda$ is asymptotically stable for $1 < \lambda < 3$ and unstable for $\lambda > 3$. Also, if $1 < \lambda \leq 3$, then $M_i \to M_\lambda$ as $i \to \infty$, provided that $0 < M_0 \leq 1$. To know what happens for $\lambda > 3$, let us see what happens at the bifurcation point $\lambda = 1$; the equilibrium solution $M = 0$ which is stable for $\lambda < 1$, continues to exist for $\lambda > 1$ but it has become unstable; the new solution M_λ is the stable one.

Also $\lambda = 3$ is a bifurcation point; for $\lambda > 3$, there are no stable equilibrium solutions but instead there is a periodic orbit which, for λ sufficiently near to 3, is stable. We have thus the definition.

Definition : A periodic solution of period T of the difference equation $x_{i+1} = f(x_i)$ is a solution satisfying $x_{i+T} = x_i$ for any i. The solution has prime period T if the solution has no period τ which is smaller than T. We have another criterion on asymptotic stability.

Let $x_1, x_2 \cdots\cdots x_T$ be the values of a periodic solution of period T of the equation $x_{i+1} = f(x_i)$.

Let us define $J = f^1(x_1) \cdots\cdots f^1(x_n)$.

If $|J| < 1$, the periodic solution is asymptotically stable. If $|J| > 1$, the periodic solution is unstable.

On this basis, let us now look for a periodic solution of period 2 :

$$x_i = x_{i+2} = \lambda x_{i+1}(1-x_{i+1}) = \lambda^2 x_i (1-x_i)\{(1-\lambda x_i)(1-x_i)\}$$

Hence x_i is a solution of

$$\lambda^3 x^4 - 2\lambda^3 x^3 + (\lambda^3 + \lambda^2)x^2 + (1-\lambda^2)x = 0$$

Now the equilibrium solutions $x = 0$ and x_λ satisfy this equation and using this we have, then, the periodic solution with values

$$x_{\lambda,1} = \frac{\lambda + 1 + \sqrt{\lambda^2 - 2\lambda - 3}}{2\lambda}, \ x_{\lambda,2} = \frac{\lambda + 1 - \sqrt{\lambda^2 - 2\lambda - 3}}{2\lambda}$$

Let us note that $\lambda^2 - 2\lambda - 3 > 0$ if $\lambda > 3$. One can verify that this solution is asymptotically stable for small values of $\lambda \neq 3$ and then becomes unstable. Hence, at the bifurcation point $\lambda = 3$, a stable periodic solution appears and the equilibrium solution x_λ is unstable.

appendix III

Further ideas and definitions

Nonlinear systems cover such a continuingly vast landscape that an impression keeps on lingering that something might have been left out. Indeed, one has to be meticulously careful about the minimality of the exposure to nonlinear systems. We can, thus, hardly refrain ourselves from a brief overview of few more concepts and ideas around them, without feeling an imposition, formal, and unwieldy.

I. Flow box

'Flow' has already been talked out. Let us consider the flow ϕ_t of the C (vector field) $f : W \to E$, where $0 \in E$ belongs to W.

We know of a hyperplane as a linear subspace where dimension is one less than $\dim E$. We have already met the term 'transverse' i.e. $S \subset H$ is *transverse* to f means that $f(x) \notin H$ for all $x \in S$ and in particular, $f(x) \notin 0$ for $x \in S$.

With this, we can consider an open set S containing 0 in a hyperplane $S \subset H$ which is transverse to f and we call this open set as a *local section* at 0.

A *flow box* is thought of to provide the description of a flow in a nbd of any non-critical point of any flow using nonlinear coordinates e.g. points moving in parallel straight lines at constant speed.

Let us recall the definition of 'diffeomorphism'. Using this, we can say that a *flow box* is a diffeomorphism $R \times H \supset N \xrightarrow{\Psi} W$ of a nbd N of $(0,0)$ onto a nbd of 0 in W, which transforms the vector field $f : W \rightarrow E$ into the constant vector field $(1,0)$ on $R \times H$. Therefore, the flow of 'f' becomes a simple flow on $R \times H$:

$$\psi(t,y) = \phi_t(y) \text{ for } (t,y) \text{ in a sufficiently small nbd of } (0,0) \text{ in } R \times H.$$

Remark

A flow box is amenable to definition about any non-equilibrium point. Since x_0 is any point, we can replace $f(x)$ by $f(x - x_0)$ so as to convert to the point 0 and we hardly restrict the nature of x_0 by equaling it to zero. There are many applications of the above ideas on dynamical systems. Even Poincare-Bendixson can be proved using the idea of a local section, which, as we know, leads to the idea of a limit-cycle as a closed orbit γ such that $\gamma \subset L_w(x)$ (ω limit cycle) or $\gamma \subset L_\alpha(x)$ (α limit cycle) for some $x \notin \gamma$.

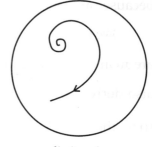

limit cycle

Fig. III.1

II. Liapunov exponent

Let us consider a one-dimensional map giving rise to a dynamical system.

Let $f : X \rightarrow X$ with $X \subset R$. Then $\mu(x)$ of a point $x \in X$, given by

$$\mu(x) = \lim_{n \to \infty} \frac{\mu |\alpha f^n(x)|}{n}$$

is called the *Liapunov exponent*.

In particular, if x is a fixed point of the map then $f^n(x) = x$

Then, using the chain rule and differentiation, we get

$$\mu(x) = \ln|\lambda|$$

where λ is the eigen value of the linearization of 'f' at x.

Thus, for $|\lambda| < 1$, $\mu(x)$ is negative and for $|\lambda| > 1$, $\mu(x)$ is positive. Hence $\mu(x)$ represents some sort of a measure.

III. Lorenz equations : Strange attraction

We have met earlier this system given by

$$\dot{x} = \sigma(y - x)$$
$$\dot{y} = rx - y - xz$$
$$\dot{z} = xy - bz$$

where σ, r, b are positive constants and whose genesis can be traced back to 1963, because of a landmark paper by the meteorologist E. N. Lorenz.

We often take $\sigma = 10$, $b = \dfrac{8}{3}$ and r can take various positive values, say, $r = 28$. There are many revealing features of the orbits represented by the above equations. One can also derive few characteristics of the system such as

(i)   the solution $\{x(t), y(t) z(t)\}$ has a symmetric counterpart $\{-x(t), -y(t), -z(t)\}$.

(ii) $\vec{\nabla} \cdot (\sigma y - \sigma x, rx - y - xz, xy - bz) = -(\sigma + 1 + b) \Rightarrow \dot{v}(t) = -(\sigma + 1 + b)v(t)$, $v(t)$ being the volume element which thus keeps on shrinking

(iii)   for $0 < r < 1$, there is one equilibrium solution $(0,0,0)$ which is found to be asymptotically stable; for $r > 1$, there are three critical points $(0,0,0)$, $\left(\pm\sqrt{b(r-1)}, \pm\sqrt{b(r-1)}, r-1 \right)$ $(0,0,0)$ being an unstable (manifold), the others leading to Hopf bifurcation, unstable periodic solutions.

        A numerical solution of the system is shown in Fig. III.2 :

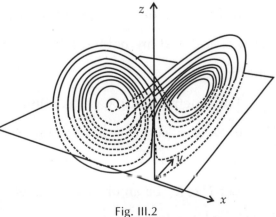

Fig. III.2

Further, if we have the Liapunov function as

$$V(x,y,z) = rx^2 + \sigma y^2 + \sigma(z - 2r)^2$$

then the orbital derivative is given by

$$L_t V = -2\sigma \left(rx^2 + y^2 + bz^2 - 2brz \right)$$

We may now discuss some geometrical concepts.

The numerical approximation shows that there is an attracting set which, as a phenomenon, was given by the mathematicians Ruelle and Takens , the terms, "strange attraction". One may also remark upon the sensitive dependence of solutions of the system on initial conditions leading to what are called limits of prediction and chaotic processes, as indicated in Epilogue.

IV. Theorem on existence and uniqueness of solutions of ordinary differential equations

Statement : Given the differential equation $\dot{x} = f(\dot{x})$, let $\varphi^t(x_0)$ be the solution $\bar{x} = (t)$-ith the given initial condition $\bar{x}_0$ at $t = 0$, $\varphi^0(\bar{x}_0) = x_0$ and $\dfrac{d}{dt}\varphi^t(\bar{x}_0) = f(\varphi^t(x_0))$ for all t for which it is defined. As already seen earlier, we often write $\varphi(t, x_0)$ in lieu of $\varphi^t(x_0)$; $\varphi^t(x_0)$ is called the flow of the differential equation. We ought to have a theorem that establishes that the solution is uniquely determined by initial conditions $\bar{x}_0$ and the time t; in fact, the notation $\varphi^t(x_0)$ shows this dependence. Normally, we refer to flows on metric spaces that are not the solutions of a differential equation and R^n . The relevant definition is :

For a metric space X, any continuous map $\varphi : U \subset R_x X \to X$ defined on an open set $U \supset \{0\}$, X is called a *flow* provided (i) it satisfies the group property $\varphi^{t_0}\varphi^s(\bar{x}_0) = \varphi^{t+s}(\bar{x}_0)$ and (ii) for fixed t, φ^t is a homoeomorphism in its domain of definition.

Let $U \subset R^n$ be an open set and let $f : U \to R^n$ be a Lipschitz function on $C^{(1)}$. Let $\bar{x}_0 \in U$ and $t_0 \in R$. Then there exists an $\alpha > 0$ and a solution $\bar{x}(t)$ of $\dot{x} = f(\bar{x})$ defined for $t_0 - \alpha < t < t_0 + \alpha$, such that $\vec{x}(t_0) = \vec{x}_0$. Moreover, if $\vec{y}(t)$ is another solution with $\vec{y}(t_0) = \vec{y}_0$, then $\vec{x}(t) = \vec{y}(t)$ in their common interval of definition about t_0.

Although the proof is not given now, we need to mention about the important inequality called the Gronwall Inequality which enables one to establish the uniqueness of the solutions.

Gronwall Inequality : Let $v(t)$ and $g(t)$ be continuous non-negative scalar functions on (a, b), $a < t_0 < b$, $C \geq 0$ and

$$v(t) \cdot \leq C + \left| \int_{t_0}^{t} v(s) g(s) ds \right| \text{ for } a < t_0 < b.$$

Then, $v(t) \leq C \exp \left(\left| \int_{t_0}^{t} g(s) ds \right| \right)$

Gronwall inequality is basically concerned about the continuity of the flow as a function of the initial conditions. In terms of the Lipschitz constant L, we can also restate this as :

Let $\vec{f}$ be defined on the open set $U \in R^n$ and let us assume that $\vec{f}$ has a Lipschitz constant in the variables $\vec{x}$ on U. Let $\vec{x}(t)$ and $\vec{y}(t)$ be solutions of the given differential equation and let (t_0, t_1) be a subset of the domains of both solutions.

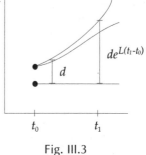

Fig. III.3

Then $\left| \vec{x}(t) - \vec{y}(t) \right| \leq \left| \vec{x}(t_0) - \vec{y}(t_0) \right| e^{L(t - t_0)}$.

where $\left| \vec{f}(x) - \vec{f}(y) \right| \leq L \left| (\vec{x} - \vec{y}) \right|$ for all $\vec{x}$ and $\vec{y}$ is U.

This is shown in the Figure III.3.

V. Reconsidering hyperbolicity

We can trace back its use much earlier when in case of linearization, we considered, the eigen values given by the characteristic equation in λ. The condition $R_e(\lambda) \neq 0$ is hyperbolicity which ensures that the local phase portrait of the original non-linear system that resembles in its significant topological features the phase portrait of this linearisation, at least in the small nbd around the fixed point so that the local scenario yielded by linearization can be fairly opposite. Then, does there exist any analogue of its periodic orbits? We can seek hyperbolicity there, too. If Γ is a periodic orbit with a period T (>0) and q is a point on Γ the $\varphi(T;\varepsilon)=q$ so that $\phi(T)$ is a mapping of R^n to itself with ε as fixed point. One of its eigen values is +1 (corresponding to Γ-direction at ε); if others do not lie as unit circle in the complex place (so their logarithms have $R_e\lambda \neq 0$) then Γ is hyperbolic. This property is independent of the choice of q as Γ and further, it can be established that in the nbd of Γ, there are local unstable and stable manifolds which meet along Γ and are such that the flow expands exponentially away from Γ and also contracts exponentially away from Γ along the respective manifolds mentioned just now.

A trajectory $\varphi(k,x)$ is called hyperbolic, if

$$\|D\varphi(k,x)\xi\|<a\|\xi\|e^{-ck}$$

$$\|D\varphi(k,x)\eta\|<a\|n\|e^{-ck}$$

where $\xi\in E_0^s$, and $\eta\in E_o^u$, a, b, c are positive constants independent of ξ, η, and k and $D\varphi(k)=A_{k-1}, A_{k-2}\cdots\cdots A_0$, $A_k=\dfrac{\partial F(x,k)}{\partial \bar{x}}$ with $\dot{x}=F(x)$; it is being assumed that we have an infinite sequence $\{E_k\}_{k=-\infty}^{k=+\infty}$ of n-dimensional spaces and operator $\{A_k\}_{k-\infty}^{k+\infty}$ such that ......, $E_k \xrightarrow{A_k} E_{k_{10}} \rightarrow \cdots\cdots$.

Let us go back to the map of the circle T^1 taken to be $\{z=C;|z|=1\}$.

where we write the map $f':T^1\rightarrow T^1$ or $z\rightarrow f(z)$. We say that a diffeomorphism $f:T^1\rightarrow \Gamma^1$ to be Morse-Smale if it has periodic points and they are all hyperbolic.

Remarks

1. One can establish that Morse-Smale diffeomorphism of T^1 is structurally stable. Moreover all periodic orbits may not attract all orbits in the nbd as $t \to +\infty$, as each may have an unstable manifold larger than the orbit itself and so, they are expanding or contracting in all directions. But we can well conceive of the entire 3-dimensional totality M of periodic and non-periodic orbits to form an attractor for a flow in some space of dimensions greater than 3 so that the orbits in the nbd would fall within the purview of M, without being able to approach the stable equilibrium or any periodic motion; there is a possibility of passing though a point in the nbd of M.

2. That individual periodic orbits are not limit cycles is well shown by what is called hyperbolic torus automorphism (HTA) and horse-shoes which essentially deal with a cross-section for a differential equation near an attracting periodic orbit.

3. In view of the above ideas, we are led to what may be called an 'hyperbolic attractor'.

4. The definition of a hyperbolic set is clear from above the definitions.

appendix IV

Miscellaneous exercise

1. Construct the Liapunov function of system $\dfrac{dx}{dt} = \alpha x - \beta xy - \gamma x^2 : \dfrac{dy}{dt} = k\beta xy - my$
   where α, p, γ, k and m are all positive constants.

   How do you investigate the stability or otherwise of the system? When can it become asymptotically unstable?

2. Investigate fully the behaviour of the system
   $$\dot{x} = \mu x + y - x(x^2 + y^2), \quad \dot{y} = -x + \mu y - y(x^2 + y^2)$$

3. What can you say about the limit cycles of the system
   $$\dot{x} = \mu x + y - xf(r)$$
   $$\dot{y} = -x + \mu y \, yf(r)$$
   where $r = \sqrt{x^2 + y^2}$, $f(r)$ is continuous for $r \geq 0$, $f(0) = 0$ and $f(r) > 0$ for $r > 0$?

4. How do you apply Poincare-Bendixson theorem to ascertain existence of limit cycles, if any, in appropriate regions of the system
   $$\dot{x} = x(x^2 + y^2 - 2x - 3) - y$$
   $$\dot{y} = y(x^2 + y^2 - 2x - 3) + x \ ?$$

5. How do you use Poincare-Bendixson's theorem to show that for a system of the kind $n'' + F(n, n')n' + n = 0$ there is at least one periodic solution in an annular region?

6.   Given the system

$$\left.\begin{array}{l} \dot{x} = y + x(c - x) \\ \dot{y} = -x + y(c - x) \end{array}\right\}$$

transform to polar co-ordinates as

$$\left.\begin{array}{l} \dot{r} = cr - r^2 \sin\theta \\ \dot{\theta} = 1 \end{array}\right\} ;$$

Does the system have periodic solutions for $c = 0$?

Justify your answer.

7.   Consider the system

$$\left.\begin{array}{l} \dot{x} = g\left(x^2 + y^2 ; c\right) + y \\ \dot{y} = g\left(x^2 + y^2 ; c\right)y - x \end{array}\right\}$$

Investigate its behaviour.

Appendix V

Some applicable aspects of Catastrophe theory

I. We consider the problem of a propped cantelever strut.

In the model, as depicted in Fig. V.1, the spring is unstretched when the strut is vertical, and the smooth sliding contact ensures that the spring is always horizontal. The symmetry requirement of the model is fulfilled, because of the uniformity of stiffness in compression as in tension of the spring. Hence for this model the P.E. (V) is given by

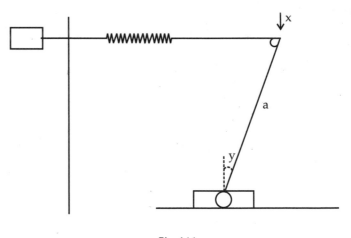

Fig. V.1

$$V = xa \cos y + \frac{1}{2}ka^2 \sin^2 y$$

$$\therefore V_y = - xa \sin y + ka^2 \sin y \cos y$$

$$= \frac{1}{2}ka^2 \sin 2y - xa \sin y$$

and $\quad V_{yy} = ka^2 \cos 2y - xa \cos y$

The equilibrium curves are now $y = 0$ and $x = ka \cos y$

When $y = 0$, $V_{yy} = a(ka - x)$, and so, the equilibrium is stable along the x-axis upto the point $(ka, 0)$ and unstable beyond it.

Again, when $x = ka \cos y$,

$$V_{yy} = ka^2 \left(\cos 2y - \cos^2 y \right)$$
$$= ka^2 \left(\cos^2 y - 1 \right)$$

So $x = ka \cos y$ gives unstable equilibrium. Equilibrium will be unstable when $V_{yy} = 0$ and this happens at the point $(ka, 0)$.

The equilibrium curve is shown below.

Now on applying increasing load vertically, we get stable equilibrium till the load reaches ka, at which point the strut collapses. This happens, because, there is no position of stable equilibrium, either central or deflected, for loads as great as ka. By altering the arrangement of the top of the strut or by changing the point of

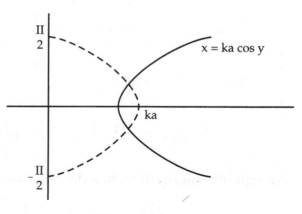

Fig. V.2: Equilibrium curves for the guyed strut

application of the load, we could always determine V, V_y and V_{yy}, so that we would have a relationship between the control variables x and a, and the state variable y.

The equation $V_y = 0$ gives the equilibrium surface in three dimensions. As is evident, the appreciation of this geometry is rather difficult. Catastrophe theory helps us to understand this more clearly.

II.   We next consider another mechanical example. Let us suppose that a mass io concentrated at the middle point P of a light elastic wire with the end point fixed at the two points A and B at a distance $2a$ apart which can sustain compression : as shown in Fig. V.3.

Suppose that the initial or rest torsion i.e. the tension when the displacement x of the mass from the vertical is T_0; a transverse force F acts on the mass.

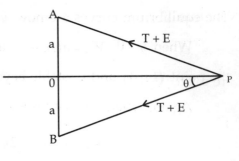

Fig. V.3

The equation of motion of the mass is given by

$$m\ddot{x} = F - 2(T+E)\cos\theta$$

where $\theta = \angle OPB$, T is the tension in the wire and E is the Euler load.

Again, $\cos\theta = \dfrac{x}{\sqrt{x^2 + a^2}}$

Also $T = T_0 + \dfrac{1}{2}\left(\dfrac{x}{a}\right)x^2 + 0\left(\dfrac{x^4}{a}\right)$

$$m\ddot{x} = F - \dfrac{2(T_0+E)}{a}x - \dfrac{\lambda}{a}x^3 + 0\left(\dfrac{x^5}{a^5}\right)$$

For equilibrium position, in a discrete case, the associated potential function is

$$V(T_0, F, x) = \dfrac{\lambda}{a}\left[\dfrac{x^4}{4} + \dfrac{1}{\lambda}(T_0+E)x^2 - \dfrac{Fa^2}{\lambda^2}x\right]$$

The catastrophe set which is associated with this kind of discontinuous behaviour may be written as $4u^3 + 27v^2 = 0$ which is a semi-cubical parabola.

The system has two stable equilibria as soon as u becomes negative i.e. as the compression in T_0 is greater than Euler load E.

For a non-dissipative character of the system i.e. for a conservative system, we have

$$\ddot{x} = x(x^3 + ux + v)$$

i.e. $-\dfrac{x^2}{2k} = \dfrac{1}{4}x^4 + \dfrac{1}{2}ux^2 + vx + s$

The maximal deflections given by

$$x^4 + 2ux^2 + 4vx + 4s = 0$$

are related to the critical set

$$V_{(a,b,c,x)} = \frac{1}{5}x^5 + \frac{1}{3}ax^3 + \frac{1}{2}bx^2 + cx$$

which is associated with a swallow-tail catastrophe.

III. Let us briefly mention a problem which deals with a possible application of catastrophe theory to social sciences. The problem takes note of the effects of changes in the distribution of public opinion on the ensuing policy adopted by the administration. The specific example chosen relates to the case of a nation deciding upon its level of action in some war. The changes influencing the public opinion are control factors. We consider, for simplicity's sake, just two control factors, viz, a = threat, b = cost whose effects on public opinion are qualitatively different; because a sense of common danger tends to mobilise opinion into a fighting mood, while a costly war usually tends to divide the population. Hence, we decide to call a the normal factor and b the splitting factor.

Let C be the control or parameter space, its horizontal space components being a, b. Any point $c = (a, b)$ is called a control. Each control point c determines a particular distribution of opinion. We define the probability function P as

$$P : C \times X \to R$$
$$\left[\left[P(c,x) = P_c(x)\right]\right]$$

Let G_c denote the set of maxima of P_c. Let X be a vertical line with probable levels of military action. Then G_c is a function from C to X. Let G denote the graph of the function G and G is contained in 3-dimensional space $C \times X = R^3$, and is defined to be the set of points

$$G = \text{closure } \{(c,x) : C \in c \times x \in G_c\}$$

G will be a surface in R^3 and it will be equivalent to the folded cusp catastrophe surface.

IV. We discuss now an application that has relevance to earth sciences. This is about phenotypes. Phenotypes of an organism are not in general susceptible to exact mathematical analysis. However, Thom's idea of structural stability and morphogenesis together with few relevant mathematical assumptions make the phenotypes more amenable to mathematical treatment and consequently, one can draw certain qualitative inferences about the change in phenotype of a population subject to natural selection in an ever-changing environment. For this kind of analysis, we need to define certain mathematical terms.

We assume that the fitness of a population with phenotype $p(p_1, p_2, \cdots, p_n)$ in an environment $e(e_1, e_2, \cdots, e_k)$ is denoted by a real number $\phi(e, p)$ where $\phi : E \times P \to R$ is a smooth real-valued function. According to Darwin's law, we know that the fitness is locally maximal or reaches a peak. Hence, if the population is in stable equilibrium with a given environment e, it has a phenotype p which becomes maximal $\phi(e, p)$ locally. This, implies,

$$\text{grad}_p \, \phi = \left(\frac{\partial \phi}{\partial p_1}, \frac{\partial \phi}{\partial p_2}, \cdots, \frac{\partial \phi}{\partial p_n} \right) = 0$$

at the point (e, p) in expression for $\text{grad}_p \, \phi$ vanishes and is called the critical set of ϕ with respect to p and is denoted by M_ϕ. This includes the local maxima of the fitness. The function ϕ, as defined above, can be identified with a potential function. In an ideal situation, the population remains stable with a steadily changing environment, there being an actual discontinuity in the phenotype immediately following the disappearance of the peak. In reality, however, there will be no discontinuity in the phenotype of the population which ceases to be in equilibrium with its environment but instead, it starts evolving from one stable form to another. Thus this discontinuity represents a comparatively sudden and substantial change in the phenotype arising from a slow, smooth change in environment. Also, the slight spread of phenotypes in a population would mean that the population starts to develop just before the peak disappears, the actual threshold depending on the variability of the population to a new optimally fit form. Just before annihilation, the peak becomes less pronounced, and just before the fitness reaches an inflection point, there should be increased variability in the distribution of phenotypes in the population. Thom's theorem enables us to describe qualitatively the significance of the above phenomena. Now if we suppose that there is just one independent environmental variable so that the environment is specified by a single real number e, then Thom's theorem implies that near neutral points in M_ϕ, the response of the phenotype is given qualitatively by the canonical model of the fold catastrophe. However, if there are two independent environmental variables i.e. when $e = (e_1, e_2)$ Thom's theorem implies that near neutral points, the phenotype manifold is qualitatively similar to either the fold or the cusp catastrophe. Both these catastrophes have already been discussed in details before. It will, however, suffice to observe that the change in phenotype with environment for a population subject to natural selection is discontinuous and complex. The time scales involved in evolution are usually very long and in general, not observable under ordinary laboratory conditions. Thus, we are free to make the assumption, acceptable to many palaeontologists, that populations with phenotypes, not in stable equilibrium with their environment, will be transient and that the change from one stable phenotype to another will be virtually instantaneous in terms of geological time. Thom's theory on catastrophes provides qualitative understanding about the great number of discontinuities in fossil lineages. The theory can also account for the diversity of species in homogeneous environments like the sea.

V. We take up the following example from physiology and demonstrate how Zeeman applied catastrophe theory to the case of heart beating and tried to explain how many of the complexities of the beat could be seen from a simple behaviour of muscle fibre. The three dynamic qualities displayed by heart muscle are

    (i) stable equilibrium

    (ii) threshold, for triggering an action

    (iii) return to equilibrium.

The above three qualities are taken as axioms. The quality (iii) is of the type 'jump return' in the case of heart beat. If the heart stops beating, it stays relaxed in diastole, which is the stable equilibrium as listed in quality (i). The global electrochemical wave emanating from a pacemaker and reaching each individual muscle fibre triggers off the action of quality (ii). Each fibre remains contracted in the systole state for about $\frac{1}{5}$ second, and then rapidly relaxes again, thus obeying the jump return to equilibrium of quality (iii). These three qualities describe the local behaviour for an individual muscle fibre and Zeeman represented this phenomenon by a differential equation in the Euclidean plane R^2. The theorem he deduced may be stated as follows :

Zeeman theorem

There exists a dynamical system on R^2 possessing qualities (i), (ii), and (iii), as dealt with earlier.

The simplest example is as follows :

$$\varepsilon \dot{x} = -\left(x^3 - x + b\right)$$
$$\dot{b} = x - x_0$$

where x_0 is a constant greater than $\dfrac{1}{\sqrt{3}}$, x, b being coordinates in R^2, ε being a small positive quantity (constant). In order to identify the variables x, b with measurable qualities, we find that x is the length of the muscle fibre, so that the action represents the contraction and the jump return, the relaxation is to be of some form of electro-chemical control. The pacemaker wave will change the control from b_0 to b_1, (Fig. 12.18.)

Rybak's experiment showed that the heart can stop beating even though the pacemaker is still on. Thus, if the tension drops, the threshold must disappear and conversely, which leads to the cusp catastrophe

$$\dot{x} = -\left(x^3 + ax + b\right)$$

where

x = length of fibre,

b = chemical control,

$-a$ = tension.

From the point of view of catastrophe theory, a and b are two parameters of control in the control space. The slow manifold M (ref. Fig. 12.18) illustrates how these two controls determine the length of the muscle fibre. The feedback on M is determined by the slow equation $b = x$. Let the chemical control b take up the values b_0 and b_1 in diastole and systole respectively.

Then $b_0 = b_1$ is the equilibrium position and the trigger moves b from b_0 to b_1 after which the slow equation returns b to b_0. Thus, during diastole, b is fixed at b_0 and during systole, b is changing, with a maximum at b_1 as shown in Fig. 12.19.